EW OEMS

BY

OWEN MEREDITH.

IN TWO VOLUMES.

VOL. I.

CHRONICLES AND CHARACTERS.

BOSTON:
TICKNOR AND FIELDS.
1868.

AUTHOR'S EDITION.

UNIVERSITY PRESS: WELCH, BIGELOW, & CO.,
CAMBRIDGE.

DEDICATION.

TO

THEODORE GOMPERZ

OF VIENNA.

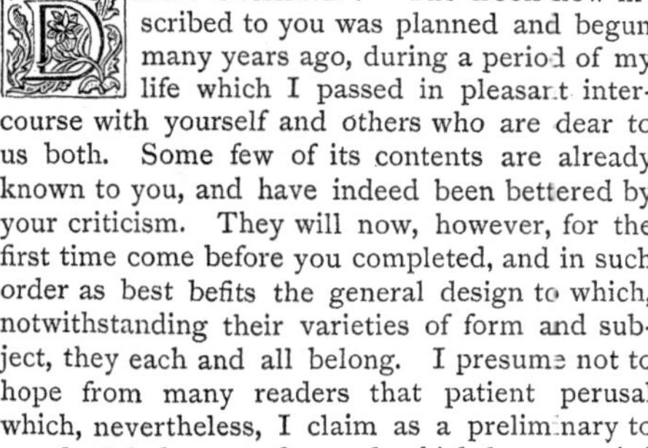EAR FRIEND: — The Book now inscribed to you was planned and begun many years ago, during a period of my life which I passed in pleasant intercourse with yourself and others who are dear to us both. Some few of its contents are already known to you, and have indeed been bettered by your criticism. They will now, however, for the first time come before you completed, and in such order as best befits the general design to which, notwithstanding their varieties of form and subject, they each and all belong. I presume not to hope from many readers that patient perusal which, nevertheless, I claim as a preliminary to any final judgment of a work which has occupied nearly seven years of my life. But, if it be honored by your own, I shall believe that it also

merits the approbation of all who, like yourself, have never held shares in any Joint-Stock Company for the formation of Opinion with Limited Liability. Many such men there are not. A few such men I know. I desire their sympathies; and, in that desire, I do homage to their virtues.

Your ever well-wisher,

ROBERT LYTTON.

CINTRA, 3d *September*, 1867.

CONTENTS.

CHRONICLES AND CHARACTERS.

CHRONICLES AND CHARACTERS.

BOOK I.

LEGENDARY GREECE.

TALES FROM HERODOTUS.

"ὥς φησιν ἐν τῇ πρώτῃ Ἡρόδοτος."
ATHENÆUS. B. xxiii.

TALES FROM HERODOTUS.

PRELUDE.

WITH fancies that, like phantoms, bear
The bodies of long-buried men,
Whose bones are dust, whose spirits are air,
Whose dwellings are the days that were, —
The suns that will not rise again, —
A bark, dream-built to drift along
The tides of other times, I throng;
And, helmless, here and there am blown
Beyond my will, by the Power of Song,
From shore to shore of regions lone
In sempiternal Even lying
Glimmeringly, girt by the moan
Of memories ever dying.
Like that bewildered Cretan crew
These old-world-wandering fancies are;
Whose course, unsteered by chart or star,
With tugging sail and slanted deck,
Latona's newborn offspring blew
Where'er he willed; nor could they check
In the plunging prow the spirit that knew
Whose sudden hand his speed obeyed;

As ever about in the billowy dip
And briny dance of the beakéd ship
  A golden dolphin flasht and played,
While fast through shallow foam they flew
  Along the shore-locked seas, and fast
  Beheld the Elean port slide past,
    And many a wisht-for haven fade,
      And many a slowly-sun-flusht bay,
    Till faint their staggering keel was stayed
      Off Crissa; when the crimson day
    In lights and ardors manifold
      Was burning all the west away,
      And, bright beyond the harbor bar,
    Brimmed his blue baths with fervid gold:
      Then, o'er the seaborn mountains far,
    And far in Even's inmost hold,
      The weary mariners (thus they say)
    Saw white walls hang in a rosy air;
    For so the god had built them there.

I.

OPIS AND ARGE.*

(HERODOTUS, iv. 35.)

PAST Ophiusa sailing, long ere morn
Had stolen beneath the summer stars from where
About the waters' verge in paler air
The stars are fewest and most large, near land
The Ortygian mariners their sea-drenched bark
Moored on the shallow sea, a weary band,
By Delos, waiting for the dawn; and there
(While broken winds, among the mountains born,
Scarce heaved — the sighing stillness of the dark)
They heard, along wild shores of capes forlorn,
The Hyperborean virgins, hand in hand,
Sing loud, from lands beyond the wind o' the north,
With mystic music moving down the seas
Toward Greece, this hymn, whose latest notes drew forth
Full-crownéd sunrise from the Cyclades:

* In the two succeeding poems the narrative of Herodotus has been literally followed; but in the present instance his passing allusion to the supposed introduction into Greece of the images of the gods, wrapped up in wheaten straw, by two Hyperborean virgins, has been taken only as a text for the utterance of some thoughts concerning what is owed, on behalf of human culture, to the mythology and art of the Greeks.

"Sister Arge, sister Arge, shake thy tresses to the wind,
Till the life that floods them overfloat the lone air with delight!
And tread swiftly down the shadows of the starry hills that bind
To the bases of the darkness the high silence of the night.
Virgin, watcher of the veilèd forms, to whom hath been consigned
The divinity enshrined,
Thou that bearest on thy bosom all the beauty, all the might,
Of the yet-unheard, the yet-unseen, whence floweth sound and sight;
Dost thou tremble at the nearness of the time that we are touching?
Doth the whitefire leaping in the stars that lead us scorch thee blind?
Art thou wary of the sly and wishful winds that would be clutching
At the shut heart of the blessing we are bearing to mankind?
Show not! show not!
Let men know not
What is coming. For the mind
Of the world is undefined;
And the dark not yet the daystar doth release.
Wherefore watch ye well, and ward,
Sister, hold ye fast, and guard
The sacred straw
From bruise or flaw,
And the mystic veil from soil or crease,
Whilst, unseen but aware

And awake, we bear
The high gods safe to their home in Greece."

"Sister Opis, sister Opis, I am moving at thy side
In the power that is upon us: I am treading stride for stride
Down the wonder of the world with thee, undaunted by the throng
Of the startling stars that, brightened by the breath of thy clear song,
Give in glory heaven's gladness forth. But O, the way is long
From the distance of the darkness to the distance of the light!
And, like a shipman eying
Along a shoreless sea
That sliding rippled lane the lucid moon hath paven bright,
Which to sunder, and escape from, all the livelong laboring night
His patient keel is trying;
But, with a fond denying,
It doth ever seem to be
Where it first was on the waters, and yet, o'er the waters ever
Gliding silent with the ship is still beside it, so that never
Is that watcher any farther from the light that leaveth dark
The last wave it leapeth out of ere 't is broken by his bark;
So my spirit, striving forward, yet doth never find release
From the still-pursuing splendor of the thoughts that pass in peace,

Passing swift from sweet to sweeter,
Strange to stranger, through completer
Indications of the stature
Of the beautiful in nature,
To the perfect form and feature
Of the godship of this Greece.

"I heard a gryphon yelping for his gold across a dim
Blue frostbitten mountain gully, where the rock-stream would not flow:
I outsped the Arimaspian that was outspeeding him,
Whose one eye, when he beheld me, shrivelled blinded in his brow
With a knowledge premature
Of what, knowing, to endure,
Not yet the gods had granted his incompetence-to-know.
And not even so much sound
As doth lisp around, around,
In a little whisperous whirl of windy snow,
My flitting footstep made,
As it traversed unbetrayed
The silent iron-colored floors of frozen lakes below
Those bitter pale Cimmerian skies,
Whose ghostly suns with blood-red eyes,
Thick wrapt in frosty film, make wan
The whited desert of lean plains,
Where hornless beeves in wooden wains
The Scythian and the Sindian
Drive, streaking, as unheard they go,
The echoless white waste with slow
Dark dotted trains,

As silent as, through light that lies
Lone on the verge of evening, flies
A troop of long-necked cranes.
And the bald-head Argipæan,
Beneath his black bean-tree,
Sat bareheaded in the sun to judge the people, as
I passed.
But to-night from bowers Eubæan
Blow sweet odors up the sea,
And the Grecian beauty breathes into my being
at the last.
Yet I show not,
For I know not,
What is coming to mankind.
White the wheat lies on the faces of the folded
Images:
And other hands
In other lands
Are destined to unbind
The veil of this Invisible by slowly-sweet degrees.
Wherefore aye in watch and ward,
Sister, hold I fast and guard
The sacred straw
From bruise or flaw,
And the mystic veil from soil or crease,
Whilst, awake and aware,
Together we bear
The high gods safe to their home in Greece."

A wind, that all night long in Rhodope,
Waiting release, had crouched with casual thrills
Of power but half repressed, now leaping free,
His kindred from the high Keraunian hills
Called to him athwart the dark Ægean Sea,

And swept from Athos and the rocky fringe
Of many a mountain-builded promontory
Beyond Pallene, those high vapors hoary
That, soon as Morn swings out on silent hinge
Her golden gates against the eastern skies,
Do travel the dim air in search of glory.
Whereat they rose (graybearded companies,
Whose paths above the peakèd mountains are),
Leaving the moonless night upon the wane,
In haste to fill their floating urns with flame,
And midway meet the Light that loves to rise
On Delos, where his mother dwelt. There came
A change across the skies, and in the strain
Of that strange music, that now dropped from far
Fresh, clear, and cold, as drops of driven rain
Dasht on dark summits from the morning star:—

"Art thou near me, Sister Arge?"
"Sister Opis, I am near."
"And dost hear me, Sister Arge?"
"Sister Opis, speak, I hear."

"From the cold to the warm, from the dark to the light,
From the wish to the will, from the part to the whole,
To the deed from the need, to the day from the night,
From the brute in the body to the god in the soul,
Man grows.
For, the gods having first morselled Man into men,
Men by growing together must grow into Man;
Who grows outward at first, to grow inward again,
Thus outgrowing the point whence his first growth began;

Till (who knows ?)
Point by point in successive ascensions, perchance
The high gods, on his being upborne, shall go higher
Up in Heaven, to leave scope for the search of his glance,
And large space for the love in his life to aspire
To the air that feeds fire :
Still, as more and more godlike he grows, to discover
More and more in the godhead, above him forever ;
The wider he reaches, more reachlessness ; over
His highest attained, still a higher to endeavor
In the Ever-near Never."

Light rose in response mild a lovelier voice
Along the morning air, like a spring wind
Whose benediction bids old earth rejoice
Because of violets it is come to find.

" Sister Opis, I hear thee,
And, near thee,
My heart, with thy song in it, glows ;
And the fulness of sweetness o'erflows,
While thy soul from thy lip
All a-tremble doth slip
As a dew-drop in light from a rose."

And, higher thought in higher tone to pour,
The music of that mystic voice intense
Rose on the tingling dark, and more and more
Was felt like light within the listener's sense.

" Blind and mute no more,
As, for ages and ages old,

Upon Time's storm-beaten shore
  It dwelt in the dark and cold
Of error, and shame, and wrong,
  Man's race, erewhile forlorn,
With speech that is now made song,
  And sight that is beauty born,
Shall see, and speak, and be heard;
  And the lion, and wolf, and leopard,
As tame as a mountain herd
  That follows at morn the shepherd,
By a music and a light
  To a fairer land afar,
Charmed out of the caves of night,
  Shall follow man's dawning star;
Where the force, refined to grace,
  Of Strength and Beauty mated
Shall give birth to a lovelier race
  Of men to gods related;
Till there beat in the old brute world
  A human heart that knows
Where the Spirit of Love lies curled
  In all that breathes and blows;
And a peeping face shall flit
  Through the leaves of the forest lone,
And the mountain wells be lit
  By the limbs of a Naiad known,
And the orbs that brighten heaven
  Shall be no nameless glory,
But the beauty and splendor given
  To a breathing human story."

Anon together, like two butterflies
Born of one flower that gave to both its hue,
Which sport around each other in warm skies,

Yet all the while their upward flight pursue
Through summer's liquid lights and melodies,
Those voices twain on intertwinéd wing
Of woven music mounted, hovering: —

"Blessèd art thou, O man, at thy lowest,
O thou lord of the hand and the thought!
For thou livest in that which thou doest,
And thou makest thyself out of naught.
Now to thy cradle we bear thee
The Teachers, the bright, the benign,
That out of earth's dust shall uprear thee
An altar, a temple, a shrine,
And forth of all things that be near thee
(By the touch of a tenderness fine)
To guide, to sustain, and to cheer thee,
Shall summon a Presence Divine.
Beauty, the wave-born, the flowing,
Shall rise, and in rapture give birth
To Love, the man-maker, the glowing
Boy-bringer of Beauty to earth.
Lo! I weigh thee the weight of thy worth.
All things are thine:
All things combine
In a strenuous design
To make thee divine.
Name them, and claim them!
None dare decline
In aught to fulfil
The behest of thy will.
Choose them, and use them!
The moving, and the still,
The upright, the supine,
Take them, and make them

(Both the color and the line)
Ministers all at the marvellous shrine
Of the strong-bodied, spirit-wedded,
Hundred-handed, myriad-headed,
Mighty, wonder-working Skill!

"The wave shall render thee
Its intricate harmony
Of movement multiform, and gliding swerve
Of shadowy curve;
The mould of Music visible, the free
Lip o' the eloquent sea:
The vine shall fix forever
For thee her fond endeavor
Of drooping leaf, and tendril-twine,
To richly deck the rigid line
Of limitary law, that lies
Unseen, endeared by love's disguise:
The milk-white marble pale,
To tell thine eyes the tale
Of what thy thoughts discern
Beyond them, shall avail
Olympian speech to learn;
And, for thy sake, forthwith forego
The formless face of his smooth snow
For novel features, sweet or stern,
To fit thy fancy, gay or grave,
And in unmoved memorial save
The falling leaf, the flowing wave,
From death, that doth their beauty crave:
And, as both stock and stone
To thee their uses lend,
Thou too, in turn, shalt these befriend
With better beauty, not their own;

And every tender slope and turn
Of sumptuous form, well-featured face,
Or pure proportion, pleased to deck
This mortal mould, shall flow to grace
Some calyxed vase, with curling neck,
Fine-eared, or fluted urn.

"Now, therefore, new-grown,
Come forth, and be known,
Thou poor hewer, thou blind-handed breaker
Of wood and of stone!
Henceforth, in thy might, as the maker,
To the ages be shown!
And the gold shall break out into glory,
And the ivory be pallid with awe,
At the frown of the god high and hoary,
That liveth alone in the law
Of himself; when, in splendor strong-zoned,
Zeus, sovran in Elis, sits throned.

"Blesséd art thou, O man! for thou growest
(O thou lord of the thought and the hand!)
In the growth of whatever thou doest,
And the ages await thy command.

"Life's image, born of the brain,
In the form which the hand hath fashioned,
Shall forever unmarred retain
Life's moment the most impassioned;
All power, that in act hath been
Put forth, shall perish never;
And life's beauty once felt and seen
Is life beautified forever."

In that high tone the mingled music shrill
Of those triumphant voices, ceasing, left
The silence tremulous with a solemn thrill,
As one whose troubled sense is sharply cleft
By sudden knowledge of undreamed-of good.
And, for a while, there was no other sound
Than the sea's murmur on the solitude,
And the light winds that sighed and whispered
round
The dawning headlands. Then, with altered tone,
Was poured from the pale hills one voice alone:

"Sister Opis, sister Opis, thou exultest in thy
song;
For to thee the god speaks certainly, and there-
fore thou art strong.
But me a sorrow moveth in the midst of much
delight,
For the grief that 's growing in the joy, the
weakness in the might,
Of this twofold nature, each way growing into
depth and height;
Whereby more strength more strongly feels more
weakness, in despite
Of more strength yet in sight.
For man, from the moment when man
Feels a power in his soul to conceive
Of a power surpassing the span
Of the life he hath power to achieve,
Must be wretched; perceiving, both ways,
The abyss of a boundless Beyond;
With, as more imperfection may gaze
On perfection, more cause to despond.
Evermore must the life of the many,

That in Art is completed alone,
Transcending the mere life of any
One creature, leave hopeless that one.
And no shepherd shall stand on the mountain
As stately as Phœbus the fair;
And no maiden shall move by the fountain
As radiant as Hebe the rare;
And Niobe's marble bereavement,
In anguish made beauty forever,
Shall immortally mock the achievement
Of grief's merely mortal endeavor.
Then say, if thou seest, — for I see not,
What hope is in man that he be not
The architect merely — as, stone
Upon stone, it ascends — of his own
Mortal life's monumental despair?
From insolent heights never ending,
In immutable forms ever fair,
Conception transcending, offending,
And mocking Experience, — declare
What shall comfort the poor life of each,
When, fixt far beyond the soul's reach,
Though confronting the sense, — ever there
In completion, abasht, it must gaze
On the full-imaged life of the All?
What shall reconcile shame? and upraise
To man's greatness mere men, that are small?
Ay me! for man's sake my tears fall,
Not seeing whence comfort to call."

Whereto, in answer, the hill-tops along,
That other voice, clear, confident, and strong: —

"Sister Arge, sister Arge, dost thou falter? But to me

The god hath given certainly to utter what shall
be.
Wherefore listen."

"I am listening, with my spirit turned
to thee."

"List, and see!—
Base wert thou, O man, though thou buildest
Halls higher than ever the emmet,
And poor, though thou purplest and gildest
Thy pomp: a fly's wing would condemn it.
But to measure thy weakness, and know it,
Is the crown of thy strength. Wherefore speak,
And come forth, O consoler! O poet!
Thou whose song giveth strength to the weak.
Thou doer, aye unguessed among
Things done: deceiver of the throng
That 's ignorantly thine; whose life,
Living through all, unheard proceeds
Amid the noise of mortal deeds,
And shapes of passing things, and strife
Of changing times, which, when thy presence
Their emptiness and little strength
Hath filled and interpenetrated
With its own divinest essence,
Grow great and calm, take breadth and length,
And height and depth, and rest related
To those immortal verities
That change not with the changing skies,
And reel not with the rolling years:
Thou Destiny, whose thoughts are seers,
Come forth, controller of the shears,
The spindle, and the rock!

Hero, whose words are victories all,
Enlarge man's life: leave nothing small,
  Inconsequent or fractional:
The world's shut heart unlock.
Do thou with beauty stop the chinks
  And flaws of uncompleted man,
And with music brim the brinks
  Of nature: filling out the plan
Of the life man yearns to live,
  And strives to seize, but never can,
Till thy help to him thou give;
  Putting space within his span.

"Life's flower hath many springs:
  Leaves fallen feed its root:
Camps, nations, courts, and kings
  Murmur, and soon are mute.
But over the bloody plain
  Where a nation's life lies lost,
From the bodies of many slain
  Doth arise but a single ghost.
Nor chance nor change can mar
  The beauty of her pale brows,
Whereon the pilot star
  Of the wandering Future glows:
She, that is all pure essence,
  Can no more suffer wrong:
Men call her name The Presence
  Of the Past made theirs in Song.
And this most beauteous child
  Of a Past that cannot die,
Whose spirit doth reign strong-willed
  O'er the realm of Futurity,
By means of her mighty sons, that are

The makers of man's thought, fair, and far
From the perishing Present's fitful strife,
Upbuildeth the beautiful dome of life;
All thronged with lucid shapes that be
Clothed each in the calm of eternity;
Those mighty memories of mankind,
Whose home is the universal mind.
Wherefore yet I praise man at his lowest,
  Being lord of the living voice.
Hark, O wind, through the reeds where thou
    blowest,
  Pan cometh! I bid thee rejoice.
The ægipans, satyrs, and fauns,
  To his shrill pipe trooping after,
Trample over the lanes and the lawns,
  With timbrel and tipsy laughter:
But after Pan cometh Apollo,
  Whose music is sound made fire,
And the gods and the heroes follow
  The loud twang of his golden lyre."

Down swept a rushing sound, across the lone
And melancholy mountains clothed in cloud,
As of the multitudinous hurrying on
Of unseen feet, and murmurings of a crowd,
With music, cymbals faint, faint flutes; as when
On festal days, with pomp processional,
And minstrelsy, and dancing maids and men,
Some merrymaking city pours through all
Her gaping gates a jubilant swarm; whose sound
Among the humming hills is sometimes heard
Where gorges open, and then shut again,
Sudden, i' the shifting vale, with all its train
Of mirthful tumult manifold, and drowned

In such deep silence that the hooting bird,
That haunts by mountain tarns, is audible
Far off once more, and audible alone,
In the reinstated stillness, with stern tone
Chiding the solitary air. So fell
Down vaporous precipices, soon almost
As heard, those sounds of things unwitnessed lost
Along the dreaming gulfs, and rolled away.
Anon once more, against the dawning day,
The former voices; shrill distinct, as darts
That, clashed against sonorous metal, sing,
Sharp tune; whereto clear echoes from the hearts
Of hollow caves rang response, vibrating: —

"Sister Opis, sister Opis, on a silver wave of song
Sweetly streaming,
Dim as dreaming,
The deep melodies among,
By thy singing,
Bliss is bringing
All my being. Yet prolong
The loved rapture!"

"Listen, Sister!
For my spirit on the throng
Of the ages rushes strong.
When the strong archetypal moulders
Of mortal clay
Have bequeathed to unborn beholders
The forms that stay
Fixt and fast
In the flux of time,
For man's thought, cast
In a mould sublime;

And the few fine Spirits first needed
  To build up the walls of the world
(From the Protoplast freshly proceeded),
  Having, each from his fortress, unfurled
The standard of man's realm, made fuller
  For all men by one man alone, —
Over marble, or music, or color,
  Or language, — are gathered and gone
From the sun's sight, like stars of the morning,
  Lost in level enlargements of light,
Where the world needs no longer their warning
  Or witness to steer through the night,
Then the men that come after, not equal
  In height, but more spacious in span,
Shall combine and complete in the sequel
  Each sublime isolation: and man,
Grown compacter, shall gather together
  His faculties, full-grown before
Each up to the length of its tether,
  But scattered and single of yore.
No piling on Ossa of Pelion,
  Leaving valleys uncultured and lone:
But the whole world in high perihelion,
  Breathing light, shall set broad to the sun!
And for this I praise man, at his lowest,
  Being heir to heights higher than his;
For, when even his march is at slowest,
  He is ever beyond what he is.

"The form of the shining present,
  By the shade of the past controlled,
As the curve of the young moon's crescent
  Is shapen about the old,
In the self-completing orb

Of a life, that in its own light
Doth the shade of itself absorb,
Man lifteth through time's lone night.
In the present his future he feeleth,
Formeth and holdeth it fast,
And himself to himself revealeth
Himself by himself surpast.

"But see! the great light is beginning
Up yonder; with sharp silver thinning
The thick night, and peeling away
The black shell that shut down the day.
Leave we here on the high promontory,
That is toucht at the tops with the glory,
Each great Form, folded fast head and feet,
And swathed in the sweet yellow wheat;
Best befitting for symbol and sign:
For man's first need is merely to live,
His next to make mere life divine;
And the corn-crownéd Ceres must give
The first gift to the god-crownéd shrine.
With the hard hand that hacks out the harvest
From the solid resistance of things,
Poor peasant, a portion thou carvest
Of ease for thy sons that be kings!"

By this, severe cold amber-colored light
Was sharpening the dark edges of the sea:
From shadowy summits, slowly stolen in sight,
Through the still air the voice came, carolling free:

"Come, Sister, come down
The deep meadows unmown!
Down, Sister, deeper and deeper down,

Through the lone bright lands
Not ours, where hands
Happy and fair, in the years' unshown
Of boy and of maiden,
Shall our sepulchres crown,
Flower-decked and gift-laden,
With green myrtle coronals oft.
Light let us stray
Down the valleys away,
And where shadows wave soft
Through dim olive-woods, sighing
With the low undertone
Of a life ever dying,
Ere her crownet of dew the pale cistus hath doffed.
Leave the High Ones alone
And aloft, fitly lying
In the light that lives lonely aloft.
Down! down!"

Whereto, with mimic echo, from a cloud
Brightening upon the impenetrable peak
That his dim head in heaven did highest shroud,
An answering voice far off came faint and weak: —

"Down, down,
And deeper, Sister, and deeper down,
I come, I come
To our long-sought home!
And, lightly stepping, my step unknown,
Not a print, as we pass, ever presses
From the blossoming grasses below.
We, the breath of the morn in our tresses,
And the beam of the morn on our brow!

Nevermore to the fierce wildernesses,
And the hollow rocks heavy with snow,
Nevermore to the storm-beaten beaches,
Whose black gulfs their chafed surges churn
Into bleak foam, the bitter wind bleaches,
Shall our god-guided footsteps return.
But here, at the last, our life reaches
The limit, and drops in the urn,
And passes complete,
At the touch of a hand
Whose touching is sweet,
To a sweeter land."

The louder voice then, with a sudden cry,
Pealed from the lower heights imperatively: —

" Wherefore stir not a straw
From the sacred Awe,
And the mystic Veil neither crush nor crease,
But, awake and aware,
Hid in Delos, there
Leave the High Gods o'erlooking their home,
sweet Greece!"

Whereat both voices, fainter grown, did seem
Strange as the ebbing music of a dream:

" Hush, O hush, within the sense
Of their own wise reticence,
Thoughts too sweet for song to sing
Even where none be listening!
Breathe, O breathe, no sound less light
Than a lizard's startled flight
Through the leaves, when lovers pass

O'er the silent summer grass!
Leave the dreaming world to waken,
Wistful of the mystic numbers
Of the music that hath shaken
With prophetic sound its slumbers.
Let the patient Many fashion
Into common use the true
Substance of the solemn passion
Of the sudden-minded Few.
Stay not, singer! song will stay
Where who sung it sings no more.
Doubt not, doer! love will pay
Life's deed done when life is o'er.
Haste! away, before the day
Show by shadows where we stray!
Violets that are not bowed
By the shadow of a cloud
Laden with midsummer thunder;
Eyes down-lidded in dim sleep,
'Neath whose fringes dare not peep
Any dream that passeth under;
Be, O earth, more still than those,
Where our unseen footstep goes!"

And, like a flock of swallows on swift wing,
Before the falling of the rain in Spring,
Light-wavering o'er a whisperous lowland green;
That suddenly, from none knows whence, are seen,
And in and out the maze of their own making
Inextricably wheel, and wink, and find
And lose themselves, but at the last, forsaking
Their momentary haunt, do leave behind
In the gray light upon the grass beneath

Not any shadow; so the scattered breath
Of those melodious voices, here and there
Along the desultory morning air
Dispersing, left at last within the wind
Not even a wandering echo, as it ceased
Against the startling stillness of the east;
Where now conspicuous, by no cloud confined,
But stern, in steadfast skies, with serious light,
Lay bare the starless forehead of the Dawn.
The sparkle of a golden sandal shined
One moment on the mountain peak. A white
And vaporous hem of eddying vesture, drawn
Across a saffron-colored cliff from sight
Slowly, left all along the mountain lawn,
Among the tawny grass and camomile,
A tremulous streak, soon quenched in day's strong
    smile,
Of waning splendor. Then those mariners all
Rose up amazed, and drew out of the deep
The hookéd anchor, and drove out to sea
Their little bark beneath a shadowy shore.
But, while they set the sail, and plied the oar,
Full-lighted on the heavenly mountain wall
Leaped the large Sunrise, and all round shook free
His flamy wings: when lo! on every steep,
Wrapt with the auroral vapor rolling high,
An august image stood, majestical,
With lifted arm, far off, 'twixt earth and sky.

II.

CRŒSUS AND ADRASTUS.

(Herodotus, i. 35.)

FORTUNE, that walks above the heads of men
I' the rolling clouds, the witless denizen
Of airy Nothing, by Necessity
Among the unsteady Hours with hooded eye,
Subservient to a will not hers, is led:
And, as she passes, oft upon his head
That, underneath heaven's hollowness, doth stand
Highest of men, her loose incertain hand
Lets fall the iron wedge and leaden weight.

Crœsus, the lord of all the Lydian state,
Of men was held the man by Fortune best
With her unheedful blind abundance blest:
Because all winds into his harbors blew
Opulent sails; because his sceptre drew
Out of far lands a majesty immense;
Because to enrich his swol'n magnificence,
The homage of a hundred hills was rolled
Upon a hundred rivers; because gold
And glory made him singular in the smile
O' the seldom-smiling world a little while.
To him, in secret vision, at the deep
Of night, what time Fate walks awake through Sleep,

The gods revealed that, in the coming on
Of times to be, Atys, his best-loved son,
Untimely, in the unripe putting forth
Of his green years, and blossom-promised worth,
By an iron dart must perish.
Then the king,
Long while within himself considering
The dreadful import of the dream, — in fear
Lest any iron javelin, lance, or spear,
Left to the clutch of clumsy Chance, should fall
On Atys, — gave command to gather all
Such weapons out of reach of him he loved,
Safe in a secret chamber far removed.
And, — that the menaced prince no more should take
His wont i' the woods, with baying dogs to break
The rough boar's ambush, nor the lion wound,
Nor flying stag, with dexterous darts, — he found,
And wived to Atys, the most beautiful
Of Lydian women : lovelier than the lull
Of summer eves in lands where Summer fills
With slumbrous light the slopes of snowy hills
Flusht by a fleeting sun. So fair was she
Whose claspéd arms should gentle jailers be
To Crœsus' chiefest treasure.
This being done,
The king was comforted about his son.

But while the nuptial feast, at 'mid of mirth,
O'erflowed with festival the golden girth
Of the king's palace, — while, with fold on fold
Of full delight, the mellow music rolled
From Lydian harps a heaving heaven of sound
In the gorgeous galleries, and garlands crowned

Warm faces in a mist of odors rare, —
There came before the king at unaware
A stranger from beyond the storm-beat sea:
A man pursued by pale Calamity,
With hands polluted; on whose countenance
Was fixed the shadow of foregone mischance.
His slow steps up the hymeneal hall
Struck sounds that sent deep silence on through all
That swarming revel. Music's broken wing
Fluttered and strove against the checked harp string:
And he that poured stood, holding half-way up
The two-eared pitcher o'er the leaf-twined cup,
While the wine wasted: he that served leaned o'er
The savorous fumes of anice-spicèd boar,
With trencher tilted: they whose limbs were dropped
At ease on purple benches, elbow-propped,
Half rose, and, stooping forward, shocked awry
From jostled brows, sloped one way suddenly,
Their slanted crowns, blue-bossed with violet,
Or dropping roses; each with eyes wide-set
In unintelligent wonder on the wan
And melancholy image of that man.
He, moving through the amazement that he caused,
Approached, unbid, the throne of Crœsus; paused,
And there, with groans from inmost anguish brought,
The hospitable-hearted king besought
His hands by the Lydian rite to purify
From taint of blood.
To whom, when presently
He had his asking granted, Crœsus said:

"Whence art thou, stranger? and whose blood hast shed,
That doth so fiercely clamor at the porch
Of Heaven's high halls? What burning wrong doth scorch
Sweet rest from out the record of thy days?"

To whom that other:
"But that Judgment lays
Foundations deeper than Oblivion,
I would my shadow from beneath the sun
Had passed forever; being the most forlorn
Of men! A Phrygian I, and royal-born;
The son of Gordius, son of Midas; who,
Ill-starred! unwittingly my brother slew.
For this, my father from his much-loved face,
And all the happy dwellings of my race,
Me into wide and wandering exile drave:
Whence, flying on the salt white-edgéd wave,
Cast out from comfort unto stars unknown,
My hollow ship, before the north wind blown,
Fate to these shores directed; where I stand
A friendless man, sea-flung on foreign land.
In thus much learn, O king, from whence I came,
And what I am. Adrastus is my name."

The monarch smiled upon him, and replied:

"Thy friends are ours: thy land to ours allied:
If not with kindred, here with kind, thou art.
A frowning fate to bear with smiling heart
Is highest wisdom. In our court remain.
Cease to be sad. Nor tempt the seas again."

So in the Lydian court Adrastus stayed,
Eating the bread of Crœsus : and obeyed
The kindly king, well-pleased to roam no more.

Now, at that time, a horrible wild boar,
By hunger driven from his lair, below
The dells dark-leavéd, lit with golden snow.
Where Mysian Olympus meets the morn,
Made ravage in the land ; despoiled the corn,
The tender vine in many a vineyard tore,
Each sapling sallow olive wounded sore,
And oft, about the little hilly towns
And stony hamlets, where high yellow downs
Pasture, among cold clouds, the mountain goat
That wanders wild from wattled fold remote,
His fierce blood-dripping tusk foul mischief wrought.
For this, the sorely-injured Mysians sought
At many times the ruinous beast to slay ;
But never yet at any time could they
Come nigh him to his hurt. For he, indeed,
Slew many of them, and the rest had need
Of nimble feet in fearful flight to find
Unworthy safety. Thus was ruin joined
To ruin.
Therefore, unto Crœsus now
They sent an embassage ; that he should know
The damage done them by this savage thing ;
Entreating much, moreover, that the king,
With certain of the Lydian youths, would send
Atys, the prince, to help them make an end.
For of all noble youths in Lydian bound
Atys the most high-couraged was renowned,
Nor matched in martial vigor.
Crœsus then,

When he had heard the message of these men,
Made answer to the Mysians :

" For our son,
Ye shall not have him. Think no more upon
That matter. For, indeed, the crescent light
That was newborn to gild his nuptial night
Is yet the unfinished circlet of a moon.
And shall a husband leave a wife so soon,
Ere the first spousal month be sped, to lie
On hill-tops bare, beneath the naked sky,
Neglecting wedlock young, and the sweet due
Of marriage pillows, Mysians, for you ?
But since (touching all else) we love you well
And fain would see the huge beast horrible,
That hath such havoc made of your fair land,
Defeated, we will send a chosen band
Of our best valors ; men that shall not miss
What is to do. Be ye content with this."

But, when the Mysians were therewith content,
The son of Crœsus, hearing these things, went
To Crœsus, and said to him :

" In time past,
Father, or in the chase, or war, thou wast
The first to wish me famous ; who dost now
To me forbid the javelin and the bow.
Wherefore ? For yet I deem that thou hast not
In me detected any taint or spot
Of fear, dishonoring one to honor born.
Yet think how all men from henceforth must scorn
Thy son, whom, being thy son, they should revere,
In him revering thee, when I appear
Among them in the agora : I alone
Of all men missing honor to be won

From this adventure! For what sort of a man
To the coarse general (that is quick to scan
Faults in superior natures) shall I seem?
Or what to my fair wife? How shall she deem
Henceforth of him, who in her white arms lay
No less than as a god but yesterday?
Wherefore, lest I some memorable deed
Now miss to do, I pray thy leave to lead
The honorable ardors of this chase,
True to my noble name and princely place;
Or, this denied, vouchsafe, at least, to say
For what just cause I must remain away.
Since I, in all things, would my heart convince
The king must needs be wiser than the prince."

But Crœsus, weeping, answered:
"Not, my son,
Because in thee aught unbecoming done
Displeased me, nor without sad reason just,
And strict constraint to do what needs I must
(Not what I would, if what I would might be!)
Have I thus acted. For there came to me
A vision from the gods, upon my bed,
In the deep middle of the night, which said
That in the days at hand, an iron dart
Thee from my love, and from thy life, must part.
For this, thy marriage have I hastened on:
That, with occasion due, thou shouldst, my son,
Awhile withhold thee from thy wont to seek
The haunts of lions, or with dogs to break
The rough boar's ambush in the rooty earth,
But rest, companioned, by the pillared hearth,
To one new-wedded a befitting place:
For this, did I forbid thee to the chase:

For this . . . . O stay, my son, by thy fair wife,
And, in prolonging thine, prolong my life!"

And his son answered:
"Wisely, since the dream
Came from the all-wise gods, as I must deem,
Wisely, dear head, and kindly, hast thou done;
Thus, with forethoughted care, to hold thy son
Back from the far-seen coming of the wave
Of Fate, — if him forethoughted care could save!
But I, indeed, as touching this same chase,
Can see no cause for fear. In every place
Death's footsteps fall. Nor triple-bolted gate,
Nor brazen wall, can shut from man his fate.
Yet, had the vision prophesied to me
That, or by tooth, or tusk, my death should be,
I had been well content to stay at home;
Leaving the coming hour, at least to come
By me not rashly met in middle way.
But since 't was said an iron dart must slay
Me, to black death appointed, I might fear
An iron dart as well, though staying here,
As there, in open field, among my friends.
For who can lock his life up at all ends
From charméd Chance, that walks invisibly
Among us, to elude the dragon eye
Of Policy, and the stretched hand of Care?
Wherefore, I pray thee yet that I may share
What honor from this hunt is to be won,
Before death find me. Since a man may shun
Honor, yet shunning honor all he can,
He shuns not Death, which finds out every man."

Then Crœsus, overcome, not satisfied,

From under moistened eyelids, doubtful, eyed
The impatient flushing in the brightened cheek
Of Atys. And, because his heart was weak
From its vague fears to shape foundation fast
For judgment, "Since, my son," he sighed at last,
"My mind, though unconvinced, thy words have
shaked,
Do as thou wilt."
But, like a man new-waked
From evil dreams, who longs for any light
To break the no-more-tolerable night,
Soon as, far off in the purple corridor,
The sandal clicking on the marble floor
Ceased to be heard, and he was all alone,
And knew that Atys to the chase was gone,
He started up in a great discontent
Of his own thoughts, and for Adrastus sent.
To whom the monarch thus his mind expressed:

"Adrastus, since, not only as my guest
But as my friend, thou hast to me been dear,
If aught of natural piety, and the fear
Of Zeus, whom I by hospitable rites
Have honored, honoring thee, thy heart delights
To harbor, heed thou well my words. For I,
When thou, pursued by pale Calamity,
Didst come before me, thee, upbraiding not,
Did purify, and, as a man no spot
Of blood attainted, to my hearth received,
And there with ministering hand relieved.
Now, therefore, follow to the chase my son,
Nor leave him ever till the chase be done;
His guardian be; prevent him in the way,
And let no skulking villain lurk to slay

The son of him that hath befriended thee.
Moreover, for thine own sake, thou shouldst be
Of this adventure; so, to signalize
A noble name by feats of fair emprise;
Since thy forefathers of such feats had praise,
And thou art in the vigor of thy days."

Adrastus answered:
"For no cause but this
(Since Crœsus' wish unto Adrastus is
Sacred as law delivered from above)
In this adventure had I sought to move.
For 't is not fit that such a man as I,
Under the shadow of adversity,
Should with his prosperous compeers resort;
And, not desiring this, from martial sport
Among the Lydian youths, with spear or bow,
I have till now withheld myself. But now,
Since I am bid by him I must obey,
Bound to requite in whatsoe'er I may
Kindness received, this chase I will not shun.
Thou, therefore, rest assured thy royal son,
Dear Paramount, so far as lies in me,
His guardian, shall unharmed return to thee."

Meanwhile, the huntsmen had with leathern thongs
The lean hounds leashed, and all that fair belongs
To royal chase appointed, as was fit;
With pious rites around the altar, lit
To solemn Cybele, at whose great shrines
On wooded Ida, 'mid the windy pines,
Or Tmolus, oft the Sardian, to invoke
The mighty Mother, bade the black sheep smoke;
And Artemis, the silver-crescented,

Adoring whom, a white kid's blood was shed,
And crowns of scarlet poppies, intermixed
With dittany, among the columns fixed,
Or hung, fresh-gathered, the high stones upon.

And now the Lydian youths (with whom the son
Of Crœsus and the Phrygian stranger) blew
The brazen bugles, till the drops of dew
Danced in the drowsy hollows of the wood;
And the unseen things that haunt by fell and flood,
Roused by the clanging echoes out of rest,
Shouted from misty lands, and, trampling, pressed
Through glimmering intervals of greenness cold,
To hang in flying laughters manifold
Upon the march of that blithe company:
Great-hearted hunters all, with quivered thigh,
And spear on shoulder propped, in buskins brown
Brushing the honey-meal and yellow down
From the high-flowering weed, whilst, in their rear,
The great drums throbbed low thunder, and the clear
Short-sounding cymbals sung; until they came
To large Olympus, where the amber flame
Of morn, new-risen, was spreaded broad, and still.
There, for the ruinous beast they searched, until
They found him, with the dew upon his flank,
Couched in a hollow cold, beneath the dank
Roots of a fallen oak, thick-roofèd, dim.
And, having narrowly encircled him,
They hurled their javelins at him. With the rest
That stranger (he that was King Crœsus' guest,
The Phrygian, named Adrastus, purified
Of murder by the monarch), when he spied

The monster, by the dogs' tenacious bite
And smart of clinging steel, now maddened quite,
Making towards him, — hurled against the boar:
Which, missing, by mischance he wounded sore
Atys; through whose gashed body, with a groan
The quick life rushed.
Thus fates, in vain foreknown,
Were suddenly accomplished. For those Powers
That spin, and snap, the threads of mortal hours,
Had willed that Crœsus nevermore should hear
The voice of Atys; unto him more dear
Than fondest echo to forlornest hill
In lonesome lands, more sweet than sweetest rill,
Through shadowy mountain meadows murmuring cold,
To panting herds: nor evermore behold
The face of Atys; unto him more fair
Than mellow sunlight and the summer air
To sick men waking healed. Now, therefore, one,
Having beheld the fate of the king's son,
Fled back to Sardis, and to Crœsus said
What he had seen: — how that a javelin, sped
By that ill-fated hand, to nothing good
Predestined, from the blot of brother's blood
By Crœsus purified, yet all in vain,
Since still to bloodshed doomed, — had Atys slain,
Fulfilling fates predicted.
Crœsus then,
Believing that he was of living men
Most miserable, who had purified,
Himself, the hand by second slaughter dyed
In the dear blood of his much-mourned-for son
(Since by his own deed was he now undone)
Uplifted hands to Heaven, and vengeance claimed

Of Zeus, the Expiator; whom he named
By double title, to make doubly strong
A twofold curse upon a twofold wrong:
As God of Hospitality, — since he
That was his guest had proved his enemy;
As God of Private Friendship, — since the man
That slew his son was his son's guardian,
To whom himself the sacred charge did give.

Therefore he prayed, "Let not Adrastus live!"

But, while he prayed, a noise of mourning rose
Among the flinty courts: and, followed close
Out of the narrow streets by a dense throng
Of people weeping, slowly moved along
The Lydian hunters bearing up the bier
Of Atys, strewn with branches; in whose rear,
Down-headed, as a man that bears the weight
Of some enormous and excessive fate,
The slayer walked.
Full slowly had they come,
With steps that ever slackened nearer home,
And heavier evermore their burden seemed,
As ever longer round their footsteps streamed
The woful crowd; and evermore they thought
Sadlier on him to whom they sadly brought
His hope in ruins. When they reached the gate
The western sky was all on flame. Stretched straight
Through a thick amber haze Adrastus saw,
As in a trance of supernatural awe,
The high slant street; that lengthened on, and on,
And up, and up, until it touched the sun,
And there fell off into a field of flame.

He knew that he was bearing his last shame;
And all the men and women, swarming dim
Along the misty light, were made to him
Shadows, and things of air, for all his mind
Was passed beyond them. So, with heart resigned
To its surpassing sorrow, he bowed down
His head, and followed up the columned town
The bier of Atys, without any care
Of what might come: because supreme despair
Had taken out the substance from the show
Of the world's business, and his thoughts were now
In a great silence, which no mortal speech,
Kind or unkind, might any longer reach.
Meanwhile, with melancholy footsteps slow,
Slow footsteps hindered by the general woe,
Those hunters mount the murmurous marble stair
To the king's palace.
He himself stood there
To meet them; knowing why they came; with eyes
Impatiently defiant of surprise.
But, when they set their burden down before
The father of him murdered whom they bore;
And, when the inward-moaning monarch flung
His body on the branchèd bier, — there hung
With murmurings meaningless, and dabbled vest
Soaked in the dear blood sobbing from the breast
Of his slain son, — there, dragged along the flint
His bruisèd knees; and crushed, beneath the print
Of passionate lips, groans choked in kisses close,
Poured idly on those eyelids meek, and those
White lips that aye such cruel coldness kept,
For all the hot love on them kist and wept;
And when the miserable wife, whom now

The sudden hubbub from the courts below
Had pierced to, through the swiftly-emptied house,
Flew forth, and, kneeling o'er her slaughtered
spouse,
Beat with wild hands her breast, and tore her hair,
And cried out, " Where, you unjust gods, O where,
Between the stubborn earth and stolid sky,
Was found the fault of my felicity ?
That such a cruel deed should have been done
Under high heaven, beneath the pleasant sun ! "
Then he, that was the cause of that wide woe,
Came forth before the corpse, and, kneeling low,
Stretched out sad hands to Crœsus ; upon whom
He called, to execute the righteous doom
Of death on him, deserving life no more.

When, therefore, Crœsus heard this, he forbore
To groan against the edge of his own fate ;
But judged most miserable that man's state
Who, evil meaning not, had evil done, —
First having slain his brother, then the son
Of him that gave him hospitality.
So, letting sink a slowly-softened eye
To settle on Adrastus, who yet knelt
Before him, his hard thoughts began to melt,
And he was moved in mind to tolerate
The greatness of his grief ; which, being less great
Than his that caused it, stood in check, to make
This tolerable, too.
Sadly he spake :
" To me," he said, " thou hast requital made,
Most miserable man ! on thine own head
Invoking death. Wherefore, I doom thee not.
Nor deem thy hand hath this disastrous lot

From the dark urn down-shaken. Rather, he,
That unknown god, whoever he may be,
That long ago foreshadowed this worst hour,
Hath thus compelled it to us. Some veiled Power
Walks in our midst, and moves us to strange ends.
Our wills are Heaven's, and we what Heaven
intends."
Then Crœsus caused to be upheaved foursquare
A mount of milk-white marble; and did there
In trophied urn the holy ashes heap
Of his loved Atys. And, that fame should keep
Unperished all the prince's early glory,
Large tablets wrought he, rough with this sad story.

But when the solemn-footed funeral,
With martial music, from the marble wall
Flowed off, and fell asunder in far fields;
And silenced was the clang of jostling shields,
And the sonorous-throated trumpet mute,
And mute the shrill-voiced melancholy flute;
What time Orion in the west began
Over the thin edge of the ocean
To set a shining foot, and dark night fell;
Then, judging life to be intolerable,
The son of Gordius sharply made short end
Of long mischance: and, calling death his friend,
He, self-condemned to darkness, in the gloom
And stillness, slew himself upon the tomb.
This to Adrastus was the end of tears.

But Crœsus mourned for Atys many years.

III.

GYGES AND CANDAULES.

(Herodotus, i. 8.)

I.

FOR the lute whereon Apollo played
At Love's own marriage! or the ecstatic string
That ransomed thy too-soon-recaptured shade,
Renowned Eurydice, from Hell's hard king!
O for one warbled strain of those that made
Ulysses long to leave his voyaging,
That in my song might now be felt and seen
The beauty rare of King Candaules' Queen!

II.

In old Mœonian Lydia, lord of all
Between the blue sea-floors and snowy brows
Of ancient Tmolus, where, by many a wall
Red with the bloom of ripe pomegranate boughs,
From bridge to bridge, the Golden Tide did fall
Through silken Sardis, with his bright-haired spouse
Dwelt that soft monarch, slave to her sweet eyes,
In gardens green 'neath costly canopies.

III.

For he was so enamoured of his wife,
So sunk in love's soft sea without a shore,

That he no longer lived save in the life
  Which her full-flowing loveliness did pour
On his dim passion : all his thoughts were rife
  With her red kisses : ever he forbore
State business, and let all things fall asleep
That he might dream, and dream, of beauty deep.

IV.

There was no sweetness under the sweet sky
  That to the heart-sick king was half so sweet
As all the languorous summer days to lie,
  Faint as a fallen rose-leaf, at her feet ;
To loose his spirit o'er her in a sigh ;
  And feel, like sunny light and odorous heat,
The bounteous influence of her looks and lips,
And touchings fine of her faint finger-tips.

V.

And he would break from solemn council hall,
  To breathe within the comfort of her face ;
And he would steal from flaring festival,
  To sit within her smile in private place ;
And oft in midst of grave discourse would fall
  To musing mute upon her matchless grace,
Then hurl wild words of passion into air,
Vaunting her perfect limbs and lustrous hair.

VI.

But oftenest he with Gyges would discuss
  Her unimaginable excellence ;
— Gyges, his friend, the son of Dascylus,
  A man in honor, and of soberest sense

To disapprove the over-garrulous
  Ill-counselled king; whom he, with deference,
Rebuked not seldom, pacing pleasant hours
Among the palace halls and garden bowers.

VII.

Yet this Candaules, in his foolishness,
  (Mad as a man foredoomed to misery!)
Was angered that his friend should aye repress,
  With slant cold speech, his fervid ecstasy.
And once he said, "But you would wonder less,
  Since man's ear is less credulous than his eye,
That I so boast the beauty of my Queen,
If you her unrobed whiteness once had seen."

VIII.

But Gyges cried: "Forbid it, gods on high,
  That I should see a sight to shame my king!
For woman's robe is woman's modesty.
  Surely, a man should only heed the thing
Which only him concerns. And therefore I,
  That would my Queen to no dishonor bring,
This wisdom from the words of sages spell:
'Let no man wish what is to no man well.'"

IX.

This Gyges answered; and forevermore,
  Fearing lest harm unto himself should be,
The foolish king with cautious words forbore;
  But evermore the foolish king, for he
Was as a man the Nymphs have frenzied, swore
  That his too-much-mistrusting friend should see
The thing he would not. Therefore he replied:
"Have thou no fear lest mischief hence betide.

X.

"Her shalt thou see, thyself by her unseen;
  For in the purple draperies of the door,
By night, what time the unsuspecting queen
  Lone, as her wont is when our cups flow o'er,
Moves to the nuptial couch, behind the screen
  Of broidered Tyrian that is drawn before
The inner portal, thou, close-hid, shalt see
Her smooth-limbed beauty breathing bare to thee.

XI.

"Fast by the royal couch forever stands,
  Under a silver lamp, a golden chair;
And, when she comes, she with her own white hands
  Lays down her light of gorgeous garments there;
And smoothly slips from out their jewelled bands
  Her lustrous shoulders; and beams shining fair
In the amazéd mirror, ere is slid
Her snowy sweetness 'neath the coverlid."

XII.

Then Gyges, when he found not any way
  The monarch's mad design to set aside,
With groaning heart prepared him to obey,
  Though cursing deep his king's unkingly pride.
And, when night came, from out the banquet they
  With guilty steps, like stealthy ghosts, did glide
Through wondering chambers dim with woven dyes,
And listening lengths of empty galleries.

XIII.

Thus to the nuptial chamber did they steal.
  And in the portal's purple curtains there

The king himself did Gyges close conceal,
  And bade him watch behind the golden chair
Whereby the queen her beauty should reveal.
  Then to the banquet back, without a care,
Went King Candaules, pleased with folly done;
And Gyges with his thoughts was left alone.

XIV.

And first self-scorn shut all his sullen sense
  Within himself: but soon the odors sweet,
Streamed from the misty lamps, and that intense
  Rich-scented silence, seeming to entreat
Some sound to ease its sumptuous somnolence,
  Lured out his thoughts, and made his pulses beat
With wondrous expectation. The dim place
Seemed aching to be filled up by her face.

XV.

Meanwhile, the music out of distant halls
  Hummed like the inland sound of hid sea-shores,
And ghostly laughters lapsed at intervals
  Along the faint-lit, cold-walled corridors;
And portals oped and shut, and then footfalls
  That wandered near, and, over other floors
To other silence, wandered off again,
Kept up continual throbbing in his brain.

XVI.

At length, deep-down the opposing gallery,
  From out the long-drawn darkness flashed a light;
And, peering from his purple privacy,
  He spied, with red gold bound and robed in white,

Sole as the first star in a sleepy sky,
   That, while men watch it, grows more large and bright,
The slow queen sweeping down the lucid floor;
And in her hand a silver lamp she bore.

XVII.

Before her, coming, floated a faint fear
   Into his heart who watched her whiteness move
Swan-soft along the lamp-lit marble clear,
   And, lingering o'er her in the beams above,
The winged and folded shadow shift and veer,
   Her airy follower, fraught with fretful love.
Through all his shaken senses rose vague heat
From the sweet sounding of her sandalled feet.

XVIII.

Anon, she entered, and her lamp down-laid
   By the smooth-metalled mirror; and awhile
Stood, slanting low the glory of her head,
   And dipped her full face in its own warm smile;
Then looked she sidelong through one loosened braid
   Of her rich hair, as though she would beguile
Some love-sick spirit on the air to linger,
Twining a gold curl round her glowing finger.

XIX.

But soon she all that twisted gold outshook,
   Till over either shining shoulder streamed
The sudden splendor; and began to unhook
   From those white slopes the buckled gems that beamed

Deep in the mirror's kindling dark, which took
Her mellow image to itself, and gleamed
With soft surprises, and grew bright and warm
With the delicious phantom of her form.

XX.

Her Gyges watched, as one that helpless hears
The cataract call him downward. His heart made
Such passionate pealing in his fluttered ears,
That by his fear he feared to be betrayed.
And, but that ever greater with his fears
His raptures grew, he had not so long stayed;
But, having stayed so long, he still must stay,
And, having looked, he may not look away.

XXI.

Last, she with listless, long-delaying hand
The golden sandals loosed from her white feet,
And loosed from her warm waist the golden band.
The milk-white tunic slided off its sweet
Snow-surfaced slope, and left half bare her bland
Full-orbéd breast. But, in the fainting heat
Of his bewildered heart and fevered sight,
Here Gyges in the curtain groaned outright.

XXII.

She started, as a Nymph of Dian's train,
Surprised, when bathing blithe in forest pool,
By some chance-straggler from the purple plain,
Ere she, quick-flashing through the fern-fringed cool,
Her golden darts can from the green weed gain,
Wherewith to pierce the rash low-fronted fool;

And where he cowered, she, in superb surprise,
Levelled the lustres of her angry eyes.

XXIII.

Then, more with wrath than shame, from breast to brow
  Each snowy surface passed to rosy red,
The rosy redness passed again to snow;
  Scornful she sprang into the purple bed,
And plunged her globed and gleaming limbs below
  Their silken-fringèd sheath. Forth Gyges fled,
As from the god profaned some mad wretch flies,
Stricken and scorched, beneath indignant skies.

XXIV.

All down the hollow gallery, after him
  The loud stones shouted at his heels: behind
The unseen Fury, sailing fast through dim
  And dreadful space, breathed like a burning wind
Upon his hair: swift fire in every limb
  Seethed up and down: night's blackness broke and shined
All round with restless eddyings of the glare
Of that strong vision, flooding the hot air.

XXV.

Nor did he, chased by stony echoes, mark
  The silly-smiling king, with tumbled wreath,
Stretch hands wine-stained to stay him in the dark,
  And waft wild whispers thick on heated breath
To win him back. More desperate than the bark
  Unruddered in the storm, and blind as death,
He rushed to waste himself in some unknown
Mad morrow, from that wicked midnight grown.

XXVI.

But when at last clear-crested Dawn upbroke
The seeming-endless trouble of that night,
And Gyges out of sleepless dream half woke
To wonder at himself, and loathe the light,
And groan beneath the unaccustomed yoke
Of wrong recalled, whilst yet on his sick sight
Swam floating gleams of all that glory seen,
And the wished image of the much-wronged Queen,

XXVII.

Even then, whilst smouldering fancy strove, like flame
Choked under kindled weeds, some rainy night
Leaves moist at morn, a sudden summons came
From her whose eyes still scorched him. O, what might
Of dreadful dearness now was in that name,
To mingle sick dismay with mad delight,
And O, with what shamed knowledge now must he
Loathe to be seen by whom he longs to see!

XXVIII.

Unconscious by what power his powerless feet
Were moved within the light of her deep eyes,
He sank beneath them, smitten by the heat
Of their slow scorn; and, poured in agonies
Upon the pavement, did not dare to meet
Looks that grew large and larger, to comprise
The slowly-widening circle of some doom
That deepened ever in their sultry gloom.

XXIX.

Long while she spake not; and through every limb
He felt the silence straining at his heart;
Whilst her remorseless eye, still searching him,
Went to its aim like a dividing dart:
But still faint nearness to the fragrant rim
Of her warm robe dissolved his inmost smart
In dear delight, and still in sumptuous dread
Swift lives of joy seemed dying. Then she said:

XXX.

"Rise! and remember that thou *wast* a man,
Though most unmanly hast thou shamed in thee
Earth's universal manhood. Dare to scan
The monstrous measure of thy wrong to me,
Then find whatever expiation can
Make life not all intolerable. We
Are made one shame together. I that bear,
And thou that didst, this wrong, this wrong must share."

XXXI.

But he, that longed into her arms to leap,
And, lost in too-completed life, die there,
Swift as a fountain flashes from the deep
Up into sudden sunshine and sweet air,
Sprang, shivering, to his height; and, from its steep
And restless poise 'twixt rapture and despair,
His long-pent passion overflowed, and he
His full heart, gushing into speech, set free.

XXXII.

Then, when he flung into fierce words and few
Recital of the monarch's mandate base,

Wherewith he strove, and strove in vain, there grew
   Strange anguish in the changes of her face.
"Enough it seemed," so moaned she, "when I knew
   Myself, though most unmeriting disgrace,
The fool of outrage. Must a husband's name
Stay ever at the summit of my shame?

XXXIII.

"Yet, half my knowledge of the king divined
   In last midnight's intolerable deed
The ignominious madness of his mind.
   And, but that Nature would so sharply plead
With that unnatural thought, all human kind
   (For such wide warrant such wild wrong must need!)
Of human kindness had seemed emptied quite,
Since love could in such loathly deed delight.

XXXIV.

"For thou hast seen what, so to have been seen,
   Leaves an eternal blush between us twain.
My blood yet burns where'er thine eyes have been:
   And insult unavenged in every vein
Makes memory mad. Me miserable Queen!
   Where shall I turn? To whom do I complain?"
"Nay but," said Gyges, "injured Beauty's child,
Indignant Love, slew him whose gaze defiled

XXXV.

"His mother's image. That wrong-doer lives
   No more in me, that am Love's votary all!"

"Yea, so?" she answered. "But the king survives,
And this round base of earth is made too small
To hold such shameless husbands with shamed wives.
The very stones beneath men's heels will call
Disgrace on things so graceless, and express
Scorn of this king of all unkingliness!

XXXVI.

"But words waste anger weakly. Therefore choose:
There is no room beneath the all-circling sun
For me, and thee, and him, wherein to lose
The knowledge of the thing which hath been done.
Wherefore to us naught rests but to refuse
To live ourselves, or not let him live on.
Judge thou for both. Die, and I follow thee:
Or, slaying him, live on sole lord of me."

XXXVII.

She ceased with a long sigh; and looked, less scorn
Than sad self-pity, and dejection deep,
Lowering faint eyelids over eyes forlorn.
But Gyges cried: "O that the tomb should keep
In that oblivious night, which hath no morn
To call obstruction cold from senseless sleep,
The silenced sweetness of so fair a face,
And no breath leave of all its breathing grace!

XXXVIII.

"Or that those lustrous limbs should ever fade
To fleeting shadow by the lampless shore

Of Orcus, or that lovely form be laid
In urnéd ashes to be seen no more!
But might the half of this dear debt be paid
By hecatombs of lives and seas of gore,
And had the king a hundred lives to lose,
To reach thee through them all I still must choose!"

XXXIX.

She mused a little; and her intricate eyes,
Orb within orb, grew dark with cruel light.
Then she said slowly: "On the place he dies
Where he designed dishonor yesternight.
But we must risk no rescue, hear no cries;
Sleeping, we slay him swiftly. Briefest fight
With fate is safest counsel. That must be
This night. The headless kingdom falls to thee,

XL.

"To thee whatever rests of woman here
Not made the food of Furies such as rise
From deeds like this. And so, from year to year,
We two must learn to bear each other's eyes;
Nay, cling the closer to shut out pale Fear,
And smother Horror up in Love's disguise.
For never now for us, ah nevermore,
Love's chaste auroras! Dewy dawn is o'er.

XLI.

"This sun of passion, fed with guilty fire,
Leaps blood-red from the womb of blackest night.
Yet call it lovely names! I must desire
Thy love, and love thee, ay in scorn's despite!

Since my hate help of thy hate doth require.
It were less base to be united quite
Than in this shameful nearness to remain,
One in dishonor, though in honor twain.

XLII.

"So kiss this crime off!" Suddenly she fell,
A blinding gush of beauty upon his breast.
Thereafter all day long, in surge and swell
Of whirling thoughts, he chased his own unrest
About wild places, till heaven's purple bell
Was dropt with stars, and reddened round the west;
Then in dark precincts, where the palace shone
New-lit, he paced the impatient hours alone.

XLIII.

Ere midnight, through the dusky doors he slid,
Drawn like an evil dream adown the dark;
And in the penetralian purples hid
His wicked knife, and crouched where he might mark
The stealthy signal, which his steps should bid
To their bad goal; and soon from slumber stark
The King's hard breathing on the silence spread,
And the Queen beckoned from the treacherous bed.

XLIV.

There, bent beneath the winking lamp, those two,
With hearts hard-edged as was their glittering knife,
The senseless King in silken slumber slew,
And, with no moan, from his misuséd life

He fleeted down to Orcus. Then they drew
The dead reluctant weight, through silence rife
With horror, o'er the soaked and slippery floor,
And dropped the blood-red ruin at the door.

XLV.

So died Candaules, slain for deed obscene:
So fell the Heracleidæ's fated tree:
So Gyges took the kingdom and the Queen:
So wrong was heaped on wrong, till Fate should be
Accomplished. But, by Heaven's high Justice seen,
Not unjudged went the deed. For when, to free
The realm from that usurping hand, men rose,
And shook the throne, and added woes to woes,

XLVI.

The god at Delphi sentence strict proclaimed:
That crown and queen to Gyges should belong,
Since queen and crown the murdered King had shamed;
Albeit, because wrong is not healed by wrong,
Therefore sharp retribution Fate had framed
Far in the folded years, and curses strong
To plague the cankered brood as yet unbred
From the base getting of that guilty bed.

END OF BOOK I.

BOOK II.

IMPERANTE TIBERIO.

THANATOS ATHANATOU.

"THAT was enough which long ago, while we were yet at Carthage, Nebridius used to propound, at which all we that heard it were staggered: — 'That said nation of darkness which the Manichees are wont to set as an opposing mass over against Thee, what could it have done unto Thee, hadst Thou refused to fight with it? For if they answered, "It would have done Thee some hurt," then shouldst Thou be subject to injury and corruption: but if it could do Thee no hurt, there was no reason brought for Thy fighting with it; and fighting in such wise as that a certain portion or member of Thee, or offspring of Thy very Substance, should be mingled with opposed powers and natures not created by Thee, and be by them so far corrupted and changed to the worse, as to be turned from happiness to misery, and need assistance whereby it might be extricated and purified: and that this offspring of Thy Substance was the soul, which, being enthralled, defiled, corrupted, Thy Word, free, pure, and whole, might relieve; that Word Itself being still corruptible, because It was of one and the same Substance. So then, should they affirm Thee, whatsoever Thou art, that is, Thy Substance, whereby Thou art, to be incorruptible, then were all these sayings false and execrable; but, if corruptible, the very statement showed it to be false and revolting.' " — *Confessions of S. Augustine*, B. VII. (ii.) 3.

"I set now before the sight of my spirit the whole creation, whatsoever we can see therein (as sea, earth, air, stars, trees, mortal creatures); yea, and whatever in it we do not see, as the firmament of heaven, all angels moreover, and the spiritual inhabitants thereof." . . . . "And I said, Behold God, and behold what God hath created . . . . both Creator and created, all are good. Whence, then, is Evil?" — *Idem.* (v.) 7. "O Truth who art Eternity! and Love who art Truth! and Eternity who art Love!" — *Idem.* (x.) 16.

THANATOS ATHANATOU.*

The Ninth Hour. — Darkness over Calvary.

VOICES FROM ABOVE.

OW long, O Lord, our God ?

VOICES FROM BENEATH.

O Lord, how long ?
[*A pause.*

VOICES FROM ABOVE AND BENEATH.

No answer yet ? — Woe ! woe ! no answer yet !

SPIRITS (*sinking*).

Wild in the windless dark, what sullen song
Rolls this way from the waste ? Our wings be wet
With dismal dews, bloody and salt.

* The Latin rhymes with which this poem is interspersed have not been introduced whimsically, but as the simplest means of giving to monastic sentiment a language plainly distinguishable from that of the other utterances amongst which the voice of it is here occasionally audible.

SPIRITS (*rising*).

The strong
Grief o' the gray old Earth these drops doth sweat.
The moan of old Earth's wrong
Mounts ; and we mount with it.

A VOICE FROM THE EARTH.

I have nourished my numbers of nations
On a hope that hath never been blest:
And the ghosts of my gone generations
Vex me yet with reproachful unrest.
Worn by long unrequited endeavor,
As I roll through my ages of pain,
I have listened, I listen forever,
For a word that is waited in vain!

AN ECHO.

In vain!

A VOICE FROM THE EARTH.

In temple and palace
The bread and the chalice,
Bitter with brotherless pride,
Are eaten and drunken by Murder and Malice
Crowned, mitred, and mantled, and magnified,
While brute-born Hunger, in hovel and den,
Is smiting and biting the bones of men
In whose bodies their souls have died.
One Misery goeth in gold:
And one Misery goeth acold:
And there is no difference beside,
However their dust be drest:
For the flourishing Evil is sad,
Because it is Evil at best:

And the fading Good is not glad,
  Because it is Good opprest:
And their wretchedness knoweth no rest
  From a hope that is ever belied
In a blessing not ever possest.
The children cry at the birth,
  Buds cursing a cankered stem!
Shall they live or die? What strength have I,
  The mother of miseries, Earth,
    To bear, or to bury them?
From pitiless city to city,
Passion hath hunted Pity:
    Love feedeth his funeral pyre
    On the flame of his own heart's fire:
My altars gurgle with groans,
Soaked black are my temple stones
  With the blood of my whitest ones.
    Surely, surely, O Lord,
    It is time to utter the word,
  And deliver Thyself, and Thy sons.

AN ECHO.

Deliver Thyself and Thy sons!

VOICES FROM HUMANITY.

Tristis nostra est conditio:
Qui parentis, ab initio,
Protoplasti vim in vitio,
Dum spiramus, propagamus
Usque ad finem hominum.
Nec suplicio nec exitio
Nostra subtrahit petitio
Multum quidem nos luentes,

Ob parentes, heu! solventes
Dirum debitum hominum.
Prima mali labes crescit:
Unde hominum marcescit
Genus omne. Sicut fumus
Fugit dies. Ægri sumus:
Cor humanum nihil corrigit:
Nemo nobis manum porrigit:
Quin et etiam vincit fortis
Inexpletæ hasta mortis
Dominorum Dominum.

VOICES FROM THE GRAVE.

Of yesterday's joy and its sorrow,
Of the hopes and the fears of to-morrow,
Of misery, madness, and mirth,
Of the bright and the sable spheres
Where the treasures of space are stored,
Of the wonderful world they engirth,
Azure-roofed, emerald-floored,
Of the monuments Memory rears,
And Pride, with a gory sword,
Graves, forging the name of Worth,
Of the scrolls of singers and seers
With the words of promise scored,
Words written to lull the pain
Of Doubt, from Doubt's dictating,
We have sought, and sought again,
The meaning of Life and of Birth.
We have waited, — waited in vain,
For an answer, a token, a word;
Waited, — waited for years,
Waiting, weeping, and waiting,

Till Death, to be rid of our tears,
Hid us under this handful of earth,
Where still the old hopes, the old fears,
Wait in vain for an answer, O Lord.

AN ECHO.

Answer, O Lord!

A VOICE FROM THE SHADOW OF DEATH.

Mortui non laudabunt te,
Neque in infernum
Qui descendunt, Domine!
Exibit nam spiritus:
Revertetur animus
Subter humum. Venit hora:
Sistit opus: silent ora:
Non auditur vox clamantis:
Non respondet cor amantis:
Et amores et labores
Pereunt in eternum!

A VOICE FROM THE SEA.

Slave of the Spirit of Might
Have I been in my own despite,
For ages, and ages;
But a memory yet of a ruined right
To a something lost of divine delight
Through my mid-inmost rages
For ages, for ages!
I have struck with a struggling shoulder
The sides of this stubborn star,
Till old promontories, older
Than its oldest memories are,

Began to crumble and moulder
And drop under my prison bar.
I have tumbled my sands and shells
Over cities and citadels;
Through ages and ages,
Ever moving, moaning ever;
Ever seeking, finding never,
Answer to the deep endeavor
Of the spirit that in me dwells,
Which no rest assuages
Through ages and ages.
With the voice of my waves and storms
I have questioned the million forms
That float in the molten thunder,
And drop with a voice of wonder
Down the red-litten
Ruin-smitten
Hollow and hissing dark,
When 't is suddenly, terribly, torn asunder
By the leap of the lightning-spark:
My voice the sun's mid noon,
My voice the midnight moon,
By whose silver sceptre cold
With strong moanings manifold
Are my wishful waters drawn,
Long hath heard; and the white Dawn;
And the wistful Even, too;
What time round his pavilion
Of blue, amber, and vermilion,
He, with a stealthy finger
That doth ever love to linger,
Softly disengages
From out their azure cages,
To float in fervid heights,
All those wingéd lights

That soar on winking pinions
Of white fire, and wander through
Their newly gained dominions
Of divinest blue;
Still lifted up, long ages,
Still vainly, to inquire
(For man, whose mind makes choice
Of mine, to be the voice
Of his own pining pain)
Wherefore infinite desire
Finite power doth enchain?
But, unanswered by the ages
Wherewith man's passion wages
Weary war, that doth but tire,
Waste, and break him, I again
To the sorrow of his sages
Fling their question back; in vain
Forced upon me; never nigher
To the knowledge they would gain
Of the meaning of man's pain.

AN ECHO.

Pain!

VOICES FROM THE AIR.

Hourly in a crystal cup
Do we Spirits gather up
The sounds of all the sorrows
Of the yesterdays and morrows
Of man's measured misery.
But never yet, O Lord,
Have we ever heard
On Sorrow's lip the word
That might set Sorrow free.

AN ECHO FROM THE ÆONS.

Set Sorrow free!

A VOICE ON CALVARY.

Himself, that savéd others, let him save!

ANOTHER VOICE.

Thou, if thou be the Son of God, come down!

AN ECHO FROM GEHENNA.

Son of God, come down!

A MULTITUDE OF VOICES.

Art thou a Prophet? Prophesy, we crave,

A MULTITUDE OF ECHOES.

Prophesy, we crave!

THE VOICES.

What thorns mean in thy crown.

A VOICE FROM THE GRAVE.

Put forth thy strength now, Thou that wouldest burst
The doors of my dominion! Doth the First
Daunt thee? The Second Death is yet. The worst
Hath evermore a worse beyond.

A VOICE FROM THE CROSS.

I THIRST!

VOICES BELOW THE CROSS.

Mix the hyssop with the myrrh!

DEMONS OF THE OUTER DEEP.

A cup of deadly wine
Be it ours to minister
To a thirst divine!
We are the Cruelties of Nature,
That swarm to overwhelm
The spirit in the creature
That invades her realm.
Horror, stolen from the lips
Of the livid-faced eclipse;
Terror, from the scorched earth under
The swift transit of the thunder;
Wrath from the enormous ocean;
Madness from the earthquake's motion:

DEMONS OF THE INNER DEEP.

Pallid fears, heart-harrowing cares,
From invincible nightmares;
And the stealthy day-by-day
Of what turns men's hair to gray;
And the sudden, sharp collapse
Of Courage, when the vast Perhaps
Springs at unawares in sight;
And the whisper in the night
That breaks a noble heart:

DEMONS OF THE OUTER DEEP.

Deep awe
From the abysses: vulture's claw,
Serpent's fang, and scorpion's sting,

Tiger's tooth, and dragon's wing :
All that 's hideous and unholy
  Mix we here, to make the wine
Of our mighty melancholy,
  Meet for lips divine.

TOGETHER.

Fleshly pang, and ghostly woe :
Let him drain it ! Let men know
What of God's Divinity
Dwells in Man's Humanity !

DEMONS OF THE OUTER DEEP.

Weave the web of agony,
Softly ! softly and silently
Wind the web of agony
  Round about his heart !
Delicately let it lie
On the spirit and the eye,
Meshed with finest misery,
  And in every part
Strung, by choicest cruelty,
  Strong with subtlest smart !
Draw the tightening threads together,
  Stronger each than adamant,
Lighter each than powdery feather
  Fall'n upon the florid plant
Where, all faint from fervid ether,
  To his inmost honeyed haunt
Summer's fond and wanton rover,
  The fine-wingèd moth doth creep.
Let the film of anguish hover
  O'er his senses, like the sleep

Of sick fear that settles over
Stifled lands in lurid weather,
When, beneath, pent earthquakes gather
  Forces for a sudden leap!
Let him break it, if he can,
And reveal the God in Man!

DEMONS OF THE INNER DEEP.

Through and through the strangling weft,
Drive the knife home to the heft!
Turn it in his inmost heart!
Turn it! Let him feel the smart
Of the sharpness of the whole
Of the iron in the soul!
Let him bear it if he can,
And avenge the God in Man!

TOGETHER.

Probe the wound unto the core!
  Burn and bite into the bone!
Prove we, if this man be more
Than the men that went before,
  And were swiftly overthrown.
Let him feel it all he can,
Feel as God may feel for Man:
Fleshly pang, and ghostly woe!
It is fit that men should know
What of God's Divinity
Dwells in Man's Humanity!

THE VOICE OF SATAN ON THE HEIGHTS.

Make good thy double title, Son of Man,
Or Son of God! If Son of God thou beest

More than all other sons of man that be,
Then is thy solitary deed, though done
In man's disguise, not man's: whose life remains
No loftier and no lovelier than before
His flesh was filched to test the transient play
Of a god's power which, though in him put forth,
Leaves man's self helpless as that hollow heap
Of trophied harness from whose lifeless clutch
Some passionate hero plucks the brand, to prove
How living hands may wield it. Son of God,
If thou beest only but as all men be,
Then, more than all men can thou canst not.
Named
By either title, — son of Man or God, —
I do defy thee, by surpassing pangs,
To snatch from me my old supremacy
In sorrow, my Divinity of Pain.
Vainly with me in misery dost thou vie,
Prophet of Pity! — whom I pity most,
That thou shouldst deem it possible to force
Far recompense from transient torment spent
On what thou addest to a million more
And mightier woes, — or, that oblivious Time,
Who, as he marches, all behind him burns,
Will halt his wasteful course, to count and keep
(Once dropt into the measureless abyss
Of anguish, and the homelessness of things)
The few red drippings of that dolorous brow.
Why, how now, O mine Enemy? Behold!
There is not one of thy lost children here, —
Thy children by lost heritage in Hope,
Mine by adoption and the curse of Sin, —
There is not one of these that hath not groaned
Beneath some throe as sharp as at this hour

Racks the God in thee! Count the ages up
By all their aching pulses, and consider
What power is thine, — even to contemplate
The congregated anguish and despair,
Grim ignorance, wrath, execration, fierce
Brute wrongs, and purblind, drudging wretchedness,
The heart-broken memory, the trampled hope,
The slow, cold, suffocating, creeping care,
The cankering doubt, choked longing, livid hate,
The stabbing shame, the stark, gaunt, naked need,
The weary struggle of the strangled will,
The whirling frenzy, and the wild regret,
The dim, inexplicable, shapeless dread,
The intense torture unendurable,
The sick self-loathing, and the crusht revolt
Of the excruciated flesh, — all, all
The myriad miseries crammed into the curse
Not of man only, but of all that lives:
Whose several sufferings, separate discontents,
And special curses, are summed up in man,
As man's in me, that of man's miseries all
Am the unanswered Protest against Him
That made us what, for being, we are plagued:
From puling infancy to pining youth,
From life's mid fever to its last faint gasp,
From the worm trodden by the heedless foot
To the man broken by the heavy years
He staggers under, or else caught and crusht
By the strong sudden hand in the first fray,
And trampled by his fellows: Fate's blind fool
Upon whose borrowed image he himself
Now wreaks the rabid fury of his race
Reared into endless enmity with all

That to upraise it doth in vain aspire.
What I endure, — I call, to testify,
All creatures, and all things inanimate,
Which are as pasture to my pain. Respond
From your abysses and sublunar haunts,
From viewless dens, or public paths of pain,
In earth, or air, or sea, — whatever creeps,
Or flies, or swims, or with inanimate woe
Makes inarticulate protest, — blighted growths,
Cankered, corrupted, curst! — ye prisoners all
That populate this penitential star,
And know my voice! thou ocean, from thy deeps
Where Desolation dwells, thou realm of air
Whereof I am the prince, — and all ye winds
That waft and mock the moanings of the world, —
Thou ancient earth, — and all ye habitants
Of this old lodge of anger! — Listen God!

AN INORGANIC VOICE.

I suffer!

ORGANIC VOICES.

And we suffer!

HUMAN VOICES.

And we suffer!

SATAN.

Enough! Ye suffer for my sake, as He
Suffers for yours, and suffering hath no end!
Thou lord of Love, dost thou these voices hear?
What are thy pangs to those which these endure,

And have endured for ages, and must yet
For ages more moan under? Lord of Love
Thou knowest what Love can suffer, and no more!
But men were born to hate themselves, and thee:
Love is not of their nature. Dost thou deem
That any tear thou weepest can blot out
The curse that 's scrawled across a universe
Condemned from the beginning to the end?
Few were thy mortal years, and counted soon:
In thine Immortal, — nothing! Short thy strife,
Soon quenched its agony! Yet, if the thirst
Of this soul-parching Hour might drain the dregs
Of all the tears of all the centuries,
Lost were thy labor! For, if man thou art,
More than all men have done thou canst not do;
But more than all must fail, who more than all
Hast dared. If thou beest God, why then, as God,
Conquer thou canst: but in that conquest, man,
That hath no part, can no more profit claim
Than some poor savage, in a barbarous isle
Half brutish born, could boast of, did he know
That otherwhere, in Athens or in Rome,
Some being, like himself, of woman born,
Formed, like himself, of flesh and blood, like him
Mortal, hath learned the lore of Samian seers,
Or won the Cæsar's crown. God's strength is God's;
Man's at the best can be but man's: who fails
Though God, as God, succeed; and thy success
(If thou succeedest) is not man's, but His
Whose power, in thee, is but superfluous proof
Of a foregone conclusion. Man, or God,
If man, hope nothing to man's hope denied,

If God, though thou God's conquest claim, I claim
Man's failure; most in thee; who mock'st him most
With what he might be, if, like thee, he had
A god's strength in him, by a god's will plied.

A VOICE FROM THE CROSS.

WHEREFORE, MY GOD, HAST THOU FORSAKEN
ME? [*A pause.*

INORGANIC VOICES.

Is God no longer in Humanity?
Then masters of Man's godless world are we,
Peopling its pale impersonality.

EVIL SPIRITS (*gathering*).

Darknesses, Silences, Strangenesses, waken!
Ye, that forsake not whom God hath forsaken,
Take the Untaken!

THE SILENCES.

By the sweetness of music slain
Is the soul of our silence fed
On a pang surpassing sound.

THE DARKNESSES.

And our darkness' dearest gain
By the ghost of a glory dead
With a sharper shade is crowned.

THE DEEDLESS ONES.

From the lonesome places,
Unseen, untrod,

Where no life traces
 In seed or sod
The love that chases
 The steps of God;

THE DEFEATED ONES.

From the twilights sunk in the nether dens,
Where Madness and Death are denizens;
From the wildernesses of wasted dreams,
 Where pale-faced Failure strays, and feeds
Her footless flocks by the frenzied streams
 Of desires dragged down among broken deeds;
From the shipless shore where no bird flies,
 But old wrecks choke the sobbing tide,
And the stranded wretch, that beheld our eyes
 Where the storm-wave cast him, crazed and died;
From the red high-road to the sudden end,
 Which the blood of its lone wayfarer streaks,
Who, dogged by the fear of himself, doth wend
 Till the suicide findeth the knife he seeks;
From the flint-bound cells, where a strong heart breaks
When the maniac's chain in his last gasp shakes;
Where from milkless nipples unmated mothers
Pluck the nameless babes the unblest earth smothers,
 And the Memories God remembers not
 In the charnel houses of Hope do rot;

TOGETHER.

We come! we come!
In the frustrate strife
Of the vanquisht life,
On the course misrun

To the goal unwon
By the faith, self-cheated
Of the deed defeated,
To claim our home.

DENOUNCING VOICES.

Thus far rose the race of man,
Thus low doth it lie.
Worlds that in man's faith began
In man's failure die.

EVIL SPIRITS OF THE HEIGHTS (*descending*).

The plain we have left unmolested
Where low things low lie, still.
The dust in the dust lay, and rested
Where the wind had wreaked on it his will;
Though the plumes of the purple-crested
Thunder throbbed on the hill.
For what can be done, or undone,
With the filth that is filth forever?
So we spared our pain
To ruin the plain,
And, leaving it safe in its baseness alone,
Made wing for the higher endeavor.
It is but an atom of earth,
A grain, a speck most small;
But the place of it gave it worth,
For this summit was highest of all.
So for ages and ages long
We Spirits had no such bliss
As to watch, with our eyes upon it,
Waiting to do it wrong:
Since the Devil had need of this.

And, lo you! at last we have won it.
A grain, — no more: but it grew
Where all things fall if it fall.
A speck: but a summit too,
— The highest summit of all!

EVIL SPIRITS OF THE DEPTHS (*ascending*).

In the deepest deeps of Night
Swam the star of a far-off day.
A Spirit in bondage there,
Chained fast to the sullen slope,
Sat watching the lonesome ray
Of that star's incertain light,
With an agonizing stare.
Let him grieve and grope as he may
Henceforth, that Spirit blind,
Whose name, not Patience now,
Shall by men be called Despair;
But he never again shall find,
However he grieve or grope,
'Neath Night's eternal Nay,
Any light on the deeps below.
For the star he was watching is Hope,
And that star we have stolen away.

DENOUNCING VOICES.

Tempters of the height,
Darkners of the deep,
Midway now unite,
Man from God to keep.
Thus far rose the race of man,
Thus low doth it lie.
All that in man's life began
In man's death doth die.

SPIRITS UNITING.

Where bare of sepulture
 It hangs on the rock,
To the carcass the vulture
 And eagle do flock:
Scenting the carrion,
 The raven and kite
Follow the clarion,
 And feast on the fight:
To his prey leaps the leopard:
 The wolf on the lamb
That is left by the shepherd
 His hunger doth cram:
Round the spent swimmer,
 With eyes peering pale
Through the green glimmer
 The lean shark doth sail;
The owlet by night spoils the nest in the tree;
 The bat tears the moth: God, that seeth it done,
Sayeth never a word: as He made us are we:
 And so seize we our own!

THE VOICES APPROACHING.

Ye that forsake not whom God hath forsaken,
Spirits of evil, awaken! awaken!
 Shake the Unshaken!

SATAN.

Mine Enemy, could I accuse thee now,
Hell from her deep foundations should send forth
A shout to shake the highest porch of Heaven
With most infernal thunder! Enemy,
Could I accuse thee, all the Potentates

Of Pain would rise to welcome to his throne
My peer in condemnation!
                                        Hearken all,
You sightless Essences that have no voice
Under the silence of Eternal God,
Till Nature cries — "Too late!" — and Hell responds
With all her echoes! You that spy on man,
Sit in his heart, and count its pulses up,
People the silent places of his mind,
And set your secret sign upon his thoughts,
Dog all his steps from wicked woes to woes,
Gather his deeds, and lay them in the lap
Of Accusation, — Destinies, and Fates,
Dooms, Witnesses, Informers against man,
Angels of Reprobation! — you that keep
The record-book of wrongs for future wrath,
Accusers all, — that are my ministers,
As I am God's, — in Hate, not Love, — attend!
Answer me, now, What fault is in this man?

VOICES.

We find not any fault within this Man.

A VOICE FROM HEAVEN.

Within this Man not any fault is found!

ECHO FROM THE ABYSS OF NATURE.

Fault is found.

VOICES FROM THE DEPTHS OF HUMANITY.

Is ours their fault who failed ere we began?

Born to the woes we wrought not, are we bound
By a plan we did not plan?

VOICES OF EVIL SPIRITS.

Woe to the offspring of the Fault of Man!
Woe!

ECHO FROM GEHENNA.

Woe, the offspring of the Fault of Man!

THE WORLD, THE FLESH, AND THE DEVIL.

Dance we around! around!
Man hath forsaken God: God hath forsaken Man!
The sun is dark in heaven: there is no light from above:
We must be merry meanwhile, — merry as long as we can,
Though Nature is sick to the heart, and the Angels are weeping for Love!
Hand in hand, a heedless band,
Round about the Tree,
Purple-gowned, and golden-crowned,
Merrily dance We Three!
One of us three hath a cloven foot
That *will* peep out, whatever the boot
That Use or Wont may fashion to 't; —
Which of us can it be?
One of us three hath a leering eye,
And a slippery step, and a parching sigh
On a red lip, draining men's hearts dry, —
And the Witch knows which it must be.
One of us three hath a royal gait,
And a heart of scorn, and a brow of hate,

And nathless he lifteth his head elate
Though he looketh upon the Tree.
This is an ancient dance:
And long ago we danced it,
Round a god of another stamp:
In the heart of the Chosen Camp,
Heedless whatever the chance,
We danced it, and we pranced it,
With a mad and a merry tramp,
While nobody heeded what God said,
Though the thunder was talking overhead,
And the sun turned sick as a languished lamp
Whose last light sinks unfed.
With a merry song, and a merry laugh
Round about the Golden Calf,
We danced it all together,
And the populace, at as merry a pace,
High and low, all joined the race,
In turban, robe, and feather:
Women, as mad as mad could be,
Little children, bare to the knee,
Priests and elders of high degree,
All in the stormy weather!

VOICES FROM BENEATH THE THRONE.

How long, O Lord, must we endure? How long?
Avenge the perfect patience of thy Saints
Whose blood cries out o' the earth against Earth's
Wrong.

A VOICE FROM THE EARTH.

Avenge not, God, thy Holy One on me,
Whose latest hope in His life's darkness faints.

VOICES FROM HADES.

Release, O Lord, thy prisoners, that to thee
Make moan, long-fettered in the bonds of Night,
Unransomed captives of unconquered Sin!

SPIRITS IN THE BOSOM OF ABRAHAM.

Celestial Shepherd of the Flocks of Light,
Descend, descend the moaning deeps among,
And draw thy lost sheep in!

THE VOICES IN HADES.

How long shall Darkness hide us, Lord? How long?
When shall the Dawn begin? [*A pause.*

A MULTITUDE OF VOICES.

Alas! no answer yet!

VOICES OF ANGELS, WATCHING ROUND THE CROSS.

By the awe on Olivet,
By the darkness on the day,
By the earth that now is wet
With the blood of Him they slay
Knowing not, — by all the debt
Which thy Son doth die to pay,
Lord, no more thine oath forget,
Nor thy right hand stay!
Ransom, Lord, thy quick and dead,
By the blood which now is shed
For them . . . .

A VOICE FROM THE CROSS.

IT IS FINISHÉD!

A VOICE FROM THE ABYSS OF NATURE.

Amen!

EVIL SPIRITS.

Haste! Away!
[*Thunder and earthquake.*

ANGELS, BEARING UP THE WORD.

Earth has heard, and Heaven hath heard,
And the Ever-living Lord,
What was uttered doth record!
Caught upon the blackened lips,
Of the lightning-seamed eclipse,
Echoed by infernal thunder
From the earthquake groaning under,
Answered from the hearts of men
By a yet unvoiced Amen,
Bear we up the Word!

A VOICE FROM THE TEMPLE.

The Mystery of the Vail is rent! is rent!

EVIL SPIRITS DEPARTING.

Ariel! Ariel!
Thou Lion of the Lord armipotent,
Tried and invincible!

VOICE FROM THE TEMPLE.

The Mystery of the Vail is rent! is rent!

ANGELS IN AIR.

Ariel! Ariel!

The covenant whereto He did assent
  Our God hath disannulled with Death and Hell.
Thou Lion of the Lord Omnipotent
  In thee henceforth the heart o' the world shall
      dwell!

VOICE FROM THE TEMPLE.

The Mystery of the Vail is rent! is rent!

ANGEL VOICES.

Ariel! Ariel!

ELDERS BEFORE THE THRONE.

Blessing, blessing, and thanksgiving,
  Glory, glory, rule and reign,
To the Dead One that is living,
  The Death-slayer that was slain!
In the Life is sown the seed:
  From the Death the fruit is wrought:
Beauty buried in the deed
  Re-arises in the thought:
From the transitory Act,
  Which shall perish with the past,
Springs the Faith, the Living Fact,
  That forevermore shall last.
To the teaching of the Word,—
  To the Uttered Law,—succeed
Yet a Second and a Third.
  First, the teaching of the Deed:
— Of the Deed, which is the Example,
  In the Life which is the Love:
These ennoble and make ample
  What to perfect and to prove,

(Heir of all) doth man inherit,
  Help of Him that cometh Third:
And the teaching of the Spirit
  Shall complete the Deed and Word.
Amen! blessing and thanksgiving.
  Amen! glory rule and reign
To the Slain One by the living
  Of whose dying Death is slain!

A VOICE OUT OF THE SANCTUARY.

    The earth doth quake,
    But cannot shake
This corner-stone of mine:
    The steadfast stone,
    The only one
That never shall be overthrown,
For, graved by God, doth shine
    His Name thereon
    That is the Son
Of God and Man; whose Name alone
    Is Human and Divine.

THE ELDERS ABOVE.

Amen! Amen! God that gazest
  On thine image in Man's Son!
Man that man to God upraisest,
  Human and Divine in one!

SAINTS ARISING.

  Sing ye, singing out of dust,
  Buried Spirits of the Just,
For now i' the deadest dark of Death the light of
    Life doth shine.

We arise, each bidden guest,
From the chambers of our rest.
Open, Zion, open to us, all those solemn gates of thine!
A sound, a sound of voices, and of harpings, and a light
As when a great solemnity is holden in the night!
For the vintage of the vineyard, for the gathering of the vine!
And sing ye, and sing ye to the Lord a holy ditty:
The song that David sung to us upon the harp with might:
A vineyard, a vineyard, a vineyard of red wine!
The lord thereof is Lord of Life, whose love is infinite:
For deeper than the plummet drops in Him are depths of pity,
And in Him is mercy more than may be measured by the line,
And the judgment that is in Him is not reckoned by the rod.

A VOICE FROM JERUSALEM.

Enter, ye Saints, into the Holy City!

VOICE OF A CENTURION.

Verily, this man was the Son of God!

VOICES OF ARISEN SAINTS (*growing fainter as they pass*).

Fire among the thorns that burnest!
Star that heaven around thee turnest!

Living star of love, whose light
  From the breast of the Divine
Brightest glows in blackest night,
  Down this human darkness shine!
   Ignis inter spicula:
  Umbrâ sidus in nocturnâ:
  Jesu tibi sit superna
  Gloria in sempiterna
   Seculorum secula.
Voice the winds and waves obey!
Spirit summoning this clay!
Life-creative Word of God,
Trumpet whose triumphant breath
Calls the soul from out the clod,
  And awakens life in death!
  Audivere quos nox tegit;
   Tremuitque gens infausta
  Inter umbras; quæ mors regit
   Fracta audivere claustra!
Hostage found we none to take
Death upon him for our sake.
Bondsmen of the Night, to thee
  Made we moan from underground.
Thou, descending, didst set free
  From their bonds the prison-bound.
  Liberati sunt ligati,
  Et soluti condemnati.
  Ubi mors sedebat, ibi
  Venit vita. Gloria tibi!
Dayspring, of whose light is born
Mortal life's immortal morn,
Thou from the Beginning wast
  God with Very God alone:
Man, with very man, thou hast

In the Flesh the Godhead shown.
Eque Deo Deus, numen
Verum tu de numine,
Et divinum vivens lumen
In æterno lumine.
To the right hand of the Father,
Where Thou sitt'st in glory, gather,
Out of darkness, death, and doom,
Son of God, the sons of men.
Shine upon us in the tomb,
Light us into life again!
Fac ut quando morietur
Corpus, nostræ sit victoria
Animæ. Fac ut donetur
Tecum paradisi gloria!

[*The voices die out in the passing of the eclipse.* — *Evening falls, and moonlight, over Calvary.* JOSEPH OF ARIMATHEA, *the two* MARYS, *other Women, and Disciples, bearing away the body of* CHRIST.

Hush! for the soldier's spear:
Hush! for the high priest's scorn:
Hush! lest the haters hear:
For we are sheep forlorn.
Dead is our shepherd dear,
Dead, and the wolves are near.
Hush! lest we, too, be torn.
Brothers, tread light, breathe low:
With no loud voice of woe
Must the loved burden we bear hence be borne.
Ah, that, of all for whom his blood did flow
None left to mourn him be,
None left, save only we,
Alas, that left him once whom now we mourn,
And could not save him, though we loved him so!

Peace! he hath died, but is not dead.
Stoop! ere he lie in earthy bed,
With crusht cassia strew,
For savor sweet, his winding-sheet.
And, from his holy head and feet
Kiss off the cold death dew.
We will never more forsake him.
To our human hearts we take him:
In our human hearts we make him
A deep grave, that he,
Buried in our love and pain,
Thence may rise to live again
In the lives of ransomed men
Whom he died to free.
Lord, until this Human die
Into Thy Divinity,
(So made wholly Thine!)
Deep in our Humanity
(So made wholly ours!) shall lie
Buried Thy Divine!

VOICES OF ANGELS PASSING.

Blessèd are ye forlorn,
For whom The Lord is dead!
Rejoice all ye that mourn,
Ye shall be comforted!

[*The Mourners move down the hill with the body of* CHRIST. THE ANGEL OF THE WATCH *descends.*

THE ANGEL OF THE WATCH.

Peace upon earth! Good-will to men. All 's well!
[SATAN *approaches.*

THE ANGEL.

Satan, I warn thee hence. Whence comest thou?

SATAN.

From walking to and fro upon the earth.
Thou liest, Angel! Nothing here is well,
For I am here.

ANGEL OF THE WATCH.

Yet must thou hence.

SATAN.

"Must," Cherub?
I will not.

ANGEL OF THE WATCH.

Not thy will, nor mine, decides
Our places. Here, I guard the Cross of Christ.

SATAN.

I also. Hearken, Angel of the Watch!
Hath Sorrow any right unto this Cross?
If so, I claim it by my right in Sorrow.
Or Sin, thou Angel, hath it any right
Unto this Cross? Then, by my right in Sin,
I claim it. If not Sorrow, if not Sin,
What, then, hath rights upon this Cross? Not thou,
Nor all the hosts that share with thee God's joy;
For these He died not, and for these no cross
Was needed. Sorrow's place, and Sin's, is here.
Therefore my place is here, with Sin and Sorrow.

The body of thy lord, Humanity
Hath taken to itself. O I have heard
Those woman-wailings! Verily I have heard,
And laughed to think what sort of love was theirs
That sang of love so loudly!
Mark me, Angel!
Already I foresee, in the new time,
How men will crucify this Christ again
Daily and hourly, in their hours and days:
How they will crucify him in their faith,
As, in their doubt too, they will crucify him!
How, in their knowledge and their ignorance,
How in their love as in their hate, their hope
And their despair, their wisdom and their folly,
Still they will crucify him!
Enemy!
Thou knowest that the mind of man is warped
From the beginning of the world. Thou knowest
That men will choose the evil, not the good,
Their nature being evil, and the True
Still crucify, still crown the False, and still
Shape knowledge into ignorance.
Henceforth,
This stone of stumbling, where it falls, shall grind
All things to powder. Neither day, nor hour,
Shall pass, but what, disputing to the death
Thy substance, and thine elements, man's mind
Shall waste man's life about a wilderness
Of miserable, innumerable folly.
Pedants, and pedagogues, and busybodies,
Schools, councils, doctors, disputants, divines,
Shall stretch contentious hands to scribble still,
Even as erewhile, their Hebrew, Greek, and Latin
Over thy murdered head, and write thee wrong

In every language learned by Ignorance!
In thy name, men shall slaughter, and torment,
Desolate, ruin, and destroy each other!
In thy name, scaffolds shall be smeared with gore;
In thy name, dungeons shall be crammed with groans;
The bloody whip, the branding-iron, the stake,
The fagot, and the sharp two-handed axe,
The torturing engine, and the toothéd wheel,
Shall owe thy name no lack of work to do.
In thy name, men shall brutalize God's gift
Of life, ill-comprehended, till they rot,
Howling, or, mad with stupid silence, pass
Out of Humanity, to crawl to death,
Beast-like, through bestial filth, foul sores, and scum
Of self-neglect, in desert dens and holes!
In thy name, men shall utter blasphemies
Undreamed of yet by devils damned in Hell!
In thy name, Fraud and Force and Violence
Shall prosper in the prejudice of all
That hath till yet made patience possible
Under huge wrongs! . . . . Till thou, mine Enemy,
The infinitely-often crucified,
Even in the heights of thy felicity
Yonder, and by the right-hand of high God,
Shalt drain the cup of bitterness, — erewhile
Half-tasted only, — to so deep a depth
Of wrath and anguish, that thyself shalt curse
Thy new-adopted, even as they curse thee!
Meanwhile, my place is here, beside this Cross,
With Sin and Sorrow. Therefore stand aside,
Thou Angel of the Watch! Here will I rest.

ANGEL OF THE WATCH.

Angel of Accusation, here or elsewhere
Neither thy power nor mine prevails, but His
That suffers us, — each in his several sphere,
Me to obey, and thee to contradict,
And both to serve his purpose equally.
The meaning of thy mystery, and the end
Foreseen from the beginning, and foreseen
By wisdom infinite for endless good,
Thyself, thou knowest not. Neither do I know
The meaning of my own. Thou canst but view
The single act of God's eternity,
Which is to partial senses sensible
In partial action only, by the eye
Of thine own nature, as by mine I view it.
And, thy perception being limited
To evil only, to thee only evil
Is still perceptible, as still to me
Good only, and good everywhere.

SATAN.

Enough,
Angel, I know, at what I know to mock,
And marvel at this huge ado for that
Which, when 't is done, is nothing, — or, at least,
Nothing in the diminishment of all
The misery and the wretchedness in man,
To which God said, — "Increase and multiply!"
The ages to the ages, and the hours
Unto the hours, shall add themselves, and men
Shall multiply, and ever with more men
More misery! Meanwhile, my place is here,
And here I stand, — beside this Cross of Christ;

Where Sin shall come, and Sorrow come with Sin,
And Sin and Sorrow still shall find me here,
Still ready to accuse them. And, when men
Shall learn, like thee, to talk theology
Most eloquently with the Devil himself,
Dispute with him his nature, proper place
And fit relation, in the latest plan
Of general self-complacency, — at least,
His presence shall they feel, as thou dost now,
Here, in the shadow of this Cross of Christ!

ANGEL OF THE WATCH.

Mocker! Scorn ever was the sign assured
Of impotency.

SATAN.

And of ignorance,
Such tearless self-complacency as thine.
Is man's praise challenged? Be man's right to blame
Thereby accorded! What is changed for man?
Or how is man's case bettered? What man was
He is, and shall be, and so must have been,
So being made. The mutable images
Of Good and Evil in the minds of men
May change from age to age. But man himself
No nearer and no farther than before
Stands, where he stood, between them. What man names
Evil to-day, to-morrow he names good:
And, contrary, what he names good to-day,
To-morrow he names evil. What of that?
He changes not his nature, but a name.
Good men, or men so called, have been erenow,

And evil men, or men so called, shall be,
In like proportion, to the end of time.
At one time this thing, at another that,
Man studies to become, and calls it good:
His power to be it, whatsoe'er it be,
Is through all time the same as it hath been;
In the strong somewhat, nothing in the weak,
Not much in any.
Cherub, know me. Prince
Of this world, thou hast heard it, am I called.
Prince of this world I am. But in this world
I have no power save on the mind of man;
Whereby whatever God for man made good
I for man turn to evil. Storm, eclipse,
Deluge, and the exterminating fire,
Earthquake, and pestilence — God's works, not mine —
Obey me not. But me my works obey,
Which are the fears these fashion in men's minds,
The fearful deeds which, through man's life, these fears
Shape themselves into. Look on me. I am
Man's mind's eternal protest against Law,
— Man's life's eternal protest against Love.
A time there may be, though it must be far,
When men, by Knowledge reconciled to Law
In things material, shall convert to good
All that for ages I have made to them
Material evil. In that time my voice
Shall no more in man's life, as now, be heard,
Protesting against God's material law.
But what of that? Still heard my voice shall be
In man's heart, still against himself protesting.
And, till that protest hath in man no place,

Where man's place, mine is, Cherub; nor canst thou
Here, or wherever else man comes, to me
Cry, "Enter not!"

THE ANGEL.

Nor needs it, bitter fiend,
That I forbid thee. For thou canst not pass
The limit of thy nature, which God's love
Surpasses, here. Obey not me: thou still
Obeyest God.

SATAN.

Cherub, what more dost thou?

THE ANGEL.

Love Him.

SATAN.

Thou lovest, hypocrite, the gain
That 's got for loving.

THE ANGEL.

Ay. Love's gain is love.

SATAN.

Hated or loved, here will I rest. Away!

THE ANGEL.

Not by the length of my authority,
But by the narrowness of thine, is fixt
Thy kingdom, Satan. But when He, by whom
Thy passing protest against permanent power
Is heard i' the incompleteness of man's life,

Shall, in man's life completed, have vouchsafed
Its complete refutation, then . . . .

SATAN.

Ay! *then?*
Count me, prophetic Spirit, if thou canst,
How many wrinkles to the brow of Time
Shall ere that *Then* be added? And what then?
Thou knowest no more than I. When man no more
My work provides, thine own shall lack provision;
Whose task on earth is but the consequence
Of my procedure: temporary both.
Enough! I stand by my necessity,
Which is not of eternity, but time.
I know no Then nor There. I am Here and Now.
Standing beneath the glory of God, not in it,
Man casts upon this earth, whereon he stands,
The formidable shadow of himself:
The Spirit of that Shadow, which, where'er
Man goes, goes with him, darkening earth, am I.
Unto what end man's steps are bound, whose course,
Making it marked by darkness, everywhere
I dog protesting against light, or when
That end may be, I know not. But I know,
Nor care I to know more, that he and I,
I with my protest in man's life, and man,
Man in God's glory, in man's shadow I,
Have yet through time no journey short to make
Together; taking with us this day's deed,
Which yet is mine to deal with.

THE ANGEL.

If, in truth,
Spirit of Discontent, the unknown time

Of God's endurance doth, as thou dost boast,
Accord such leisure thine to meditate
Thy place in his incalculable scheme
Of pure perfection, and thy power thereon,
By him permitted, — study this first law
To which all power is made conditional: —
Hate creates nothing.

SATAN.

Nay, but Hate destroys.

THE ANGEL.

For Love to still create.

SATAN.

And Love creates
For Hate to still destroy. Paid eulogist
Of unintelligible authorship,
I am the only critic of God's works
That do not praise them. And, for this, I think
It likes him well enough to let me be,
And give me hearing with a certain zest
Which mere monotony of praise like thine
Would surfeit else. Moreover in this world
We tolerate each other, He and I,
Better than you surmise. I set men's wits
To question what they scarce would notice else,
And so find out what, having so found out,
They all the more admire. I keep alert
The Maker's pleasure in his works thereby,
To prove me bungler. Yet I praise him best,
In my own way; and unto me he owes
Man's worship, which was ever born of fear.

Do I not manifest to men his power,
Whereof a part, nor that the least, in me
Put forth, completes the vast Two-fronted Will,
Against whose everlasting Yes and No
Man's frenzied being breaks, and moaningly
Grovels in abject terror ? Which to him
Is joy, — the joy of feeling himself felt
By what he made to feel him ; therefore made
Weak in all ways, but not withal so weak
But it can bear his foot upon its neck,
And, feeling what his strength is, worship it,
While the bruised head the bruising heel adores.
We rule, then, each, — both he and I, — by fear :
And he is strongest : but I still am strong.
Spake he not to his Prophet of old time :
"I form the light, and I the darkness : I
Make peace, and create evil : I, the Lord,
Do all these things" ? But half of all these things,
What hand but mine the doing of them moves ?
The Evil I, and I the Darkness ! Both
His work and will : then of his will and work
The great one-half, made manifest, am I !
If I could be aught other than I am,
I would be he : and in that wish, methinks,
I own him for my God, and worship him —
Him — not this Other ; that resembles not
In aught the God I am content to serve.
Nor serve I only, but I honor him ;
Keeping in honor those that serve him here
Strong kings, shrewd priests, and mighty men of war,
And all that upon earth is honorable.
But I can neither praise nor tolerate,
What I protest against, — this latest change

Of purpose in the Ever-changing One.
Here, for the first time, I seem set aside;
And, could I ever weep, I should weep now
For the perversity of this new plan,
Perceiving what must happen presently.
Like some long-trusted counsellor, displaced
And discontented with the times, am I;
Who sees the young prince pulling down the props
He spent his utmost pains on, to uphold,
Based on the popular fear, the father's throne.
I, that have been about the world so long,
Methinks should know it; and, if aught I know,
Men are not to be governed but by fear.
When they shall lose the wholesome dread, now theirs,
Of kings and priests, what next? Why, men will cease
To fear me even; and, ceasing to fear me,
Will cease to fear Jehovah. Heed the event!
But meanwhile men shall win their license hard,
To laugh at what now scares them. I remain
In spite of the new-comers. Long shall Love
Red-handed walk the world with Hate's own sword,
Nor plant one forward footstep, save in blood.
Therefore I stand here, Angel of the Watch,
Watching with thee. Whose watch I grudge not. Wait.
For vigil long must be both thine and mine,
And we will watch together.

THE ANGEL.

Wild, as waves
That wash no shore, words wander. If between
Yon throbbing lights that round us roll and burn,

No radiant interelemental thrill
Made response to their restless hearts, perchance
The leaping lightsprings of the Sun himself
Might blaze in sempiternal blackness, dark
To orbs beyond the never-beaten bound
And blank engulfment of his barren globe:
And all the kindred sovereignties of space,
His starry peers whose now fraternal fires
Flash mutual rapture, then would wanly ply
Pale incommunicable pulses, filled
With ineffectual fervor. Even so,
Between us twain, — spirits of spheres that move
In no same elemental sense of things,
No corresponsive impulse interchanging
From simultaneous impact of the Power
That keeps in commune all the souls it sways,
— Thought, like a beam that heats not, lights not, beating
On unimpressive absolute nothingness,
Visits in vain the waste and void of what
Holds thee and me asunder.
Obscure Power,
Which, in the ever-fleeting substance pent
Of all that passes, all that perishes,
The Eternal Fire eternally consumes,
What time from age to age, from hour to hour,
From soul to soul, burning, it proves itself
And all things else that Time, as fuel, flings
Into the furnace of transforming Love,
Leaving Hate's pile in ashes, — pass thy way,
And ply thy transitory task! Which is
To feed the fervor of the fire of God,
And speed its issue through the body and form
Of all experience, which it animates.

Ply thou thy task! accumulating Time's
Perversenesses, obstructions, enmities,
And unintelligent antagonisms;
Therewith, as fagots for the burning, bound,
To satisfy the everlasting flame
Whose altars are the ages: whence it glows
To spirits of men, — a beacon light; to thee,
Whose ever-dwindling substance, in that heat
Of Heavenly Love, from age to age assumes
Slow transformation, — thine own funeral pyre!
Dull Fiend, the more thou on this Fire of Love
Hast leave to heap all hideous hatreds, all
Denials, contradictions, cruelties,
Fables, and fears, and frenzied shames, — the more
Shall it, by all such stimulations stung
To intenser force, burn from the souls of men
Those multitudinous mischiefs that are made
Its sacrificial sustenance.
Enough!
Put forth thy hand.

SATAN.

Where art thou? feebly sounds
Thy voice, vain Angel: strong in word, but weak
In act to hold what now I seize. Thy voice
Floats to me, fainter, fainter! and thy form
Fades farther, farther, farther, from my ken.
Thou flyest, Cherub!

THE ANGEL.

Self-deceiver, no!
Here, where I was, I am: and what I held
I hold. But thee thine ever-changing place
Hath changed already. Prince of passing ills,

Already in the Past thy footstep strays,
Seeking the Future.

SATAN.

What I seek I find
In thy despite: and what I find I win,
This Cross of Christ.

THE ANGEL.

The Cross of Christ wins *thee.*
As suns draw forth the vapors they dissolve,
So Love draws Hate, Truth, Falsehood, to itself
Whose touch annuls them; ever doomed to seek
Their destined dissolution. Take thy road,
Destroyer, to destruction! Seize thy time,
And all thy power expend; whose time is brief.
Brief shall thy time be, Satan, by so much
As most thy power is in that time put forth.
Do thou This Tree the dismal standard make
Of all the hosts of Darkness. Hither call
The legioned lies, and wraths, and wrongs, that lurk
In life's yet dubious twilight. Here, where Christ,
For man's sake, was by man's hand crucified,
Let Christless churches crucify man's heart:
Where pity bled, let pitiless priests proclaim
Bloody dominion: man's oppressors all,
Where hung man's Saviour, here their sceptres hang.
What then? O all unwise in wickedness!
The faster thou, to quench this kindled fire
Of deathless love, devouring deathful ills,
Shalt heap together from the tangled tracts
Of thorny Time all stubborn-hearted hates,

So much the sooner, Satan, shall all these
Be blasted, burned, obliterated, borne
Into oblivion, — and, with these, thyself
(The fleeting shadow of a faded shape
Of darkness in a universe of light,
Like Sodom's burned-out guilt in gathered smoke
Above her smouldering ashes, which anon
Left stainless the eternal heavens) depart
I know not to what place of unrevealed
Employment in the Perfectness of Power
That perfects all things.
Thou, and what is thine,
All pomps, all powers, not legalized by love,
All forms of faith that fall as faith exceeds,
All bonds that bind, all burdens that oppress,
Conventions, sects, exclusions, enmities,
Earth, as Hate makes it, — but the porch of Hell;
Heaven, as Fear sees it, — but a heartless eye
Fixt in the forehead of a frowning Fate,
Shall surely pass, and haply pass away;
But not the Word that Heaven and Earth this day
Recorded. Therefore, All is well, I say.
Peace and good-will — God's Will — to man!
Amen.
God's will be done on Earth — good will to men —
Even as in Heaven.

SATAN.

Angel, ay! But *when?*

[*Human voices of those that bear the body of* CHRIST *faintly heard in the distance, dying away.*

Courage, O friends! endure:
Bear all things: even as He:

Live — as He taught us — pure :
  Die — as He left us — free.
Freed from the world that bound us,
  Let the new life begin !
What know we of aught around us ?
  We know but what is within.
Not of the world was He
  When out of the world He chose us :
And not of the world are we :
  And what, if the world oppose us ?
Struggle we must, and strive,
  Sorrow, and suffer pain :
Die ever that we may live :
  Lose often that we may gain.
Say ye not unto the soul,
"Rest, soul ! it is over." Lo,
Beyond us is ever the goal,
  And forever before us the foe !
The strife that on earth is begun,
  Not on earth is it ended, sure.
The cause is eternal, one
  With the Godhead. Wherefore endure.
By the evil here and there
  Try we, and test we, the good :
And O, what if the evil were
  Good, only misunderstood ?
For, knowing not what is below,
  We know not what is above :
But that all is well we know,
  Knowing that all is love.

END OF BOOK II.

BOOK III.

LOWER EMPIRE.

ROMANCES.

"Quid salvum est si Roma perit?" — HIERONYMUS, Ep. 91.

LICINIUS.

PART I.

THE TIME.

I.

T was the fall and evening of a time
In whose large daylight, ere it sank, sublime
And strong, as bulks of brazen gods, that stand,
Bare-bodied, with helmed head and armèd hand.
All massive monumental thoughts of hers
Rome's mind had marked in stately characters
Against the world's horizon. These, at last,
Fading, as darkness deepened through her vast
Dominion, Rome became mere space, spread forth,
Confused and shapeless, east, west, south, and north;
And, the whole homeless earth thus made her home,
Rome now might nowhere rid herself of Rome.
The heavens were all distempered with the breath
Of her old-age. She, very nigh to death,
Paced through her perishing world in search of air

Unpoisoned by herself; but everywhere,
Like that Greek giant to whose frenzied frame
The blood of his slain foe clung fast as flame,
Withering the mighty limbs he could not free
From their disastrous trophy, so did she,
Choked by her own ensanguined purple, pant.

II.

Rome, in all places earth's inhabitant,
In no place earth's possessor any more,
Was thus by Rome pursued from shore to shore.
And, in that vast and sombre universe
Which was her dying chamber, 't was Rome's curse
To see the shadows change to substances,
The substances to shadows: and all these
Mocked her dim eye with their delirious train.
For now, from Power decayed, in the dull wane
And woful wasting out of her spent day,
Sick vapors rose that, rolling vague and gray,
Unshaped the face of everything that was.

III.

That severe Senate, once by Cyneas
To gods in synod likened, was become
Mere kennel for the curs that crammed in Rome
(Rome, — robbed in turn by Goth, Hun, Vandal, Gaul,
And, having all devoured, devoured by all!)
Earth's offal, — the filched filth of every land:
Mongrels, they licked each new-made master's hand,
Snarling at one another. Gorged with gore,
The purple gluttons of the globe, — no more

They, whose tremendous sires were fain to tug
For savage nurture at the she-wolf's dug,
With Mavors marched, beneath the Bird of Jove,
To scale the shaken walls o' the world. Craft
throve
As courage failed. Nor, now, the People rose,
And clamored, but the Courtier, plotting close,
Bided his time, and stabbed. Thus tyrants, dying,
Made room for tyrants: tyranny thus vying
With tyranny: to suit which slavery
With slavery, and fear with fear, did vie;
While Roman swords, for daggers used, were red
With murder, not with conquest. At the head
Of Rome's worst rabble (ill revering it!)
A new Religion's weird labarum, writ
On Rome's red ensigns by a Faith unknown
To Rome's rude sires, from Tiber, now, to Rhone,
Replaced her Senate's and her People's name:
Claiming whose sanction, in contempt of shame,
Blood-smeared Brutality with grim Disgrace
Coupled, like dogs, upon the public place.
Slander, the stylus, Treason plied the knife:
And, preaching peace, Religion practised strife.

IV.

Old things had ceased, nor new things yet begun,
To justify their place beneath the sun.
The Future and the Past, contending, wrought
To wreck the Present, for whose faith they fought:
And, in the barbarous bosom of the new,
Grimly the worn-out old world's vices grew.
Some pure Patrician, in whose veins yet ran
The scornful blood of sires Etrurian,

Saw, newly shrined, as, frowning, past he trod,
The Mother of the Galilean God,
And cursed her: some hook-nosed Antiochene,
Whose great-grandfather Paul's first prize had
been
Among the Rabbins, on the other side
Passing, beheld stark naked, wanton-eyed,
Stout-bodied Venus in her ancient place,
And spat, devoutly brutal, in her face:
Some half-bred Cæsar, waiting for his chance,
Bowed to both goddesses, and, with a glance
Behind him, passed, suspicious, on his way.

V.

Rome, in the main, for her part, like some gray,
Bedridden beldam, petulant and weak,
That from her own stout firstborn's sunburnt
cheek,
And brawny arm, turns, captious, to caress
The sprawling grandchild on her knees, and bless
With mumbling lip the unswaddled infancy
Whose manhood will not dawn before she die,
Less loved whatever rested of her prime
Than the loud childhood of the later time:
And the new creed, as babes are by the nurse,
Fondled and scolded, and both ways made worse,
Babbling, clenched baby clutches to destroy
Both sun and moon. An empire was its toy.
Donatus, with fierce fingers dipped in gall,
Dragged down Cicilien through the councils all:
From sultry churches Carthagenian
To convents cold in Arles the echoes ran
Of curses, all pure Christian, in bad Greek:

Cicilien damned Donatus. Shriek for shriek,
And stab for stab, with gladiatorial gust,
And, clamorous, scattering cumbrous clouds of dust,
The well-matched theologic athletes strove,
While Cæsar, smiling, eyed them from above.
Meanwhile, amid the hubbub, unalarmed,
That "Christian Cicero," Lactantius, charmed
Young Crispus; and in smoothest Latin praised
Those Christian virtues on whose work he gazed;
Discomfited the Polytheist sore,
And smote the fall'n Olympians by the score;
Slaughtering, with finely pointed periods
Of borrowed Ciceronian, Cicero's gods.

VI.

Then, when Licinius, Rome's last Roman, saw
The gods, his sires had worshipt with grave awe,
By slave, and savage, pimp, buffoon, and priest
Scorned and insulted, "Unavenged, at least,
The great gods die not!" groaned the gray old man.
And, breaking bound from wilds Pannonian,
He, with a remnant rallied to the name
Of Jove the Avenger, crossed the world, and came,
Camping on Hebrus, to confront the Sign
Of that new Creed proclaimed by Constantine.

PART II.

THE MAN.

I.

EVENING. At morn the battle. Met at last,
Stood, face to face, the Future and the Past.
Under the wild and sullen hills of Thrace,
Ominous, wrathful, ruin in his face,
On the last day of his own deity
The sun sunk. Mystic lights, from sky to sky,
Shot meteoric through the startled stars,
O'er regions named from him that, born of Mars,
First reigned among those snowy mountain-tops,
What time gray Saturn by the sons of Ops
Was, in his turn — as, by himself, had been
Cœlus, his sire — dethroned. For Power, not e'en
In Heaven, one hand holds ever. There, while o'er
Rome's antique ensigns, Jove's own Bird once more
Spread his broad wings upon the gloomy air,
The robed Haruspices, with silent care,
Prepared the victim, and asperged the shrine
Mysteriously with sprinkled meal and wine
And frankincense, till all together gleamed
The altars of the Twelve Great Gods, and streamed
With fragrant fumes. A shout of pride: a sound
Of shields in closing circle clasht all round
The central camp: where martial cymbals clanged

Applause, as old Licinius thus harangued
The legions loyal to the gods he loved:

II.

"Romans, whose pride is by your name approved,
The immortal gods, that to your fathers gave
The empire they now call their sons to save,
From yonder altars on those sons look down,
And all Olympus deems our cause its own.
With us the gods to battle go: with us
Whatever rests of Rome yet virtuous,
Yet Roman: all of manhood left on earth,
Of godhood left in Heaven. From every hearth,
Where Roman sons revere heroic sires
Our hearts have caught hereditary fires.
Each Roman here, to rescue Rome her laws,
Her gods, her memories, her manhood, draws
The sword Rome gave her children. Friends, our foes
Not us alone, but the great gods, oppose.
False to the faith of their forefathers, they,
To change Rome's laws, and chase her gods away,
Have armed Dishonor. Such their cause. Our own
To serve, and save, the old worth, the old renown
Of all that made Rome, ROME. A cause so just
I, with just faith, to the great gods intrust;
Whose cause it is. But if, O friends, in truth,
All we now fight for, — all that to our youth
Was sacred, all that to our age is dear,
The greatness of the gods that we revere,
The manful Past, that manly minds admire,
The immortal name of Rome's immortal sire,

The urns wherein our fathers' dust is laid,
The shrines they built us, and the laws they made,
Ay, even the banners that they bore in war! —
Were all these things less noble than they are,
Yet where, in fortune's poorest state, is he,
So poor in spirit, that can endure to see
Fouled by the rabble on his own hearth floor
The meanest garb that his dead father wore?
Or what man breathes, though born of humblest
birth,
That hallows not whate'er remains on earth, —
Each frailest relic, and each feeblest trace,
His reverent love can rescue from disgrace, —
Of her that bore him? Direr monster none,
Since Pyrrha's age, hath preyed on earth, nor done
More impious deed, than this unfathered Faith;
Man's memories all unmothering by a breath
Which blights the Present, strikes the godlike Past
Godless, and doth the barren Future blast
Bare of the bright presiding Powers that blest
Our great forefathers, gone to glorious rest;
They in whose names, with pure libations
Full-poured, our mothers blest their unborn sons;
Man's fair familiar Presidencies all,
Whose forms made sacred even a foeman's hall!
These, whom we fight for, are the gods that fought
For great Achilles; are the gods that brought
The wise Ulysses to his island home,
And brought from Troy the patriarch sire of
Rome.
Them old Homerus, them Virgilius, sung:
Them heroes worshipt: them we know. This
young
New-found half-god, Jew-born and bastard both,

Patron of slaves, and Power of upstart growth,
Where was he when Troy burned? Enough!
We know
Whose cause is ours, — Rome's cause! whose foe,
— Rome's foe!
Whose gods, — Rome's gods! In hands, more
mighty far
Than ours, the mighty issues of this war
Hang. If we fall, Romans, with us falls all
Romans have lived for. But we cannot fall,
Rome cannot fall, while yet of Rome there be
A score of Romans left to cry with me,
'Honor to our dead fathers!'"

III.

Proud he spake
And from that armèd auditory brake
The multitudinous echo of his mind,
In human-hearted thunder, the night wind
Rolled hoarse above the battle-heapèd ground.

PART III.

THE GODS.

I.

But afterward; when, save the steel-shod sound
O' the surly sentinel from tent to tent,
The camps were silent, and the night far spent,
Licinius, rising in the restless night,
Mused by the altars of his gods.

II.

Faint light
Streamed from the faded embers, and faint fume.
O'er all his spirit a supernatural gloom
Had fall'n, and that profound discouragement
Which seizes on the soul whose passion, spent
In stormy thought, leaves action half unnerved.
In dead cold skies the dark east, unobserved,
Waxed sallow. Dead-cold influences passed
About the old man's heart. Licinius cast
His body upon the ground, and felt a Fear
Plant its foot on him in the darkness drear,
And prayed intensely, as men only pray
When Fear is on them. Terror passed away.
A mystic wind was moving in his hair:
And hands unearthly touched him unaware.

III.

He, gazing up against the scattered gleam
Of the late stars, what time her dragon team
The night's moon-fronted maiden charioteer

Down o'er the dark world's edge was driving clear,
Saw — bright above the black and massy earth,
From cope to base — beyond the utmost girth
Of their wide-orbed horizons, the intense
And intricate heavens, with silent vehemence,
Burst supernaturally open ; as though
A bud should in a moment's time, not grow,
But change itself, into a flower full-blown.

IV.

To his sole sight was such a marvel shown.
The fair Olympians, all at once, and all
Together, in the Ambrosial Banquet Hall !
Each august countenance (vast gladness closed
In complete calm) ineffably composed
To an awful beauty. Unendurably bare
The bright celestial nakednesses were.
And, far behind those Heavenly Presences,
Heaven's self lay bare to the innermost abyss
Of the unsounded azure. Orb in orb
Of what both seemed to emit and to absorb,
In the same everlasting moment, light,
Space, silence, — sporting with the infinite !
For, to the universe, the universe
Listening, the while it answered, did immerse
The sound within the silentness of things.
Lights — meteors — mystic messengers, with wings,
Wands, trumpets, crowns — silently came and went
In the profound but lucid element
Of that unfathomable, far abysm,
Wherein (as, cloven by the crystal prism
It pierces, one pure ray of perfect light

Doth into divers colors disunite
And scatter its uncolored unity)
Life, — all the vast varieties, that lie
In Life's vast oneness, loosed. Befitting form
Each Spirit shaped itself from calm, or storm,
Snow, fire, rain, thunder, and sea-thrilling wind:
All creatures of the All-creative Mind,
That makes each moment, and each moment mars
Its own imaginings: thoughts, many as stars,
Or birds innumerable upon the wing:
Some, with congenial chance incarnating
Their restless essence, and so, brightening: some,
As soon as born, dissolved within the dome
Of that deep-lighted distance. Underneath,
The dim world, wrapt in mist of mortal breath,
Low glimmering, sea and land. And all about
The belted orb, close-coiling in and out,
Like a sleek snake with vary-colored back,
Glittered the constellated zodiac.
But, over savage peaks in lonesome lands,
Plains strewn with battle, billowy seas, blown sands
Where round the ragged bulks of broken ships
The white foam whirled, — and over leafy slips
Of sunken lawns, lone isles, and slumbrous lakes,
Where naked nymphs lured fauns from forest brakes,
To roaring cities, girt with gated walls
(Whitening whose masoned floors at intervals,
'Twixt bridges piled, and dark with passing droves,
Past milk-white temples, past green temple groves,
Tall obelisks, and statues somnolent,
Along the streeted wharves the water went
Barge-laden), slided down the silent sky,

Bearing disaster, bearing victory,
With benedictions these, as those with ills,
The viewless heralds of the Heavenly Wills,
Unmindful of the murmuring of mankind.

V.

All vague as vapor shapen by the wind
To mimic mountain, cape, or continent,
That every moment changes, came and went,
With wondrous modulation manifold,
The vision of that marvellous movement, rolled
Around the zonéd orb of Circumstance,
Revolving in the marginless expanse
Whereon the serene doors and porches all
Of that sublime god-builded Banquet Hall
Opening, let in and out Eternity.

VI.

There, midmost of his kindred godheads, high
In contemplative glory, and calm as morn
On lone Olympus (where no foot hath worn
Heaven's white snow from the summit of the world)
Sat Father Jove. From whose crowned temples curled
The locks that, shaken, shake the woody tops
Of scornful hills, and o'er the full-eared crops
Roll blighting thunders, in storms, white or blue,
Of hail and rain. Broad-browed, broad-bearded too,
In meditative mood, with slack right-hand
The cypress sceptre of his vast command

He, leaning forward, lightly held. All bare
The god's broad chest and ample shoulders were:
For gods, in company with gods, forego
Disguises meant for men: but all below
His spacious waist, in floods of massy fold,
From his large knees the lilied vesture rolled:
Lest mortal eyes should, even in Heaven, espy
Aught save the robe that wraps the Deity.

VII.

Firm by Jove's foot, watching the heedless play
Of the low-flighted world, his purblind prey,
Perched on the sheavéd thunders, with keen eye,
The dusky-feathered King of Birds. Hard by,
At the right hand of her great spouse, the Queen
Of scorn, majestic, with man-quelling mien,
And regnant eyes, whose large looks everywhere
Were felt in Heaven, gazed from her blazing
 chair;
Whereon, to left and right, from either side
Four crested peacocks drooped their Argus-eyed
Junonian trains. Behind, above her head
The attendant Iris, her handmaiden, spread
Her bright bow, woven from the azure grain
Of the midsummer silver-threaded rain.
That eloquent spirit of the woodland air,
Men call the cuckoo (which, being bodiless there,
Needs not, and builds not, any nest on earth)
Sat on her stately sceptre.

VIII.

Solemn mirth,
Like sempiternal summer, filled the hall

Where, round that Twain, the lesser godheads all,
At ease reclining by the ambrosial board,
In rosy circle ranged. Save one: Hell's lord,
The black-browed Pluto. Through Heaven's
cloudy gaps,
Where lurk the lightnings, no loud thunder-claps
Companion (they whose sport on sultry nights
Peoples the peaked horizon with pale lights)
His gloomy kingdoms on the nether deep
Glimmered, as dreams do through the gates of
Sleep:
From earth removed than earth is from the sun
Thrice farther: where sulphureous Phlegethon
Vomits his sullen ooze, — main sewer of sin,
That, in Hell ended, doth on earth begin.
There, dubious in the light by Hecate brewed
For ghastly uses, a vast multitude
Of shapes — all shadows of the lives of men —
Continually coming, sought the den
Man's fear digs in his conscience for his crimes:
The outcasts of all ages, from all climes,
Doomed by all creeds: Religion's shipwrecked
crew,
Barbarian, Roman, Christian, Greek, and Jew:
Who, in the glare of that disastrous light,
Gazed on each other's faces (dismal sight!)
And knew themselves, at last, for kinsmen drear,
The common offspring of one parent, Fear.
For, though man change his gods full many times,
Yet changed gods change not man, nor he his
crimes:
Still from the knowledge of himself he breeds
Fears that make Hell the helpmate of all creeds,
Or old or new. And, even already, all

The brazen bound of that Tartarean wall,
Which not the gods themselves can overleap,
In windy circuit o'er the sulphurous deep,
Half-Gothic towers, by monkish masons built,
Put dimly forth. Naught but the shame and guilt
Seemed real in the ghostly flux below
Of swimming change, that surged from woe to
woe:
So, flexile as man's ever-moving mind,
Whose masonry all monstrous forms combined
In one immense metropolis of Pain,
Though moored by Fear upon a midnight main,
Yet pace with time Hell's fluent structures kept,
From each new architectural adept
Fresh grimness winning.

IX.

But all this was seen
In fluctuation indistinct between
The gaps of Heaven, through filmy distances
Of darkness, wild as wicked fancy is:
Nor marred the mirth of that Olympian feast
More than spots floating on the sun's bright
breast
Darken his glory.

X.

Only, in the first
Amazing moment, when the vision burst
On him that saw it, Hebe, filling up
With nectarous œnomel a glorious cup,
Paused, as she poured, and stared, with open eyes
And open mouth, in half-displeased surprise,
Upon the wondering mortal. For he had,

To her, the ever-insolently-glad,
In the great human sadness of his face,
The aspect of a creature out of place:
As though into her golden cup had dropped
A sudden spider. Ganymede, too, stopped
Teasing Jove's Eagle: who, with a great cry,
Rose, roughed his feathers, seemed about to fly,
But, seeing Jove so quiet, drooped his wing,
And waited watchful of his keen-eyed king.
Venus with glance disdainful turned to scan
The old man's face: then, seeing that the man
Was chopped with battle, sun-bronzed, seamed with scars,
She, whose white arm was round the throat of Mars,
Pointed a rosy finger, veiling half
In her soft eyes a little mirthful laugh
Under delicious lids dark-lashed. But he
Looked on his worshipper remorsefully,
As some grave chieftain, when the strife is done,
Safe and unhurt himself, might gaze upon
His wounded battle-horse about to die.
Amor, that, trifling with his bow hard by,
Noticed not this new-comer of the earth
(He having both eyes bandaged from his birth)
Guessed, with that instinct arch to children given
For mischievous occasion (since, through Heaven,
The babble of the mighty banquet hall
Suddenly ceased, a moment's space) that all
The attention of the gods was occupied:
And furtively, by Dian unespied,
From her chaste quiver stole the arrows keen,
And, in their places, with mock-serious mien,
The rosy rascal-hearted child his own

Lascivious little wingèd darts dropped down.
Poor Psyche, with sad eyes, silent, apart,
Sat watching her boy-spouse: and wished his dart
Had ever been like Dian's. For, though now
The wrath appeased of Venus did allow
To her, as true wife of her truant lord,
Place by his side at the ambrosial board,
Yet on her still the great gods looked askance,
As a new-comer, of small circumstance,
And doubtful origin: and light-hearted Love
'Mid loose-zoned goddesses was wont to rove
Not seldom, with no Psyche by his side:
"For," said they all, "'t is fit that one allied
Beneath him, to his nobler native place
Returning, should consort with his own race,
Not tamely tied to a mate of meaner birth."
Such things in Heaven once, and oft on earth,
Have been. So Psyche mourned to find Love wed
Was not Love fixt: though stately Hymen said
Much to console her, whispering at her ear:
"Love comes and goes: but I am ever here:
Look in my face: am I not fair?" And she,
Sighing, said only: "O Hymen, counsel me,
If thou art wise, how souls may hold Love close!"

PART IV.

THE PAST.

I.

BUT great Apollo in his glory uprose.
And, even as when, what time strong mountains
swoon,
And tremble, in a sumptuous summer noon,
And all the under air is still, so still
That no leaf stirs, o'er some ethereal hill
Round which heaven's highest influences range
Invisibly, a cloud, with solemn change,
Begins to move; drooping his globéd glory
Slowly adown that inland promontory;
So down Olympus moved the Lyric God,
Majestic. All his serious visage glowed
With inner light, and music, mixt with fire,
Streamed from the strings of his Mercurial lyre,
Preluding prophecy.

II.

Severe he stood
Above the Roman, resting in a flood
Of radiance clear, and thus stern speech began:

"Ill counselled, and rash-spirited old man!
Learn to revere the all-wise Necessity,
That to the unceasing wheel of Time, whereby
Earth takes the shape by Heaven designed, holds
fast

Man's ductile clay; and, with the solid Past
Fusing the fluid Present's ardors, doth
The bright fantastic Future form from both.
Deem'st thou that, at thy summons, shall return
To earth the Powers whose parting footsteps spurn
Shrines where forever, since his course began,
The Names man worships are belied by man?
I will unfold the full mind of the gods,
From men obscured by Time's dull periods.
For man was on the earth ere we, that are
Not his first teachers, nor his last, were 'ware
Of his unblest condition: who, being born
Above the brutes, is but the more forlorn,
If missing consciousness of aught above
Himself, for him, in turn, to serve and love.
We, therefore, then, with gentle visitings,
To earth descended; and, from lonesome springs,
And hollow woods, lending to mountain winds,
And forest leaves, our language, with men's minds
Held commune: prompting man, by wishfulness
For the divineness of things fair, to press
Strong search for what they only find that seek.
Until, at length, from every river creek,
And winding vale, and wooded mountain, stole
Upon man's sense, in visible shape, the whole
Society of that immortal life
Which, mingling with man's own, made strong its strife,
Inspired its contemplation, beautified
Its being, and, ennobling earth, allied
Men, by gods visited, to gods, by men
Sought and perceived. Nor were we churlish then
To mortals. Wisdom, out of whisperous trees,
More sweet than whitest honey by wild bees

Sucked from Midsummer's veins, to shepherd priests
We poured in oracles; and at men's feasts
Sat down familiar, or beside their hearths;
Teaching Old Age how best the dædal earth's
Wind-sown abundance, might, by skill increased,
Be harvested, when manful Youth the beast,
That 's foe to man, had, helped of us, subdued:
Youth, whose yet earnest eyes in ours first viewed
The images of what man's life might be
By imitating gods! Neither did we
Withhold the godlike gift of glorious Song.
Brutish we found man's life, the brutes among;
Beauteous we strove to make it .... strove in vain!
Since man's low nature, failing to attain
The life of gods, but filched from gods their names
To deify what most degrades, most shames,
The life of man. Ill thanked was all our toil!
To glorify earth's clay, O, not to soil
Heaven's azure! came we from the kindly skies,
Kindling immortal fire in mortal eyes.
We gave men Beauty. But our gift, misused,
Hath wronged the givers. Have not men abused
Our very names, invoking them amiss
To deify ill deeds? Was it for this
Dian is chaste? Mars brave? and Venus fair?
And Jove just-minded? Wherefore, whatsoe'er
Henceforth men worship (whose base sense, indeed,
With its own baseness grown content, hath need—
If any price man's race may ransom yet
From bondage to its own bad life — to get,
By sharp compulsion of Heaven's highest will,
Keen knowledge of a nobler godhead, still
More potent, or more pitiful, than ours,

Whose images men's hands have hid with flowers
So thick, men's eyes no longer mark the frown
On each wronged forehead 'neath its shameful crown)
We, at the least, resign man's earth, and man,
To fates by us no more controlled. Nor can
Man's worship mock our altars any more.
Not unto us, henceforth, your priests shall pour
The victim's blood. Not ours, henceforth, the names
Invoked on earth to sanction earth's worst shames.
Not simulating service in our cause
Shall Fraud forge Heaven's approval of the laws
Devised by wicked Force to sanction Wrong.
Not ours the worshippers whose zeal shall throng
Dungeons with dying, charnel dens with dead.
Nor yet to us shall praise be sung, prayer said,
Whenever men henceforth have injured men.
Why should we bide on earth, and be again
Dishonored in the deeds whereby mankind
Profess to honor Heaven?

"Yet shall they find,
Who yet may seek, us. Not where we have been,
By thrones, on altars, seen, and vainly seen,
Through purchased incense clouding shrines profaned!
But I, that from of old this power attained, —
Having foreseen the Future, — to make fast
What in the Future man desires, — the Past,
Have wrought for man, by means of mighty Song,
A mystic world, which neither change can wrong,
Nor time can trouble. And, therein, man yet
May gaze on gods, and fashion from Regret
Fair forms resembling Hope. Wherefore, do thou

Cease to avoid the Inevitable. Know
That we, the gods, who minister no more
To man's ambition, fairer than of yore
Thy fathers found us, since henceforth set free
From all that mixt us with mortality,
Range undisturbed, beyond all reach of change,
In regions where immortal memories range,
Unvext by mortal hopes: responsible
For mortal wrongs no longer.

"Deem not ill
For man whatever betters aught man deems,
Or hath deemed, beautiful, though but in dreams.
Not by shrines shattered, not by statues spurned,
Temples deserted, altars overturned,
And incense stinted, are the gods disgraced;
But by base homage of a herd debased,
By Faith in service to a fraudful Force,
And wrongful deed by righteous name made worse.

"Nor yet, before the blaze of shrines not ours,
Fail we, or fall we. For the Heavenly Powers
Strive not against each other, as do those
Earth breeds of earth; nor can the gods be foes
O' the Godhead. Conquered are we not: since not
Contending. Deemest thou that Time can plot
Against Eternity? Fool! doth the seed
Grudge to his place the tree 't was born to breed?
The bud the blossom which it bursts to bear,
When Summer's summons through the sunlit air
Shatters the long-shut sleep, whose dreams occult
Are realized in sleep's aroused result?
Time, that returns not, errs not. Be content,

Knowing thus much: nor toil against the event
Whereto Time tends."

III.

Thus, frowning, Phœbus said.
And Jove, from high Olympus, bowed his head.

PART V.

THE PRESENT.

I.

THERE is a stillness of the upper air,
Foreboding change; when mighty winds prepare
In secret sudden war upon the world.
And when that stillness breaks, forests are hurled
Asunder, and sea-sceptring navies drowned.
There is another stillness, more profound,
Worse change foreboding; of the inmost soul,
In that dread moment when, from the control
Of life's long acquiescence in whate'er
Life's faith has been, revolted thoughts prepare
War on man's nature. When that stillness breaks,
A heart breaks with it, in the shock that shakes
Deep-planted custom, and roots up the hold
Of long-grown habit, and observance old.

From such a stillness in himself, at last,
Licinius raised his voice. The spasm, that passed
Across the quivering features of the man,
Smit by stern speech from lips Olympian,
Vext, as it rose, the staggering voice, down-weighed
With heavy meanings hard to express.

II.

He said:
"Immortal gods, by Rome revered! to me,
A mortal man, revering Rome, did she
This creed bequeath: that to all sons she bears

There is but One Necessity (made theirs
In Rome's requital for a Roman's name) —
Living or dying, never to know shame:
Never to shrink from pain: never recant
Recorded faith: never be suppliant
For life less noble than 't is man's to make
Death in the cause which, even though gods forsake,
Honor, retained, keeps sacred to the last.
This, also, in the records of Rome's Past
My life read once: and read long since, indeed,
Too far to new-live now a new-learned creed: —
That, when to all the creatures under heaven
Their severally allotted tasks were given,
On man — man only — the injunction fell,
To do, by daring, the impossible:
That he who doth, though dying, dauntless still,
Plant the pale standard of unbaffled Will
On Fate's breached battlements, and to the end,
Defeating thus defeat itself, contend
Tenacious in the teeth of tenfold odds,
Uplifts the life he loses to the gods.

"Lies! lies! all lies! Since gods live careless lives,
Concerned in naught for which man's being strives.
Justice? men deemed the image of the mind
Of gods — a mere invention of mankind!
Love? — some blind blood-beat in the veins of youth!
Belief? — man's substitute for knowledge! Truth?
— Unknown in Heaven! Why man, whom you despise,
O'erweening gods, for getting all these lies

By heart in vain, seems nobler after all,
More godlike, than yourselves.
"Nor yet, so small,
So slight, so all unworthy, first appeared
Man's race, but what you gods have interfered
Too much with man's condition to assume
This late indifference to your work, — his doom.
Since one thing have you been at pains to do, —
To cheat the chosen fools that trusted you,
False gods, and filch thanksgiving, foully gained,
For all whereto the woful end ordained
Was but betrayal.
"What! then all meant naught?
All, all, that Delos told and Delphi taught,
Though a god spake it? All your oracles,
Your priests, your bards, your sacred woods and wells?
Liars of lies! all pledged to cheat man's hope
In gods too careless, or too weak, to cope
With aught man suffers!
"Well can I believe
How man's imperfect progress might deceive,
And fail, as 't were (man's prowess, at the best,
Crippled by means inadequate confessed!)
The august hopes, by some bright periods
Of his brave promise, in the mind of gods
Inspired. But I, a man, no way can find
Among the many wanderings of my mind,
To imagine even how gods (whose godheads are
Glorious with power, each perfect as a star)
Should at the last fall short of hopes by them
In man's mind once awakened.
"Gods, condemn,
Punish man, plague him . . . . but forsake him?
No!

Not for your own sakes! Lest your godhoods grow,
From long disuse of godlike attributes,
Less lovely even than the life of brutes,
Not being so helpful.
"Yet, howe'er that be,
I, at the least, have loved ye, trusted ye,
So long that, though for me you fight no more,
Still must I fight for you. 'T will soon be o'er:
Or one way, or another. Soonest, best,
I think: nor greatly care to know the rest.
One thing 's to gain yet — death. No room to range
From what I am! The gods may change, Fate change,
I cannot. Not each casual tomb will fit
The fame a Roman's death consigns to it.
And I for this too-long-continued life
Must find fit end: hew out, with gods at strife,
Though sword break, heart break, all break, in the attempt,
Memorial — mournful, but, at least, exempt
From all incongruous contradiction vile.
Nor is life left me to lament, meanwhile,
Life's failure, — frustrate faith, and fruitless deed!
One life, wherewith to fail, or to succeed,
Is man's. One only. I, at my life's end,
Cannot go back to the beginning, — mend
What it hath made me, — unlove what I loved, —
Love what I loathed, — condemn what I approved, —
New-self myself, to suit occasion new.
The arrow, sped, must still its flight pursue
As first the bowman aimed it, though since then
The bowman shift his ground. Life speeds with men

Even thus. And few can choose, none change, what 's done.
A man hath but one mother : and but one
Childhood : one past : one future : but one hearth :
One heart, — to give or keep : one Heaven : one earth :
And one religion.
"Yet thus much, though spent
His force, and spoiled his whole life's element,
A man may do : and this, at least, will I!
Ere, quenched, the fires that still consume me, die,
I will collect their scattered heats, push all
Life's ashes, even while yet the embers fall,
Into a heap, and send the dying flame
Full in Heaven's face!
"O worthy of thy name,
Loxian Apollo! Boots it me to know
That men may see thee, as I see thee now,
Far from the life thy beauty doth but wrong,
Calm on the golden summits of Old Song?
No singer I! but a dull soldier : fit
Simply to love a thing, and fight for it,
Or hate a thing, and fight against it. Vent
My soul in song, I cannot, I! content
To do, at least, what merits to be sung :
Hold fast, when old, the faith I pledged when young :
Live up to it : die for it, if needs be.
What comfort, O Apollo, dwells for me,
Or what for any man, in leave to praise
The life of gods whose life his own betrays?
Their loves, that love him not? their power, that is
The mockery of the weakness they leave his?
Sing no more songs, Apollo, in men's ears!
Leave us, ye gods, in silence to the tears

You understand not! Spare this much-vext earth
Distracting visions of Heaven's unshared mirth!
This, also, ere I die." . . . .

III.

But there, his heart
Brake the thought in it, sharply; as a dart
Breaks, in the effort of a wounded man
To pluck it from the wound.
O'er Heaven's face ran
A tremble of white anger: like the light
Of wind-blown stars when, on a winter night,
The howling earth-born gust, that devastates
His own dark birthplace, having burst the grates
Of some grim-pillared forest (whose black bars
Release him, groaning) strives against the stars;
Their icy brilliance only kindling thus
To a keener glory. Eyes contemptuous,
Eyes cruel with calm scorn of all that pain
Which scorched his own, burned on him. The disdain
Of brows divine, in phalanx infinite
And formidable of transcendent light,
Glowed from Heaven's depths against him. But all these
Luminous and severe solemnities
He noticed not. For, when the wretched man
First to accuse the assembled gods began,
Love, from the midmost rosy Heaven, where he
Was sporting, stole a-tiptoe, curiously,
Closer at each word, by no eyes perceived
Save Psyche's, brightening while her bosom heaved
With some unwonted spasm, and her sad brow
Flushed, as a pale star flushes when the glow

Of the full-flowing sunset, sweet and warm,
Is poured upon it. With half-lifted arm,
And troubled countenance, and listening ear,
Love, thus, in pensive posture, lingered near
Whence came that voice (among their bright abodes
Ambrosial, then first heard by those glad gods)
Of Human Pain denouncing Heavenly Joy.
And, on the blind face of the beauteous Boy
The man's look lightening, as he lifted it
Defiant of whatever it might meet
In Heaven, was caught, and fastened where it fell,
By new incentive irresistible
To special indignation. Even as when
In the thronged circus, from the swarm of men
That hem and hurt him, some wild beast selects
One man, whom suddenly his wrath detects
As most obnoxious, and, in mid assault
On all the others, swiftly swerves, makes halt,
And flies at him that 's nearest; so the man,
From all that hostile cirque Olympian
Selecting Love, cried to him:

IV.

"Thou immature
And mindless god! whose smiling sinecure
Is but a blindfold childhood never grown!
Comest thou to mock at what thou hast not known,
— Man's full-grown misery at the end of all
The strivings of a life, spent past recall,
Used out, in urging, on its destined way
To dissolution, force that went astray
By struggling upwards? Such a vapor streams

From altars vainly lit; which, though it seems
To go up to the gods, goes nowhere — is
Made nothing, merged in that wide nothingness
Men take for Heaven! Thou purblind lord of all
Purblindest instincts! thee, not Love I call,
But Lust. For man's loss, Love must needs be
sad:
Lust, with no eyes to see man's loss, is glad,
As thou art. Yet, since men misname thee Love,
Loose, if thou canst, what, pent in me, doth move
Importunate, as some dumb creature curst
With such a secret as at length must burst
Its heart, endeavoring to be understood.
O Love, if thou be Love, pluck off that hood
That hides thine eyes from human grief. Revere
Love's last result on earth, — a wretch's tear!
Break silence, Love! Thee only, of the gods,
I ask .... What is it heaves earth's sullen clods
When Spring winds, wet with tears from trembling
boughs,
Breathe, and behold! in place of snows (those
snows
Themselves earth's seasonable comforters)
The abounding violet! Or what Spirit stirs
In tones and scents that bathe man's wearied heart
With fresh belief, and bid the strong tears start
For solemn joy? What mystic inmate gives
Some sense of loveliness to all that lives;
Some worth, though hindered, to the humblest
worm
That crawls; some purpose to the poorest germ
That buds unwitnessed from the meanest seed;
Some beauty to the barest rock's worst weed?
Which, through all pores of Being, everywhere

Passing, at last, into Man's Life; and there
Changing what was (till such a change it knew)
Merely, perchance, some droplet of wild dew,
Clasping a thorn, to Pity; some tost sea,
To Aspiration passionate; some tree,
That struggles with the savage gust forlorn
All night, wherein a wild bird sings at morn
Exulting, to the Fortitude of Faith;
In Man grows audible; speaks out, and saith
To Heaven, "Await me!" with a human voice
Man here, God everywhere! Which doth rejoice,
And droop, live, strive, and grieve, and grow, with
man:
And so, completing from all points, the plan
Of a god's vast experience in God's Bliss, —
Too perfect, too immeasurable, to miss
The manifold significance of tears,
Strength strained from weakness, struggle that
endears
Triumph, and failure forced into success, —
Looks down through all inferior grades to bless
Life's hopes with Love's assurance of the end
Whereto all Life, by Love inspired, doth tend!
Such a god dare not be indifferent
To man's success or failure: He, the Event,
Which man, His Means, he fashions to fulfil:
A god's means, therefore worth a god's care still!
O, such a god, my spirit whispers me,
Though nameless yet, and yet unknown, must be.
I seek His Face among your faces all,
Olympians; and, not finding it, I call
Earth's woe to witness that you do not well,
Being gods, to leave man godless. . . . . You! that
tell,

Smiling the while, as you depart serene,
Me that have loved you, me whose life hath been
Yours, though in vain, yours past recovery, here
At that life's cheated end, to now revere
What love of you hath bid me loathe . . . .
"If he —
If he, indeed, were — what ye are not, ye! —
That God — that Love, which . . . . Ah, but know I not,
Too well, with cause to curse them all for what
They are — and do — his worshippers? the late
Last form of man's forlornness . . . . men that hate
Even each other!
"Fair, false Forms depart!
Happy in ignorance of the human heart
You have deceived! Apollo, load some star
With liquid music far from earth! Far, far
From eyes worn out with weeping wasted love,
O Venus, guide whatever golden dove
Delights to draw thy lucid wheels!
"But we?
The men that loved you, and are left?
"Ah me,
What goal to us remains, whose course some Fate
Impels unwilling where no prize can wait
The weary runner?
"He, that late is come
To rule from your abandoned thrones the scum
And sewage of that rough-hewn rabble world
Wrought from the ruins of Rome's pride down-hurled,
Why comes he now, who comes so late? He too,
Hath he not all too long connived with you

At man's disaster? If he love to be
Beloved of men, why so long lingered he?
Letting men grow familiar, age by age,
With gods not destined to endure; engage,
Unwarned, to you the homage, he now claims,
And you resign; while men that got your names
By heart, have now no heart left to unlearn
The faith which, sued for ages, given, you spurn?
Is nothing sure? Must man's existence be
Bartered and bandied thus eternally
From god to god? By each new master made
Pull down in haste what each last master bade
The o'ertasked drudge build up with toil intense?
O for some voice Love's sanction to dispense
To Life's endeavor! O for one, but one,
Of all you gods, whose forms I gaze upon
With grief left godless, to assure at last
This else-wronged spirit, that, in despite the Past,
Which failed in power, the Present, by despair
Darkened, the Future, desolate and bare,
It did not ill to trust an instinct, wronged
Not seldom, oft rebuked, but yet prolonged
Through strangling hindrance and confounding chance;
Which, fronting Heaven with constant countenance,
Would whisper, 'I am love, and love is there,
And love to love is kindred everywhere!'
But which of all the gods can do this?"

PART VI.

THE FUTURE.

I.

"I!"
Love answered; and sprang forth with such a cry
As paled, beneath their golden porches, all
The rosy lords of that Ambrosial Hall.
Olympus groaned aghast beneath the sound,
Whereto the throbbing universe all round
Responded with a million echoes wild
Of awful joy.

II.

For lo! the glorious child,
By one transcendent moment's mighty throe,
Full-statured sprang into the new-born glow
Of his superlative godhead. His right hand
Wrenched from his lustrous orbs the blinding band
That had for ages held their lordly light
From flooding heaven and earth with infinite
And all-transforming splendor. Faint and wan
Waxed all the lesser lights Olympian
In the sunrise of that surpassing gaze:
Like their own orbs. Mars, with diminisht rays,
Reddening, receded to what seemed at last
A single spot of angry fire in fast-
Increasing distance. Like a happy tear
About to fall, Venus, a trembling sphere
All pale in rosy air, descended slow.
Of Phœbus rested nothing but a glow
Of solemn gladness on heaven's serene face.

Even Jove himself, in that expanding space
Love's ever-greatening glory lit, became
No brighter than his own broad star, whose flame
Burns lone on night's far frontier.

III.

In amaze,
Beneath the Face whereon he dared not gaze,
The man, prostrated, fell. In whose thrilled ears
A voice rang, musical as moving spheres :
"The sound of Human Sorrow heard in Heaven,
Immortal love to mortal life hath given :
Whereby in grief of life is growth of love.
Arise! On Earth below, in Heaven above,
Part of all creeds, and every creed surviving,
The Ever-loving is the Ever-living.
Heavenly and Human both : which, through man's eyes
Forever gazing upward, to Heaven cries,
'Behold me, Father!' and from Heaven anon
Down gazing cries to Earth, 'Behold me, Son!'
Arise, and follow where Love leads."

IV.

The man
Arose, and, guided by the Voice, began
To ascend that solemn mountain. Changed was all
Its aspect. Gone the Olympian Festival!
Gone all the rosy revellers! Rough the road
With raunce and bramble, where once breathed and glowed
The clear-cupped cistus and bright asphodel.
And lo, where last each golden goblet fell,

A grinning skull! On the sharp summit seemed,
Where late Olympian Jove's bright throne had
beamed,
Some dim stupendous image, looming through
Red morn's dull mist, and lurid in the dew,
Till at its foot the god-led mortal stood:
Then on his brow fell drops of human blood
From a great Cross, wide-armed, that o'er him
spread.

V.

He shrank, indignant.
Music o'er his head,
Like a light bird, came fluttering. And again,
To that light music lured, in mistlike train,
From rosiest air's remotest inmost deep,
Trooped — dim and beautiful, as dreams that creep
Under the sweet lids of a sleeping child,
On whose wet lashes tears, though reconciled
With trouble soon dismissed, are trembling new —
The old Olympians. Wreaths of every hue,
Fresh-pluckt from bowers of never-fading Thought
In Memory's dewiest meadow-deeps, they brought,
Wherewith to deck that darkling Cross. Whereon
The Past's pale blossom-bearers every one,
Each as he came, fresh garlands hung. Till, lo!
The Cross in flowers, — the flowers themselves, —
the flow
Of flower-bearers, — all, began to fade
In ever-deepening light.

VI.

Love, only, staid.
Yet Love's self changed. Whose form, expand-
ing, seemed,

To him on whose awed gaze its glory beamed,
To absorb into itself all things that were.
Heaven's farthest stars were glittering in his hair:
All winds of heaven his breathing loosed or bound:
His voice became an ever-murmuring sound,
The sound of generations of mankind:
Shut in his hand, the nations hummed: Time twined
About his feet its creeping growths; which took
From him the life-sap of the leaves that shook
Light shadows from his glory.

VII.

Mute with awe,
And lost in light, Licinius mused. He saw
His own life, suddenly, as when, through rain
And streaming tempest, on a blasted plain
An instantaneous sunbeam strikes.

VIII.

Even then,
Even while the vision broadened on his ken,
A sudden trumpet sounded as in scorn
From the dark camps.

It was the battle morn.

GENSERIC.

GENSERIC, King of the Vandals, who, having laid waste seven lands,
From Tripolis far as Tangier, from the sea to the Great Desert sands,
Was lord of the Moor and the African, — thirsting anon for new slaughter,
Sailed out of Carthage, and sailed o'er the Mediterranean water;
Plundered Palermo, seized Sicily, sacked the Lucanian coast,
And paused, and said, laughing, "Where next?"
Then there came to the Vandal a Ghost
From the Shadowy Land that lies hid and unknown in the Darkness Below,
And answered, "To Rome!"
Said the King to the Ghost, "And whose envoy art thou?
Whence art thou? and name me his name that hath sent thee: and say what is thine."
"From far: and His name that hath sent me is God," the Ghost answered, "and mine
Was Hannibal once, ere thou wast: and the name that I now have is Fate.
But arise, and be swift, and return. For God waits, and the moment is late."
And "I go," said the Vandal. And went.
When at last to the gates he was come,
Loud he knocked with his fierce iron fist. And full drowsily answered him Rome.

"Who is it that knocketh so loud? Get thee hence.
Let me be. For 't is late."
"Thou art wanted," cried Genseric. "Open!
His name that hath sent me is Fate,
And mine, who knock late, Retribution."
Rome gave him her glorious things:
The keys she had conquered from kingdoms: the
crowns she had wrested from kings:
And Genseric bore them away into Carthage,
avenged thus on Rome,
And paused, and said, laughing, "Where next?"
And again the Ghost answered
him, "Home!
For now God doth need thee no longer."
"Where leadest thou me by the hand?"
Cried the King to the Ghost. And the Ghost answered,
"Into the Shadowy Land."

IRENE.

"Ye have done it unto me." — MATT. xxv. 40.

I.

THE moonlight lay like hoar-frost on the earth
Outside. But, all within, the marble hearth
Made from its dropping logs of scented wood
A rosy dimness of warm light, to flood
With fervid interchange of gloom and gleam
That gorgeous chamber, — from the mad moon-beam
Curtained secure. No other light was there.
The outer halls were silent everywhere.
Midnight. And in the bed where he was born,
I' the Porphyry Chamber at Byzance, outworn
By seventeen years of pleasure without joy,
Not yet a man, albeit no more a boy,
His flusht cheek heavy on the fragrant sheet,
Slept Constantine the Porphyrogenete;
When glided in his mother leonine,
Irene.

II.

She, reluctant to resign
To her own whelp that prey beneath her paw,
The bloody Empire, stealthily 'gan draw
The crimson curtain; with keen ear down-bent
To count the breathings, thick and indolent,
Of her recaptured cub: who, sleeping, smiled,

By visions lewd of folly and lust beguiled.
Anon, she beckoned to the unshut door:
Whence, crafty-footed, down the glassy floor
Crept to her side (with withered features white
Bowed o'er a trembling lamp) her parasite,
Storax, the lean-lipped, low-browed Logothete.

III.

"Set the lamp down," the mother muttered. "Sweet
Must be his dreams. My son is smiling . . . . see
Wake him not, Storax!" Then, while softly she
Let fall the curtain, he from out its sheath
Slided his dagger, pusht the flame beneath
The weapon's point, and watched with moody eye
The heated metal reddening.
O'er the high
Bed-head (to safeguard sleeping Cæsars, slung
Slant from the golden-sculptured cornice) hung
On dismal ebon cross limbs, carven keen
In livid ivory, of a stretched-out, lean,
And ever-dying Christ. . . . .

IV.

(For, not long since, —
As rapturous Priests remember, — to evince
For God's Church Orthodox her filial zeal,
Irene's righteous regency, — with heel
Set on the heads heretical of all
Iconoclasts, had rescued from their fall
The Images of God, — assaulted sore
Erewhile by Antichrist's mad Emperor,
That "hell-born dragon," "the Old Serpent's grub,"

"Black-spotted panther of Beelzebub,"
Whom, being dead now, lodged, too, in hell's
flame,
God-fearing folks no longer fear to name
Accurst Copronymus.)

V.

. . . . His white lips set
Fast with a formidable will, while yet
Storax, who turned and turned it slowly, scanned
The reddening steel, Irene's rapid hand,
With restless finger o'er her puckered brow
Flitting, made airy crosses in a row.
Her eyes had settled sullenly upon
The superimpending image of God's Son:
And Habit, — that hard mock-bird of the mind,
Whose tongue, to chance-got utterance confined,
Memories by chance recaptured out of place
Set talking out of season, — to the Face
Mechanic response making, "*If thine eye*
Offend thee, pluck it out," she muttered. "Ay,
That is sound Gospel," Storax in her ear
Whispered. "The thing is white-hot now . . . .
See here!"
"And I am Empress" . . . . hissed Irene . . . .
"Smite!"

VI.

The armed Armenian on the guard that night
About the palace precincts somnolent,
Where, like a weary beetle, came and went
Across the flinty platform, — else dead-dumb, —
The slumbrous city's desultory hum,

Heard, pacing drowsy-cold (his watch nigh done),
Beneath the stars, through shrivelling silence run
A sudden scream, fierce, devilish, agonized,
Of quintessential pain; and all surprised
Started upon the watch, — waiting what sound
Should follow. But that dreadful cry, soon drowned
In dreadful silence, response none uproused,
Save of an owlish echo half unhoused
Among the moody towers, that down again
With churlish mumblings in her masoned den
Settled to slumber.
Then the soldier said,
Laughing at the discovery he had made
Of what, to *him* at least, that sound meant, "So!
To-morrow, and the amphoræ shall flow.
Increase of pay to all the Armenian Guard!"
Whereat he turned, and (while i' the east, black-barred
With lazy clouds, slow-oozed a watery light)
Waited, well-pleased, the trump of dawn.

VII.

That night,
In league with Hell, ere morning streaked the skies,
Left all its darkness in the misused eyes
Of Constantine the Porphyrogenete: —
The shadow of a shadow, forced to fleet
Out of the glare that gave him in men's sight
The semblance of a substance once.

VIII.

That night,
Irene, ere the Porphyry Chamber (pale

With strife wherein to triumph is to fail)
She left triumphant, glancing back, — her glance
Fell casual on the conscious countenance
Of that white Christ upon the black cross spread,
Whose eyes, into the now-close-curtained bed
Erewhile down-gazing, had beheld why those
Tight draperies round it had been twitched so close.
And lo ! where late those witnesses had been,
Instead of eyes, two gory sockets, seen
Through the red firelight, stopped her, staggered her,
And to a Fear, wherefrom she dared not stir,
Fastened and froze her.
For a while she stood
As one that, traversing a solitude
Where nothing dwells but Danger (all in haste
To reach the end, and, after peril faced
And passed, proclaim, "The deed I dared is done!")
Turns, by ill chance, midway, to gaze upon
Some hideous gulf in safety crossed ; and so,
Seeing how deep the death that yawns below,
By unanticipated terror, just
In the fresh moment of achievement, thrust
Into the suddenly suggested jaws
Of an imaginary failure, draws
Breath faint and fainter; forced to keep in sight
His own success, which, seen, defeats him quite.
But, soon returned, the exasperated will,
Still strong to scourge the rebel senses, still
Defiant though dismayed, with effort fierce
Plucked up the keen-cold Fear that seemed to pierce
Her feet, and fix them to the floor, beneath
That eyeless gaze. And at the sculptured wreath
Above the unblest bed wherefrom It hung

She, like a wounded cat o' the mountain, sprung,
And caught, and gripped, and tugged, and tore away,
And crouched with glaring face above, her prey, —
God's Image.
Still that dreadful dearth of eyes
In the dread Face!
With fierce and bitter cries
She dasht It sharp against the marble floor,
And bruised It with wild feet.
Still as before
The Eyeless Face implied .... "Do what thou wilt
Henceforth, and hug thy gain, or hate thy guilt,
Never shalt thou behold God's eyes."
She snatched
And hurled It on the smouldering hearth: and watched
The embers quicken round It: heaped up wood,
And made the blaze leap high: and all night stood
Feeding the flame: till all was burned away
To ashes.
And ere this was done, the day
Began to dawn.

IX.

Afterwards, she became
One of the world's chief rulers. Her fair name
Was praised in all the churches. God's priests prayed
God to safeguard the mighty throne she made
Illustrious.
Three times, — in the hippodrome
Once, in the palace once, once 'neath the dome
O' the high cathedral, — the Estates took oath

After this fashion .... "Witness Christ! we both
Swear, on the Gospels Four, to guard the throne
Of our Liege Lady, thine anointed one,
Irene, and swear also, bearing leal
Allegiance to her person, for her weal
And in her service, ever to oppose
Our lives against the persons of her foes."
This on the wood of the True Cross they swore.
And their recorded oath, with many more,
Among the relics of the Saintly Dead,
On the main altar was deposited
In St. Sophia.
Four Patricians, proud
So to be seen of the applausive crowd,
Held in their hands the golden reins of four
White horses, pacing in high pomp before
Her festive chariot, when Irene passed
Along the loud streets, greeted by the vast
Vociferation of a land's applause.

X.

To all the Roman world she set wise laws.
Men praised her wisdom. Wealth was hers immense.
Men praised her splendor and munificence.
Alms to the poor her hand distributed.
Men praised her bounty. High she held her head
Amid the tempests of a turbulent time.
Men praised her courage. Cruelty and crime
She scourged with scorpions. Men her justice praised.
Gifts to the Church she gave, and altars raised.
Men praised her piety. She in the West

Treaties proposed, and embassies addrest
To Charlemagne. She in the East maintained
On equal terms alliance undisdained
With great Haroun Alraschid. "For," said she,
"We understand each other's worth, We Three."
The world, when speaking of her, said, "The Great."

XI.

At last her fortune changed.
For 't was her fate
To win a worthier title. So, one night,
The eunuchs of her palace, — slaves whose spite
Her power had scorned, — conspiring its downfall,
Plucked the throne from her: seized her treasures all;
And drave her forth from power and wealth, to be
An exile and a pauper.
Meekly she
Surrendered what she had so proudly worn,
Rome's Purple. And, retiring from men's scorn
To Mitylene, lived there, lone and poor;
A careworn woman at a cottage door
Spinning for bread.
The world was sad to see
What it had done, then. Men remorsefully
Remembered, not her many evil deeds,
But her few good ones. For who counts the weeds
In any garden where, though desolate,
One rose remains? And, much admiring fate
So bitter borne so blameless of complaint,
The world, when speaking of her, said, "The Saint."

XII.

And after all these things, at the late end
Of a long life, she died.

XIII.

Then Priests to send
Pilgrims to deck her tomb made haste. They came
Barefooted, chanting hymns unto her name,
And made a noise of praise above her bones,
Which waked her spirit in the grave.

XIV.

Old tones
Of some glad tune, first heard long years ago,
When to their music life went gladly too,
If heard once more when life, after long years,
Goes not at all, but rests, in him that hears
Awaken thus the wild unwonted spasm
Of life's long-buried old enthusiasm.
Earth under earth, the earthly instinct, raised
By earthly praises in the corpse thus praised,
Returned to life.
She rose i' the tomb, and said,
"Open! and let me forth. I am not dead.
For men yet praise me, and their praises give
My joy thereat assurance that I live."
And the tomb answered, in its own dumb way,
"I neither know the living, nor obey
Their voice."
The pious pilgrims above-ground
Their rites performed, departing now, — the sound
Of human praise about that tomb waxed faint,

Then silent.
"Ay," she mused, "a Saint? . . . . a Saint
Should seek, not men, but God." She stood before
The creviced hinge of the tomb's granite door
And struck it with dead hands, and said again,
"Door of the Tomb, since I have done with men,
Show me the way to God."
The sullen door
Answered, "I am the Door o' the Tomb. No more.
Find thou the way."

XV.

Even then, an awful light,
Not of this world, through chink and crevice (bright
With brightness as of burning fire that turns
Whatever thing the burning of it burns
Into its sifted elemental worth:
Substance to spirit, ashes unto earth)
Smote all the inner darkness where she stood.

XVI.

Whereby she saw, outstretched upon the rood,
The Image of the Christ (by Human Faith
Placed there in token of life's trust in death),
And on her soul the sudden memory came
Like hope . . . . "I am The Way!"
Who said the same
Was There i' the Tomb.
To Whom she, kneeling, said,
"Teach me, O Christ (if I, indeed, be dead),
The way . . . . Thou seest . . . ."

A Voice replied, "To Me,
Woman, give back mine eyes that I may see!"
She dared not answer: dared not gaze upon
The Face Above.

XVII.

That moment's light was gone
Even as it came. Darkness returned.
The rest,
Hid in that darkness, never shall be guessed.

END OF BOOK III.

BOOK IV.

NEOPLATONISM.

THE SCROLL AND ITS INTERPRETERS.

"εἴπερ λόγος προσελθὼν τῇ ὕλῃ σῶμα ποιεῖ, οὐδαμόθεν δ' ἂν προσέλθοι λόγος, ἢ παρὰ ψυχῆς."—PLOTINUS, ii. 25.—περὶ ἀθανασίας ψυχῆς.

THE SCROLL AND ITS INTERPRETERS.

The garden of a villa near Alexandria, overlooking the sea. — Noon. — ZOZOMEN, EUPHORBOS, *and* BEN ENOCH, *meeting each other.*

ZOZOMEN.

WELCOME, Euphorbos! Welcome, learn-
ed Jew!

EUPHORBOS *and* BEN ENOCH.

Zozomen, hail!

ZOZOMEN.

Here, while we keep in view
The striving city, we evade the strife
Which, pleased, we witness. In the webs of life
Hark to the hum of those unhappy swarms
That cannot disengage their legs and arms
From out the meshes, more than flies that sing,
Caught by the crafty many-handed thing
That in the unperceived impalpable snare
Squats, spins, spies, and devours.

EUPHORBOS.

Ay, the air
Of Summer's strongest noon is ever cool

Under these myrtle-boughs, — our sylvan school.
Here breathe we Spring, while, all beneath our gaze,
The grass burns white against the stubborn blaze,
And the bruised day on rocky anvils steams,
Beat by incessant strokes of strong sunbeams.

ZOZOMEN.

Look yonder, friends, and laugh to see those four
Brown wretches sweating down the stifled shore,
To where, between the wharves, the sea-folk swarm
Round yonder galley; each with brawny arm
And straining neck outthrust, on bended back
Uppropping, as he plods, his heavy pack
Of party-colored stuff. I oft have stood
Still by the hour, and in like mirthful mood,
To watch brown beetles o'er a sandy road
Uprolling stoutly each his cumbrous load, —
(White balls of dust, they pack their eggs therein,
I fancy,) — each with hairy chest and chin
Smothered and choking 'neath the earthy globe
It costs so much to stir so feebly. Probe
The satisfaction which it causes you
(Standing in midst of their minute ado)
To watch these creatures toiling, and you 'll find
It comes not from superior strength of mind
So much, nor strength of body, as from these
Converted into consciousness of ease
By the supreme disdain with which you view
The *thing* that tasks the toiling, moiling crew.
Your nothing done, because of much perceived,
Is worth more, doubtless, than the much achieved
Towards their little seen, by creatures born

Beneath you, whom benignantly you scorn
Too much to hurt or help them.

BEN ENOCH.

The chief gain
Of life is, certes, theirs that can abstain,
And stand apart. Man first grows something, then
When first he separates himself from men.
Life's lowest and least choice results we know
And recognize in what the Many do
Together: life's augustest grace alone
Is witnessed in the achievement of the One.
Bees, emmets, beavers, to each other seem
As helpful, in their life's collective scheme,
As men to men. In this alone doth lie
Man's difference from the beasts: that man saith "I,"
Naming himself, but those "We" only.

EUPHORBOS.

Well,
The insects yet do yonder slaves excel.
For they (the insects at their toil) at least
Toil for themselves, and furnish their own feast.
But those men toil for others, whom, indeed,
They know not, or not love. Fagged hands that feed
Mouths not their own. True, Zozomen (alack
That so it is!), well pleased, the sense comes back
From chance employment on such dusty scene,
To find meanwhile, among these branches green,
His fellow senses, in full ease, supplied
By cool sounds and sweet smells with all the pride
Of a most perfect idleness. But see!

The white half-moon, by yonder old pine-tree,
In keener curve of clearer crescent now
Bites the blue air. Time to begin, I trow!
And Enoch brings us treasures in his sleeve.
Is it the scroll, Ben Enoch?

BEN ENOCH.

By your leave.
My mother's great-great-grandsire, as you know,
In your renowned Librarium, long ago,
Had charge of those three chambers, where were
stored
The Hebrew and Assyrian rolls. The sword
Of the first Cæsar on this city lay
Not lightly: but ere Rome's revolted prey,
Recaptured thus, her wrath was pastured on,
This great-great-grandsire of my mother, gone
To Thebes, in search of knowledge, — his life's end,
Was by an old Egyptian seer, his friend,
Forewarned of what was doing. Wherefore he
Returned not, knowing that which was to be.
And in the farthest East he died at last,
Leaving this scroll. Which to explain surpassed
Even his skill, though least among the seers
He was not. Nathless I, nigh fourscore years
Searching out truth, have in myself found light
Whereby to see, and set in all men's sight,
The meaning of this mystery. It is writ
All in straight strokes, like thorns. Perusing it,
I find the sense runs, not alone from left
To right, but right to left, as in a weft
Of cross-spun threads, and also vertical:
The text alliterated, duplex, all
Instinct with double import; and the tongue

That antique Syrian which survives among
Some parts of Ezra's scripture, where he cites
The letter which the Persic king indites.
Such is the text. Upon the marge thereof
I find a commentary cramp and tough
In Hebrew with no vowel points, by a hand
Unknown, which I surmise Ben Shishak's. And
All this I have unriddled, and writ out, —
The essence of it, not the form, no doubt;
For all made up of sounds too volatile
For transmutation is the antique style:
. . . . Even your elastic language locks not these
In its clear limbec, whence their light troop flees
In brilliance, bursting swift the brittle bond,
To fade i' the boundless infinite beyond,
Dispersed like falling stars. But what I deem —
Nay hold for certain — the substantial theme
Of thought that underlies the illusive text,
Here in my hand I hold, — plain, unperplext,
Set forth in current Greek.

EUPHORBOS *and* ZOZOMEN.

Read, prithee read,
Ben Enoch!

BEN ENOCH.

Then, to please you . . . . Since, indeed,
I know that, not alone, in earlier age,
Milesian Thales, and that Samian sage,
Anaximander, and Parmenides,
But not long since, Plotinus, and with these
(Not to name all those Greeks that follow them)
Latins no few, who, though of Rome, condemn
No less the dull inapprehensive scorn

Of their o'erweening West for Knowledge born
Beyond the palms, before the pyramids,
Where Earth's first Morn first oped her ardent lids,
Were fain to slake their thirst of things divine
At that same urn whence now I pour this wine
O' the old bright East. . . . .

EUPHORBOS *and* ZOZOMEN.

Read, Enoch! read to us
The parchment with less preface.

BEN ENOCH.

Well then, thus:

(He reads.) I.

"In the Beginning, God, the Unbegun,
(Dread Doer of the Deed that 's never Done!)
Made Matter: that the glory of his pure
Perfection, through this element obscure
Passing, and being thereby, as it were,
Tempered to what the strength of souls can bear,
Might make rich colors in the lives of men,
His cared-for, but yet unborn children.

II.

"Then
What he had made God gave unto The Night,
To keep till he reclaimed it.

III.

"Far from Light
Night took, and hid, God's gift. And spread thereon
Her mantle, murmuring, 'Mine!' And slept.

IV.

"Anon
The eons of the Day that hath no rise
Nor setting in the scope of mortal eyes
Flowed round about the circle of God's Will,
I' the orbit of Eternity.

V.

"Until
The Word, — which is the perfect probola
Of Power, forth issuing from the depths of Day,
Summoned The Night to God to render back
What God had made.

VI.

"Under Night's mantle black
The embryons heard, and shuddered through and
through.

VII.

"Night answered with the everlasting No
Of nothing-knowing Silence. And outspread
Her sullen solitary wings, and fled
Farther, and farther from the Light, before
The Voice of God.

VIII.

"In her brute heart she bore
Nathless, the Word, that cried inexorable,
'Obey!' whereto Night answered mute, 'Compel!'

IX.

"So that by disobedience she obeyed,
Not knowing. Unintelligently made

By lawless deed the lawful instrument
Of love she loved not. For where'er she went,
Deeper and deeper with her went her doom, —
To bring about God's glory in the gloom :
Flying with what she fled from unaware,
Compelled in her inconscious breast to bear
The conscious burden of the uttered Word,
Whose syllables are acts.

X.

"Stark Matter stirred,
Put forth a pining impulse, and 'gan rouse
Revolt all round its gloomy prison-house,
Yearning to get back to the hand of Him
That made it. Fitful in each monstrous limb
The thick life throbbed, the formidable face
Twitched, and the enormous frame in helpless case
Heaved : for, not dead, but dreaming heavily,
The giant infant breathed. But blind of eye,
Callous of ear, Darkness with Silence old
Crouched by the cradle ; and their dismal hold
Held fast Night's prey, and theirs.

XI.

"To break whose thrall,
He that is All in One, being One in All,
Raised up Auxiliar Forces : they that be,
Since man hath been, dwellers on earth, in sea,
And in the fire, the air ; though whence of old
These first had birth not even was it told
To Moses on the mountain. This alone
Is certain : not among the Angels known
Nor Elohim ; but rather of this earth,
Or elsewhere under Heaven had these their birth."

(He says.)
Rabbi Ben Shishak thinks, and I with him,
These should be numbered of those Teraphim, —
Inferior forces, visible to man,
Of the Invisible Will, — the Syrian
Worshipped as gods; whose images, when she
With Jacob fled to Gilead, privily
Rachel from Laban stole.

(He reads) XII.

"Then forth, at length,
To conflict came he that in subtle strength
Is mightiest of those ministers that serve
The Maker's Will in Matter. Every nerve
O' the intense Nature vibrated beneath
His burning impulse when, as sword from sheath,
Forth flashed the Spirit of Fire unto his aim;
Impetuous, thunder-bolted, fledged with flame.

XIII.

"He, that himself is never still, whose pride
Of prowess is not ever satisfied,
In his immitigable scorn of rest,
With searching challenge to swift Change addrest,
To do his bidding on the dangerous Deep
Roused to reluctant motion from dull sleep
Full many more and mighty ones beside,
In warfare, waged on Night, with him allied;
Whereby Night's realm was shaked and sundered
through
With an interminable to and fro.
For whatsoe'er that Spirit loathes, or loves,
To seek, or shun, his ardent contact, *moves.*

XIV.

"To run whose errands then uprose the Wind,
That sightless seeker of what none shall find,
And moved on the vext Deep, and strove with
    might
To rend the vesture vast o' the antique Night.

XV.

"Albeit in vain. For everywhere the deep
Enduring Darkness, — steadfast, even as Sleep
Is steadfast round about, above, and under
The tumult of some Dream that cannot sunder
The slumber it makes terrible, — clung fast.
And through the hollow dark the whirlwind passed,
As a thought passes through a soul, — which, go
Where'er it will, that soul still holds. Even so
The darkness held the whirlwind. And Night's
    pall
Floated thereon, forever, over all.

XVI.

"Then rolled the Waters; laboring to the light
That was not: struck the stubborn sides of Night,
And grovelled: for the wilful-hearted world
Of waters all its frenzied forces hurled,
To meet but blind bewildering reverse,
Against the solid of the universe:
And hung the hissing torrent on the arch
Of hollows drenched, wherethrough the dismal march
Of Deluge, bellowing, burst, and, with cold claw
Of clammy greed, into the hungry maw
Of monstrous movement scraped the confused
    wrecks

Of broken opposition. But, to vex
Itself in vain, the purblind element,
A rude and ravenous monster, came and went;
And, mad, with uncongenial substance mixed,
Disordered worse disorder wild; unfixed
The hinges of the gateways of the floods,
And shifted their far-fleeting solitudes
Endlessly to no end.

XVII.

"For, evermore,
The enormous Night, still motionless on shore,
Still moving upon sea, was everywhere:
Inexorable, ignorant, unaware,
But mistress still of Matter.

XVIII.

"Last, in wrath
Forth rushed Fire's self upon his reckless path.
Night's mutilated mantle kindled, shrank,
Sucked up the seething heat, and rose and sank
Tormented, yet tenacious. For, where'er
The scorching Spirit slid through, did Night repair
With instantaneously returning dark
Her ravaged shade. As when spark after spark
Runs over trembling tinder; which anon
To every fibre whence the flame hath gone
Doth — though calcined, yet unconsumed — restore
The swift-reverting blackness as before.
But through the havoc and the breach he wrought,
In rushed the audacious Force, intense as thought,
Right to the core of what Night strove to hide.
There — swallowed soon in the abysmal tide
Of Darkness — caught a prisoner by the thing

He came to capture, — made, not Matter's king,
But Matter's slave, — thereafter, might not he
From this material any more be free.
Though, discontented, unresigned to abide
Fettered in darkness and to cold allied,
The radiant captive strove, till Night was fain,
Cramped, and diminished of her dismal reign,
To camp far off upon the cloudy tract,
Half conquered, in a sort of sullen pact
With light she loved not."

(He says.) XIX.

Thus, the Principle
Of Fire, materialized, and made to dwell
Distributed in all things, — being thereby
In each confounded irrecoverably,
To all things, interpenetrating each,
Gave his own leaping life; that yearns to reach
Upward and outward.

(He reads.) XX.

"From the depths uprose
Gaping volcanoes, that with violent throes
Gasped against heaven. The strong earthquake's spasm
Jarred underneath; and split from chasm to chasm
The granite flanks of dizzy hills and isles,
And promontories rocked on tottering piles.
About whose base the round sea, rolling, went
To wrap the world with its blue element,
Locked in the calm light of the crystal air.
The buried Force, still seeking everywhere

Fresh forms of freedom in new layers of life,
Still from each hot and hidden seedling, rife
With the enraptured consciousness of power,
Put forth fantastic pomps of plant and flower
To deck the palace of his new-born world.

XXI.

"Then first the centenary palm unfurled
Broad in blue air his emerald diadem,
And thronged with feathery shafts his quivered stem.
Then spread the pillared plantain, a dim house
Of happy leaves, with shadows populous.
Then first in blaze of bloom the aloe burst
Bold-faced, and sank, and rose renewed. Then first
Slant stooped the cedars from their mountain height.
And over all the lands, in lone delight,
The forests murmuring to themselves, the seas
Sounding together, and the melodies
Of old Earth's morning song made music sweet;
Whereto the white stars, dancing with faint feet
Far off, rejoiced in golden companies.

XXII.

"And still, in glad and serious self-surprise,
The conscious being of the beauteous world,
With breath on breath, through bloom on bloom, unfurled,
Grew fair, and fairer, gathering grace, from high
To higher life.

XXIII.

"Wings wandered the warm sky.
The eagle from his mountain pinnacle

Faced the full sun, his neighbor; proud to dwell
Alone in light. The brooding vulture bald
Peered out of unsunned crags. The curlew called
From breezy bays. Crop-full in marshy haunts
Stalked the high-shouldered pouch-beaked cormorants.
The stilted stork to guard her airy nest
Stood sentinel. Down flashed with flamy breast
The red flamingo. Screamed the scornful jay.
The trotting ostrich scudded swift away.
Cold-coated wyverns flapped with spiky wing
Waste fens, in air forlornly wayfaring.
And merry bills waxed loud in leafy groves.

XXIV.

"The briny sounds began to swarm with droves
Of silent finny shapes, whose startled eyes
Peruse the serious deeps in dim surprise.
The tunny, with his troop of uncouth kin,
Tumbled all night in moony deeps. The thin
Flat-fingered starfish on the shelly sand
Sunned his slow life, or launched him loose from land,
Buoyed on blotched tangles of the salt sea-moss.
Gray squadrons of adventurous crabs across
Wind-beaten beaches crawled. I' the hollow stone
The hermit limpet lived his life alone.
Where blushed the coral branch, with unshut eye
Xiphias, in silentness, sailed, sworded, by.

XXV.

"Nor less the green earth's populace rejoiced,
Each after his own fashion. The hoarse-voiced

Hyena laughed at nothing all night long
In lonesome lands below the moon: the strong
Unwieldy unicorns, about the brink
Of reedy rivers trampling, trooped to drink:
The jumping jerboa in her wallet warmed
Her suckling brood with beaded eyes: long-armed
The lean ape chattered on the branch, and swung:
Gambolled the frolic squirrel: gayly rung
With spleenful neighings many a herded lawn
Of happy grass, where roamed at dewy dawn
The wanton horses: with embattled mane,
A citadel of strength, in grave disdain,
Majestic marched the lion: lissom leapt,
Or crouched, the wary tiger: cumbrous stept
The mountainous elephant: on sandy couch
Supine beneath the palm, with provendered pouch,
Mused the mild camel at mid-noon.

XXVI.

"The things
That sail on sunny air, with splendid wings,
Sparkled and hummed: the frugal emmets trooped
To store their sandy citadel: moles scooped
Blind chambers in the clod: the scorpion sprawled
At ease i' the hollow wood: in patience crawled
The many-colored caterpillars: bees,
The busy builders, around resinous trees
Sung ardent in the shade: the sleek, smooth-oiled,
And silvery-spotted serpent, slumbrous, coiled
In grassy twine of tangled growths: and swift
Darted the vivid lizard to her rift.

XXVII.

"For swimming thing to creeping thing was changed,

And creeping thing to flying. Life rose, and
ranged
Like ripples of running water in the sun,
Whose mirths are many, but their movement one.
And every creature, doing what the need
Of its own nature prompted, — in that deed
Delighting, — did by its particular joy
Make more the general felicity :
And, living its own life in great or small,
Promote, in part, life's purpose, summed in all;
As units in a scale of numbers stand
So placed that each gives out on either hand
His value to all others."

(He says.)

I opine
The text implies that all which was, in fine,
On each particular part imperative,
As Power's tributary, to contrive
For contribution to the Life o' the Whole
(Which, though in many bodies, is one soul),
Was by the separate will that works alone
In each part (conscious solely of its own
Especial want or purpose, whatsoe'er
That chance to be) accorded, as it were,
In prosecution of its proper joy,
Serving itself. Moreover, that the employ
Of every function requisite thereto
Was so contrived, in all God's creatures do,
As that the creature's action should produce
Pleasure, — the aim and stimulant of Use,
The motive of Life's movement. You would say
Life, wanting such things done, devised this way
Of winning all that lives to serve her end,

Serving its own; — by joy in means that mend
The salutary sense of some distress,
Which is dictatress of that happiness
The creature's faculties were formed to find.
And therefore man, that is in one combined
Both animal and intellectual,
Most specially behooves it that he shall
Secure the complex happiness of each:
Whose business, for this reason, is to teach
Himself, first to imagine and conceive
The highest happiness, and next to leave
To his soul's scorn all happiness that seems
A lesser happiness than that he deems
The highest: sparing piecemeal to employ
His faculties on fragmentary joy.
Since great joy must, greatly to be enjoyed,
Be nourished upon lesser joys destroyed.
I also deem they err who hold that Good
Is Life's aim: rather is it — to my mood —
Life's aim's benign condition: for Life's aim,
In fact, is simply Happiness. The same
Is Good i' the consequence. I say again
What of Life's end, if all the means were pain?
What if rest, sustenance, activity
Were needful and yet hateful? if the eye,
Compelled to see, were scorched by sight? the ear
Made sore by sound, though still required to hear?
And Life's necessities imposed, in scorn,
Not love, a curse to sense? The insect born,
Even while I speak, where yon stark aloes throw
Their scanty shades, — is born with skill to know
The food, and where to find the food, he needs.
What if 't were otherwise? The leaf that feeds
Might all as well destroy him. It does not.

Wherefore, perceiving how this Life doth plot
To bring her ends round, — get herself obeyed, —
By ministering to all that she hath made
To be her minister in turn, — what care,
What shrewdly shaped contrivance everywhere, —
Seeing, I say, her means all good, I must
Infer the end good also, — to be just.
Albeit not failing to observe, in all,
The means of pleasure made conditional
To a capacity for pain as well.
A possible Heaven and a possible Hell
In the employment of all faculties;
Mysterious Ezdads, welcome to the wise,
Though fearful to the fool. One asks me, Why
Is Evil everywhere? and I reply,
That everywhere there may be growth of Good.
Would I forego that growth, even if I could?
By no means. I resume the text.

(*He reads.*) XXVIII.

"There were
Two beings — of the realm that is not air,
But formed of finer element afar,
Which floweth round about 'twixt star and star,
And feeds with heat and light all orbs we view
Through ether rolling.

XXIX.

"Brothers were they, two:
Loving each other, living in God's love,
As in them God's love liveth: born above
Mortality: of burning Essence bright:
One all pure heat; the other all pure light:

Whose nature may be realized by men
Vaguely — in moments rare — and only then
When, by the Thinking-power upward brought,
Or by the Feeling outward, in his thought
Or his emotion, man approaches close
To Truth, — knows what he loves, loves what he
knows.

XXX.

"Of this ethereal and seraphic Twain
The names be Zefyr, Zafyr. . . ."

(*He says.*)

I retain
The antique nomenclature, as most fit.
Though, for the meaning, — could one render it
In the Greek tongue, 't were simpler doubtlessly
To hellenize what these two names imply
(If my conjecture be not all at loss),
Calling them Thermos and Selasphoros.
He that illumes of him that warms being brother-
Spirits, — of Wisdom one, of Love the other.

(*He reads.*) XXXI.

"'Now Zefyr, looking down the light of God,
Beheld this earth; and saw it the abode
Of beings beauteous, but unconscious yet
Of beauty: each life limited, and set
Apart from That which is the Life of All,
Shut in itself; so, fixt from rise or fall
To its own type of beauty: — there the end
And bourne of all its being.

XXXII.

"Strong to rend
And roam, the lion: bright in bloom, the rose,
And sweet in odor: where the water flows
Swift slides the fish: the bird in buoyant air
Springs blithe: each creature, acting unaware
Of all the beauty in all others, meant,
Mixt with its own, to perfect the content
Of the Creator in his creatures all.

XXXIII.

"But, what if it were possible to call
And gather up into some central soul
(The conscious consummation of the whole)
All separate strengths and beauties stored in each?
Some crowning nature graced with force to reach
Out of itself on all sides round, — return
Into itself anon, — and so discern
Its fit relation to Life's other parts;
Whereto, in each, Life tends, wherefrom it starts;
The fit relation of all parts to it;
And last its own, and their, relation fit
To the One wherefrom all come, whereto all tend,
In whom is the beginning and the end?

XXXIV.

"Could some such soul beget itself, — suppose, —
The lion's strength, the beauty of the rose,
The joy that in the sea-born creature swims
The deep, the bird's delight that soars and skims
The boundless heavens; — by power in it, as 't were,
To put its proper life forth everywhere

Beyond itself, and bring it back again
Triumphant, with a tributary train
Of other lives, made captive to its own
By the imagining of what alone
Sense notices, but knows not. . . . .

XXXV.

"Such a being
Might be i' the world the Eye of Nature, seeing
Before and after. Consecrating so
All creatures in one creature, crowned, below,
As the world's seer, conspicuous might he stand
'Twixt Earth and Heaven, upholding in his hand
The censer of the praise of all, increast
By his own joy therein: the great High Priest
Of all God's creatures before God!

XXXVI.

"'T were well.'
So Zefyr deemed.

XXXVII.

"Whereat, on him there fell,
Through all the solemn and symphonious psalm
Of seraphim that sing 'twixt palm and palm
Of Paradise, a sadness, soft, profound,
As of a silence hid within a sound.

XXXVIII.

Zafyr, perceiving that, where'er they went
Together, Zefyr's brow was downward bent,
Not upward, as of old, in council drew
His brother forth.

XXXIX.

"'T was when the evening dew
Was on the silent summer woods, the Star
Of Even smiling fair, serene, and far
Over the lone bright lands and waters wide
Of the young world. All-spying, unespied
Of beast or bird, in midst of bird and beast,
On a mountain summit in the farthest East
These Spirits sat in converse.

XL.

"Zefyr said
To Zafyr, answering as the heart to the head
Makes answer prompt, with no dull need of speech,
In some full-natured man:

XLI.

"'Look forth! and reach
With me, where runs my thought around the rim
Of this green world, that in the light of him
That made it, lieth sleeping with shut eye
And but half-beating heart; not knowing why
It is, nor in whose Hand it lieth there.
How fair to spiritual sight! so fair
That we, God's Seraphs, from our sphere descend
To bathe us in its beauty, and so send
The fuller strain of a refreshened praise
To him that made, and grants it to our gaze.

XLII.

"'And yet how ignorant! how blind! so blind
Of being, that, — albeit we, that wind
Where'er the Maker's Will through Matter moves,

Delight, therewith, to wander these warm groves,
Or from the meditative mountain-tops
At morn or even, when the sweet light drops
Or rises, watch the wondrous going on
Of God's great work therein, — means hath it none,
Nor knowledge, nor desire of any way
To speak with us, to answer what we say,
Rise and respond to that supernal sphere
Whereto, not knowing this, it lieth so near.
Of it we know : it knoweth not of us.

XLIII.

" 'What keeps the beauteous exile cancelled thus
From all communion with the Life that 's whole
In Spirit only? Surely 't is a soul
Yet wanting.'

XLIV.

" Then, an answer from Above
Was uttered unto Zefyr : 'Spirit of Love
That lookest downward, to all souls of mine
That, looking, loving, downward, — as doth thine, —
Love that which is beneath them, it is given
To follow where love leadeth ; down from Heaven
To Earth, from Earth to Hell ; and there, made one
With what they love, to employ their love thereon,
Living their life therein. That love may so
Fill all creation, up and down. Whereto
Is this condition fixt : That, nevermore
The loftier nature may its life restore,
Nor place resume, at that first point assigned

Its process in my purpose, till it find
Strength in itself to uplift there, — not alone
Itself, — but, with itself, that lowlier one
Whereto its love allies it. If in this
It triumph, then the sphere it soars to is
Diviner, loftier, lovelier than before;
Enlarged by life, not single any more,
But twofold. For, what strength the spirit needs
To painfully recover, by slow deeds
Accumulated from the clutch of Time
And Circumstance, in action, that sublime
First starting-point of Love's self-sought career,
Impels its upward impulse to a sphere
Superior even to that which, in descent,
It for Love's sake surrendered. In the event
Such spirits, my participators, win
At the Right Hand of Greatness, highest within
High Heaven's secret sanctuary, a throne
Reserved for those Experiences alone
That have advanced my purpose : which doth move
Not only to create, but to improve
Life in the highest and lowest, — life in all :
Whereof the progress is perpetual.
But if the lord o' the loftier sphere do fail,
Bound to base engines, upward to prevail
With the low consort of his choice, twofold
Shall be his failure ; failing to uphold
Himself where first he 'lighted from above,
And failing to uplift what he doth love;
And they shall sink together. And, because
What Is is infinite, all power, that draws
Upward or downward, urges up or down
Whate'er it meets with and can make its own,
Forever and forever.'

XLV.

"Zefyr heard,
Glowing and answered, 'Good, O Lord, thy word
To him that hears it, ever! Let mine be
The task with Matter to return to thee.'

XLVI.

"But Zafyr cried: 'O Brother, go not thou!
What of the load laid on thee canst thou know?
Or of thy power to lift it from beneath?
Behold! it lieth, sleeping in the breath
Of its own beauty, as thyself hast said,
This world, whose blind brute heart-without-a-head
Dreameth not aught between itself and God.
Once wake it, — make it 'ware that in the sod,
Now smiling all unconscious, stirs a soul,
And will not Matter murtherously dole
To such a troublous tenant, — if not death, —
Pain, dreadfully prolonged on every breath
That troubles Matter? What Earth's dwellers be
Is best unbettered. Bid such beings see
A life above them, better than their own, —
A constantly receding splendor shown
Never to be secured, — a point i' the play
Of power, perpetually drawn away,
Albeit perpetually present still
To life's unsatisfied pursuit, — how ill
Even to themselves must all they be and do
Then seem, confronted with the maddening view
Of such a prospect, endlessly at hand,
Endlessly distant. What contrivance, planned
For pain, more potent than such gift, whereby
The Better seen must needs incessantly
Condemn the Good possessed?'

XLVII.

"Zefyr, meanwhile,
Saw, watching wistful with a serious smile,
Among her lucid orbs, the pallid Night
Returning softly, in sad peace with light,
Over the waters to the west; and said: —

XLVIII.

"'Lo, everywhere, though pent and prostrated,
How Fire, forerunner of the force in me,
Hath vindicated in his own degree
A noble nature in base circumstance;
Whose very pain doth yet his power enhance!
What was this world, ere in it wakened those
Stupendous pangs, those passionate birth-throes
Of Beauty, the predestined fruit of Power?
Even to make possible yon bell-prankt flower
That trembles sweet i' the solitary air,
What earthquakes quickened, what mad mountains were
Cast up, crusht down: of whose so difficult
And dismal labor, lo, the last result, —
A little flower that knows not its own worth!
Ay, but the flower's mere beauty wins to earth
A Seraph. What, now, if that Seraph's heart,
Hid in this world, had place to play its part,
Express its passion, vent its vehemence?
What — of a nature nobler, more intense,
More beautiful, more complex, more complete —
Might rise therefrom the gaze of God to greet?
Perchance, some lovelier flower, of statelier life,
Sprung, not from Matter's toil, but Spirit's strife,
Might, breathing beauty from its native sod,

Win down to earth, — no seraph, but a god!
Belovéd, I descend. I shall return.'

XLIX.

"'When?'
"'When God wills. I know not. I shall learn.'
"'Too late, perchance. Thou goest alone?'
"'Not lonely
Strong helpmates have I with me.'
"'Whom?'

L.

"'Two only·
Faith-in-the-Future, Memory-of-the-Past.
And, doubt not, these Two shall beget me fast
New families of Spirits, born to know
(God granting) whence I am, whither I go:
Poets, and Martyrs. But, since I must needs
Pass lone from where thy placid Essence feeds
Its intellectual life, to lower forms,
Thee, Brother, thee, — though housed in dust, with worms,
Still let me feel not far, — where'er perchance,
Cramped in cold clasp of clay-born Circumstance,
I, from my new probationary toil,
Look upward with the love earth cannot soil; —
Still as of old, dear Spirit, in our august
And grand communion, lifting, though from dust,
Looks that in thine the love that lights them now
Shall find unchanged! And, if God's grace allow
This long-pent passion to attain in time
Some eminence of Nature, more sublime
Than Earth yet holds, — there, Spirit, if that may be,

Stoop thou to meet me, who shall rise to thee,
Nor wholly miss thee, where I soon must live,
I' the myriad moulds God doth to Matter give,
Wherein life beats : therewith my course pursue,
Trusting to feeble faculties : renew
Full many times a patient purpose oft
Frustrate : and labor to the light aloft
By many darkling, many devious ways :
And breathe, perchance in pain, vext hymns of praise
Through harshest instruments. Thou, therefore, be
Wherever I at length may lift to thee,
In some yet unborn being, eye or ear
Appealing for communion. I shall hear
Thy voice, and see the beauty of thy face,
And comfort me. Thereby shall some new Race
Take note that Heaven is glad of Earth's endeavor;
And Spirit doth to Spirit answer ever ! '

LI.

"And Zafyr, sorrowing : 'Wheresoe'er thou art,
Trust me, my being must with thine take part,
Dear Spirit, with thine my hope, with thine my will !
And Zafyr shall to Zefyr answer still,
Prompt as of old, and clear as chord to chord
Of Heaven's mid-music, if new forms afford
To ancient forces their familiar play
Of interchange, Love's mandate to obey.'

LII.

" Then Zafyr's kiss through Zefyr's being stole
Burningly. And behold ! a living soul
In Matter " . . . .

(He says.)

Something from the text is lost,
Which to recover the vain hope hath cost
To me much labor, long research, and some
Discomfiture ; for not the palindrome
Nor yet the comment, after or before,
Aids my distressed conjecture to restore
The perisht page I still am searching for.

(He reads.)

. . . . " Night answered to her august visitor :
' Spirit, my consciousness is made confused
By cross experience, and a sense, unused,
Of wants, to me not welcome. This I know :
That all things serve The All — I, even as thou.
Spirit, I know that Matter is his child.
But Matter's nurse am I. For thus he willed.
And me the infant knows and answers . . . .
see ! . . . .
Not knowing yet its Father. If to thee
'T will answer, — try ! I know not. Yet I know
Many, and mighty ones, have been ere thou :
Who came to mock, and still remain to mourn.' "

(He says.)

Here also is the cryptic writing torn
To my much sorrow. It continues thus.

. . . . .

" After that time the Earth waxed populous
With pageantries of prouder life, improved
By wider play of worthier power : which moved
Majestic in the forward march of Fate,
Through statelier periods of more intricate
Contrivance, with superior pomp. Erect

Of stature, and serene of intellect,
The august procession to a glorious goal
Rose, and confronting Heaven with human soul,
Matter, self-conscious, to emerge began
Forth from the merely mammal into Man.

LIII.

" Thus, at the last, appeared Humanity.
Whereto was given the hand of a man, thereby
To imitate the thought of an angel: fit
And supple slave o' the spirit that doth sit
Within it, ruling it: made lord and king
Of all Earth's tribes, that to the governing
Of man were given; since, in man's nature, theirs
Is gathered up, and given forth.

LIV.

" Vast stairs
Of various range, ascending to some shrine
Wherein a God is worshipt, so combine
With the whole fabric's purpose.
From below,
Who sees, up their thick-trodden labyrinth, go,
Pushing or pusht, the multitudes betwixt,
The statues and the symbols each side fixt,
Perceives not more in those thronged temple stairs
Than that each, graced with its own sculpture, bears
In its own beauty its own import plain.
But he that, mounting up them, doth attain
The godlike Image on the glorious height,
Where all parts of the Maker's plan unite
Their several uses, must perceive anon
The Temple and the Temple-stairs be one."

(*He says.*)
Friends, 't is well known to you, what from of old
Our Rabbins held, as still our Rabbins hold,
That, even as in Noë's ark combined
Lived, not alone the whole of human kind,
But also all the creatures that God chose
For patterns and progenitors of those
Which should be after, when he loosed the flood;
So also lived in Adam's life the brood,
Not only of all generations then
Yet unborn, and all families of men,
But also all the lower lives of earth,
All creatures whose creation by man's birth
as bound together, and in contact brought
Vith Spirit by the motions of man's thought.
Since man's thought lends a soul to everything
That man's thought lives in. Therefore is he king
Of all the creatures.

(*e reads.*)

LV.

"Thus man's consciousness
s troubled by the sense of More and Less.
d, even as one that bears a dubious name,
rn of high lineage, yet the child of shame,
Sprung from a monarch's loins, albeit the fruit
f a slave's womb; so, kindred to the brute,
et conscious of an angel ancestry,
lan walked his vassal world with restless eye,
Now turned impatient, or in proud self-scorn,
On his low native dust, now raised forlorn
In vext desire to his high native skies.

LVI.

"Now, therefore, Zefyr, gazing through man's eyes,

Sought his kin Seraph: from whose bright embrac
Was born a nobler and a mightier Race —
Mightier than man's, which man himself obeys —
Of beings for whose service in all ways,
And sustenance, man's race was made.

LVII.

"For these
Which are man's lords, using man's life to please
Their purpose, as man uses, to his own,
Earth's lower lives, whereof dominion
To him in turn is given, are, indeed,
Scarce bound to Matter by mere bodily need,
As man is; but have power upon man's mind
To make it ply whatever task they find
Fit for their purpose; mastering Man, as he,
For their sakes, masters Matter.

LVIII.

"These, then, be
The world's essential substances. To whom
Man's life is, from its cradle to its tomb,
Subordinated; unto whom man gives
The best part of his being: whom he lives
To serve, and perishes to please."

(*He says.*)

Thus far
The text. The comment here . . . .

(*He reads.*)

"For men's lives are
To these as sustenance. Mark how, of old,
Men held what I, alone of moderns, hold,"

(*Says.*)
Ben Shishak's known philosophy in this
I recognize, and know the gloss for his.

(*Reads.*)
"Namely: that this thrice-complicated world,
Whereof man stands i' the centre, holds enfurled,
And superposed as 't were, three orbs distinct
Of Life. Each diverse, though together linkt
By Life's one law for whatsoever lives,
Whereby of each Earth gains, to each Earth gives,
What helps in turn, the End-all, and the Be-all:
One Animal: one Human: one Ideal:
Three circles of one sphere. Of these, the least
And lowest, is the kingdom of the beast,
Which man commands: who holds the middle place
Between Earth's lowest, and her highest, race.
But that which is the loftiest of the Three,
Sole region of Ideas, I take to be:
Which man, in truth, subserveth and obeyeth,
As him the brute beneath him. Whoso sayeth
A man's ideas to a man belong,
Knoweth not what he saith, or argueth wrong.
Far rather, I imagine, doth the Man
Belong to the Idea. For neither can
The Man command the Idea, nor deny
Submission to its mandate. Can he fly
From its pursuing? or its path dictate?
Or summons, or dismiss, or bid it wait,
Or hasten, — here advance, and there stand still, —
Now active be, now passive — at his will?
And, if it live not servile to his whim,
Say, can he slay it? Doth it not slay *him*,
Inexorably, with no mercy shown,

As he would slay a beast that is his own,
If his death, rather than his life, promote
That end whereto the Idea doth devote
The Man it uses? All as well my mule,
Whose footsteps I by staff and bridle rule,
Might think he rules me, — goeth by the road
His choice, not mine, selects, nor own the goad,
As that, for my part, I should boast to be
The lord of that ideal lord of me
Whose force I follow, and whose burden bear,
Not as I will, but as I must, where'er
He goads me. And, if this brute mule of mine
Should lord it o'er his fellow mules, — opine
Himself the sage whose way is Wisdom's track,
Because he bears *my* wisdom on his back,
Were not his folly all the worse? 'What then,'
One asketh, 'arguest thou, apart from men,
Ideas can exist? doth not man's mind
Create the Ideal?' Nay, friend, for I find
Ideas make men, not men ideas. They
The dwellers of the ideal world, I say,
Are independent of mankind so much
As man is of the brutes. No more. For such
As is mankind's requirement of a race
Beneath it, born to serve it, — in like case
Is man. . . . . O, not by any means the lord,
But sturdy servitor, of that dim horde
Of dwellers on his brain; which, truly, need
And freely use, — to bear them, or to feed, —
For pasture, or for burden, as may be —
Man, for their sakes created. Nathless he
Doth commonly consider and declare
That he is Something Great, because aware
Of Something Great within him. In like way

I dreamed the dial to the beam did say,
'Lo, I am Time!' A little wind was waked,
Across the sun a little cloudlet shaked,
And the vain index of the heedless hour
Relapsed to nothingness. In many a flower
The moth and grub their dubious egglets hide.
Can the flower choose, or doth the flower decide
What to the summons of the sun shall rise
From her chance treasures to amaze men's eyes?
This launches, sapphrine-mantled, mailed with gold,
Some warlike wyvern beautiful and bold,
Fit for the Persic fay that rides to woo
His shy queen, gayly, in her globe of dew:
That sends forth, barely fit to browse on burs,
A monster hateful as the imp that spurs
His sooty flank, and hums a hell-born hymn,
Forth venturing darkly when the air is dim.
I can but laugh, not seldom, in my sleeve,
When I look round the world, and there perceive
How men have builded monuments of brass
To others on whose brains the whim it was
Of some Idea, on its sightless way
About the world, to settle, seize, and prey.
Why should the beasts, man scorns, not also raise,
After their fashion, some such baaing praise
About the sure-foot horse man drives, the ox
He ploughs with, or the fatlings of the flocks
Man kills for his best banquet? Now, I deem
That in the purpose of the One Supreme
Man is not, as he holds himself to be,
The highest necessity on Earth. But he,
Born for the service of Ideas alone,
Is for their sake, as they are for their own.
Notice, which most concerns, most occupies,

That Providence whereby man lives and dies:
Men or Ideas? An Idea hath need
Of growth, — full scope to satisfy its greed
Of power, and multiply, and propagate.
To meet which, man is there i' the mass. Now wait.
What happens? mark the issue. Men must perish
Wholesale, it may be, or piecemeal, to cherish,
Enrich, and ratify the otherwise
Starved and pent life this one Idea tries
To nourish at men's cost; itself or these
Succumbing. Which doth the World's Ruler please
To rescue or confirm? Why, horde on horde
Nature, to serve her supernatural lord,
Of her selectest human children gives
Little accounts she their mere deaths or lives!
'T is but a race to ravage, but a realm
To wash away in blood, expunge, o'erwhelm.
Doth Nature shrink from, — Providence impeach, —
The sacrifice required? Men's bodies bleach
On bloody battle-fields uncounted. Men
Born to be used thus: ended there and then,
Their use being over. Dead and done with, they!
Yet not in vain, do after-comers say,
Lived they or died they, since their lives and deaths
(Else vainly born and buried in vain breaths)
Have served to manifest, make eminent
The Idea for which they lived and died, content.
But to themselves, who doubts these men's lives seemed
Of all-surpassing value? Each was deemed
By the dead owner of it something worth

The special cherishing of Mother Earth.
And if to save and foster man's life were
Earth's, or Earth's Arch Disposer's chiefest care
We must, for those men's sakes (whose life, poured forth
Like water, seems mere waste of what was worth
Such frustrate forethrift, care so balked of gain,
In the fine fashioning of nerve and brain),
Attribute failure vast, or drear neglect,
To Earth's great Justicer and Architect.
But He — that wrecks man's life i' the sharp ordeal
Which rescues life's pure essence from the unreal,
The false, the fleeting — heeds not how it fare
With the mere Human, born for death: whose care
Is for the Ideal that doth never die.
The human swarm swims, in its season, by:
Races on races rise and roll away:
The generations flourish and decay.
What laughing Phantom leads, and mocks, the dance
Of these blind mummers through the Masque of Chance?
Lives on the life that from their lips it drains,
More glorious waxes as their glory wanes,
Brightens its deathless eyes in that fine air
Whose ardent essence man's prolonged despair
Feeds with the fires that waste it, and doth dwell
On dead men's graves, deathless, impalpable,
Made of immortal element, the pure
Result of man, — man's life that doth endure
Above the dust man drops in? What survives
Save this, the ceaseless dying of men's lives?

Egypt and all her castes, — bold Babylon,
Beautiful Hellas, — Rome's Republic, — gone!
What rests, on earth, the lone result of these?
The airy, but immutable, images
Of their Ideals, in the life that lies,
To light our own, above us. Starrier eyes
Than ours are on us. Egypt's Thought, the Grace
Of Hellas, — now no more to render place
To Rome's strong Will, — the stout town-stealer.
. . . . There
Behold man's bright pall-bearers, — they that bear
On their calm brows, for costliest coronal,
The symbols of the summed-up ages all.
Much musing on these things, I doubt not, then,
Ideas are of more account than Men
In that grand purpose which to further here
Each of Earth's tribes was, in its several sphere,
Created."

(*He says.*)
Here the text, whereto I turn
Again, grows dubious, dark. Let him discern,
That can, its meaning!

(*Reads.*) LIX.

"Thus Ideas grew
With human growth. Thus heavenly heralds blew
The trumpet of the triumph of the Earth.
For Fire, at first, with Matter mixt, gave birth
To breathing Life in beauteous flesh and blood.
Wherefrom anon (by its blind beauty wooed
With clay to keep celestial company)
The Angelic Essence wrought, and raised on high
Man, Earth's immediate monarch. Thence, through man,

Soon as the Earth-Spirit to commune began
With his unearthly kindred (lest forlorn
Of Heavenly love should be Earth's life) was born
The race of Earth's Ideal denizens,
Monarchs of men, whose life is more than men's.
Then, last of all, through these, — as, first of all,
Through Man, was Matter in the Animal
Made 'ware of Spirit, — did man's self (the abode
Of Spirit) wax in the Spirit aware of God.

LX.

"And man, scarce started on his glorious race,
Seemed nigh to touch the goal, when . . . . What
strange face
Of deathful beauty, with disastrous eyes, —
The wanton nurse of woful destinies,
Rose on the road before him, unforetold,
To flatter to his fall him overbold
In passion, — him by fairest form beguiled
To foulest worship? What portentous child,
From the accurst incongruous union bred,
Of what Ideal to what Bestial wed,
Arrests man's course yet? For behold it there
In the world's midst, arisen at unaware,
With its brute body and its brow divine, —
Man's curse, — the Ever-fatal Feminine!
The beautiful abominable one,
The watcher on the threshold, in the sun,
The lion-woman with the 'luring eye,
The inhuman riddle of humanity,
The weakness that is more than strength, the beast
That hath the brows of Power, and the breast
Of Beauty, and the body of Disgrace,
The Eternal Discord, with the dubious face!

LXI.

"Not causeless came the Curse of Sense. For when
The ideal world was felt i' the world of men,
From its strong action this re-action rose
(As first, most fruitful, offspring of the throes
Of Spirit in Matter made parturient),
The consciousness of Beauty. Ill content
With merely being, man aspired to make
Man's being beautiful; and, for the sake
Of beauty, with unbeauteous circumstance
Contended. But, incompetent to advance
Except by sensuous aids, he halted there
Where his five guides, the Senses, cried, 'We fare
No farther.' There, soon satisfied to rest
With these, he built him temples, altars drest,
And statues shaped, and incense burned . . . . and lo,
From out the incense fumes, with eyes aglow
To catch him, rose that Curse! Whereat . . . ."

(He says.) LXII.

O friends,
Suddenly, sadly, here the writing ends. —
Or rather, not the writing, as first writ
By him, whoe'er he was, that fashioned it
Of old, — but all, alas! that time and fate
Have spared of this torn scroll; at what sad date
Thus mutilated, I divine not. Long
Hath been my labor to repair the wrong
By some rash hand, to me unknown, done here.
And all in vain! though many a weary year
My wandering search hath been most diligent.

Byzantium, Athens, Rome, — where'er I went, —
Thebes, and the ruined cities in the sand,
And wheresoe'er report from land to land
Denoted any learnéd Greek or Jew,
Studious to store all crumbs of knowledge, who
Might haply help me . . . . nowhere have I found
The missing text. So that on broken ground
I seem to stand, as one that, with full heart
And lightly bounding step, erewhile 'gan start
Bold on his journey to some far-off spot
Reached only by untrodden ways, — some grot
Hewn high up in a mountain land, — the occult
Abode of that rare sage, whom to consult
On things of weight the man sets forth in scorn
Of peril by the way; and finds, though torn
To bleeding, hand and foot, by stone and brier,
The secret clew; and, taking heart, yet higher
And higher, clambers on 'twixt flint and stub,
Escapes the wild beast's paw, the robber's club,
(For bandit hordes infest the rocky height,
And from the thickets wild beasts roam by night,)
But night and day he, chanting hymns, fares on,
Surer and surer of the road. Anon,
Some dawn, at sunrise, hath he reached the peak
Where dwelt the sage he fared so far to seek,
And lo! the hermit strangled at the door
Of his own cave. That man shall nevermore
Have his doubts answered. No result remains,
But pure conjecture, after all my pains.
Much hath been saved, though much is lost; and more
Even than enough to make me much deplore
That so much saved, because of so much lost,
Should leave so unrequited care that cost

Such time and toil to save it. Question vain!
Shall Zefyr, helped of Zafyr, yet regain
His native element original?
How shall it fare with man? What end of all
That Spirit's incarnation? Tell me you,
Whom well I deem this city's wisest two,
What think you is the import of the words
Where my conjecture halts?

ZOZOMEN.

What 's saved affords
No indication of what 's lost. Divine
Who may what means that "Fatal Feminine,"
I cannot. And methinks no such strange phrase
Was needed to imply, what none gainsays,
That woman, ever since the world began,
Hath been a beauteous mischief unto man.

BEN ENOCH.

No. I dismiss that meaning.

EUPHORBOS.

And elect
What other?

BEN ENOCH.

One, which doth, indeed, deject
And sorrow me most sorely. For I see
That man, being twofold, body and soul, must be
Against himself divided evermore;
Never at unison with life; so sore
The strife is 'twixt the body and soul. In just
So much as, discontented with mere dust,

Which is its native, natural element,
The body, prompted by the spirit pent
Within it (which — a prisoner — doth conspire
Against its hapless jailer), may desire
To pacify the querulous spirit, and do
Its mandates, run its errands to and fro,
In search of joys not for the body meant,
The soon-tired body's certain discontent
Dismays the spirit. And man fails that way.
Whilst, in so much as, willing to obey
The bidding of the body, heard in turn,
And humor thus the helpmate it would spurn
But cannot, the compliant spirit spares,
To deck the burden its associate bears,
Some casual grace, some flying flavor lends
To spice the joys whereon the body spends
Its fleshly appetite, — the spirit's soon
Enkindled scorn of its own wasted boon,
And prompt disgust of what it deigned to do,
Dismays the body. Man fails this way, too.
But, say the spirit triumphs. And what then?
Death. For it kills the body. Or, again,
Suppose the body triumphs? Again, death.
It kills the spirit. Whilst, with hindered breath,
The two conspire each other's failure, life
Endures, indeed: but how endures? At strife.
But in this scroll a hope, methinks, — nay, more,
A promise, seemed vouchsafed. What I deplore
Is that, enough remaining of the scroll
To testify that, could we read the whole,
Fulfilment of that promise would be shown,
The missing end, which cannot now be known,
Leaves, by extinguisht founts, desire awaked
To fiercer thirst, with all that thirst unslaked.

So bright the opening promise! But just here,
Here where both text and comment disappear
In a great gap of doubt, ... man's prosperous march
Seems stopped by Sense, just where through Time's near arch
First gleams the Spirit's glorious goal. As when
That Carthaginian host, with Rome in ken,
At Capua caught, forewent the long-wisht end
Deserved by toil thus far endured, to spend
On pleasure premature, upon its way,
Forces first armed to seize a nobler prey.
The conquered, thus, the conquerors captive take.
Thus would-be Cæsars turn, with worlds at stake,
By captive Cleopatras captured fast,
Let worlds escape them, and are lost at last
Thus, the Ideal Beauty, by the sense
Itself hath kindled into vehemence
O'ertaken, is in sensuous fetters fastened:
Thus man's defeat his first success hath hastened:
Thus, the old question vain returns again;
And, just where all seemed gained, all 's lost for men.
Which things perplex me.

EUPHORBUS.

Hush! we are o'erheard.
Who is yon stranger?

ZOZOMEN.

Not a leaflet stirred
Among the myrtles: on the path no stone
Cried out: and through the gates not any one
Can passed unchallenged. How, then, came he here?

BEN ENOCH.

A man of most strange aspect.

EUPHORBOS.

He draws near.

ZOZOMEN.

Mark him!

THE STRANGER (*approaching*).

Peace be unto you, brethren. Much
I marvel, O Ben Enoch, that on such
A mind as thine, inquisitive of all
Light's rays, such mere interposition small
Should cast such shadow. A man's hand, no doubt,
Is not so small but what it can shut out
God's sun, if only through a single hole
The sunlight enters. But to thee the whole
O' the world is opened. Seest thou not, although
The conquered do the conquerors conquer, slow
But sure from out such conquest comes a new
And nobler triumph born of both? Thou, Jew,
Were not the Roman master (as he is)
Of all thy race, how should thine master his
By knowledge, veiled from Lars and Lucumon,
Yet viewed by Israel ere the Roman won
A rood of barren earth for that first plough
Beneath whose yoke the world's self labors now?
The Ideal thus, though by the Sensuous held
In bondage for a while, doth work and weld
All to itself, till form be filled with soul.
And, if indeed the story of thy scroll

Holds ancient warrant, as thou dost believe,
Deem'st thou the toil of Matter could so grieve
A Spirit's nature as therefrom to get
Most pitiful participation, yet
The toil of Spirit — stronger far than this,
And nobler much — receive of him, that is
Father of Spirits, no assistance meet,
Even from the fugitive semblance of defeat
Securing future triumph? . . . . triumph missed
By man in Adam, won for man in Christ!
Which, though, indeed, for all achieved by one,
Must yet again by each be made his own,
In his own fashion, after his own kind,
Ere all possess the gain of each combined.
Meanwhile, one man's life marks where life may reach.
One ripple only touching on the beach,
Thou say'st, "The whole sea spreads thus far." But one
Of the chain's many links holds fast the stone
The mason's engine lifts: yet say'st thou not,
"The whole chain's motion moves the stone?" I wot
Thou hast much to learn, Ben Enoch.

[*He passes.*

EUPHORBOS (*after a pause*).

Come and gone!
Incredibly! and with announcement none,
More than the sudden shadow on the grass
Of a cloud passing.

ZOZOMEN.

Thou didst let him pass
Too lightly.

BEN ENOCH.

There was that upon my mind,
Whilst yet his eye was on me, I could find
No answer to his speech.

ZOZOMEN.

Nor I.

EUPHORBOS.

Didst scan
His face?

BEN ENOCH.

I think it was no living man.
I think it was Elias.

EUPHORBOS.

Could he speak
Our language, Jew? For this man's speech was Greek.

ZOZOMEN.

What if it were — once more vouchsafed to us —
He of Tyana, that taught Ephesus
Things inconceivable . . . . since of his death
No man is certain?

EUPHORBOS.

Such-like rumor saith
The same of Heavenly John, whom Christus told
How God to him had granted to behold,
Whilst yet on Earth, the coming of the Day

Of Renovation. For that man, some say,
Is yet among us : and at sundry times,
Of sundry folk, in many different climes,
Hath certainly been seen. And whensoe'er
The man hath shown himself at unaware,
Great things have happened. Him I think it was
That hath been with us, and is gone. Because
Did he not name the man, or god, whom we
From some of the new Jews have heard to be
The founder of their sect, — bowing his head
The while he spake ? Moreover it doth spread,
This sect, already, even amongst ourselves
Who walk with Plato : even on mine own shelves
I keep a book — 't is barbarous Greek, indeed —
About that self-same Christus and his creed,
Ascribed to this same John. . . . .

BEN ENOCH *and* ZOZOMEN.

We 'll follow him.
Went he this way ?

EUPHORBOS.

No. Where the air is dim
Deep in yon tamarisk thicket.

BEN ENOCH.

Would I knew
What he would have us think he knows !

ZOZOMEN.

I too.

EUPHORBOS.

Hark !

A DISTANT VOICE.

Kai to pneuma kai hê nymphê . . . .

EUPHORBOS.

There!

THE VOICE.

Legousin Elthe . . . .

ZOZOMEN.

Yonder! where the air
Is dim . . . .

THE VOICE.

Kai ho akouon eipato
Elthe!

EUPHORBOS.

That voice again! in tones, as though
The man's hand beckoned while his mystic hymn
To us he chants.

BEN ENOCH.

Shall we not follow him?

OMNES.

Most certainly.

ZOZOMEN.

But if it be, indeed,
Only a phantom which the air doth breed
Not seldom, near the setting of the sun,

Out of the womb of Eve, — an eidolon
That hath no substance save what it hath power
To suck from mortal sense at this dim hour
Which ushers in the night, ... all search were
vain.

EUPHORBOS.

And I am bidden . . . .

THE VOICE.

Elthe!

BEN ENOCH.

Hark, again!

EUPHORBOS.

I cannot. Follow, you. I cannot. I
Am bidden to the great festivity
Which What's-his-name, — the new-made Consul's
choice, —
This very night . . . .

THE VOICE.

Elthe!

BEN ENOCH.

Again that voice!

ZOZOMEN.

By Bacchus! I too must away. To-night
Myself am one of those his friends invite
To hear our bran-new poet, Proteus, read
His bran-new Epic . . . .

BEN ENOCH.

And for me, indeed,
Philemon, the Librarian, waits by this,
To overlook that learnéd work of his
Which crowns the labors of Ben Shittag, who
Reformed erewhile the Kabala, — a Jew
Whom the Greek justly honors. Yet 't is sad.
I would have followed.

EUPHORBOS.

I too, if I had
The time . . . .

ZOZOMEN.

And I.

BEN ENOCH.

But weightier matters . . . .

EUPHORBOS.

Then
Farewell, Ben Enoch. Farewell, Zozomen.

ZOZOMEN.

Farewell, Euphorbos. Farewell, worthy Jew.

BEN ENOCH.

And, gentle friends, a like farewell to you.
[*They disperse.*

TIME (*passing in the silence*).

Go, fools! It tasks a century's search to espy
What oft a moment drops in passing by.

END OF BOOK IV.

BOOK V.

MAHOMEDAN ERA.

LEGENDS AND ROMANCES.

"We journey in the path of Parivaha." — *Sakoontalá.*

MOHAMMED.*

MOHAMMED THE DIVINE, ere yet his name
Blazed in the front of everlasting fame,
Withdrew into the Desert, and abode
Hard by Mount Hara, long alone with God.

But from the solitude his soul swept forth
And viewed the world, — east, west, and south, and north:
Weakness without, and wickedness within:
And how the people murmured, as in Zin,
Yet lacked the heavenly food; how, on each side,
The Roman, and the Persian, in their pride,
Were perishing from empire; how the Jew
Defamed Jehovah; how the Christian crew,

* It is needless to mention that this has no foundation whatever in fact. It is told by Vanini in one of his Dialogues, "De admirandis Naturæ," &c., and there used by him, as here by me, without scruple, to serve a purpose by way of illustration. As regards Mohammed himself, it is a gross calumny. But, as regards every form of Religious Authority founded on *fear* of the Supernatural, whereof Mohammed is here the dramatic representative, it is no calumny, but rather the feeble illustration of a formidable fact.

Wrangling around a desecrated Christ,
Blackened the Light of God with smoke and mist
Of idol incense; how, in midst of this,
Confusion crumbling down to the abyss,
A void was, day by day, and hour by hour,
Forming fit verge and scope for some new Power.

And he perceived that every Power is good
First, — since it comes from God, be it understood:
But, after resting many years on earth,
Power dwindles from the primal strength of birth,
Grows weak, then gets confused, and, last, goes
mad.
So that it is the weakness that is bad,
And not the potency, of creeds, and schools,
And kings, and whatsoever reigns or rules.
For, howsoe'er the ruler wield the rod,
His right to rule is by the grace of God,
Not the disgrace of man, which they that cause
By wrongful rule, are rebels to God's laws.

And, whilst he thought on this, and thought beside
How nothing now was wanting to provide
That novel Power which should regenerate
Mankind, renew belief, and re-create
Creation, but one bold man's active will,
Mohammed's secret thoughts were troubled, till
They made a darkness on his countenance.

Then Amru timidly raised up his glance
Upon the Prophet's face. Amru, his friend,
Who, through those solitudes to watch and tend
Upon him, stole from Mecca, when the light
Was fading out, and, footing the deep night,

At daybreak found him in the wilderness;
And, all day long, beneath an intense stress
Of silence, breathing low, was fain to lie,
Just tolerated by the kingly eye
Of his great friend, endeavoring to become
Like a mere piece of the rock's self, — so dumb,
And gray, and motionless. Amru at last
Looked up; and saw Mohammed's face o'ercast,
And murmured,
"O Mohammed, art thou sad?"

But still the Prophet seemed as though he had
Nor seen nor heard him.

Amru then arose,
And crept a little nearer, and sat close
Against the skirting of his robe, and said,
"Mohammed, peace be with thee!"

Still, his head
Mohammed lifted not, nor answered aught.
Then Amru said again,

"What is thy thought,
Mohammed?"

And Mohammed answered:
"Friend,
A sad thought; which I think you will not mend.
For, first, I thought upon the mighty world
Which lies beyond this wilderness, unfurled
Like a great chart, to read in. And I saw,
How in all places the old power and law
Are falling off. Again, I thought upon

My Arabs in the ages coming on;
The weakness, and the wickedness, of all
The ancient races; our own strength; God's call;
And all we might be, if we heard but that.
But if, I thought, I tell this people what
God, who speaks to me in the solitude,
Hath bid me tell them, the loud rabble rude
Will mock me, crying, 'Who made thee to be
A teacher of us?' If I answer, 'He
Whose name is Very God, and God Alone,
He, and none other,' surely they will stone
Or tear me. For though I, to prove the Lord
Hath sent me to them, should proclaim his word,
They will not heed it. Men were never wise
(And never will be yet!) to recognize
God, when he speaks by Law and Order: since
In these there's nothing startling to convince
The jaded sense of those that day by day
See law and order working every way
Around them, — yet in vain! And still God speaks
Only by law and order; never breaks
The old law even to fulfil the new.
But men are ever eager, when they view
Some seeming strange disorder, to exclaim,
'A god! a god!' They think they hear God's
name
In thunder and in earthquake, but are deaf
To the low lispings of the fallen leaf,
And the soft hours. As though it were God's way
To make man's mere bewilderment obey
Some one of his immutably fixed laws
By breaking of another, — for no cause
Better than set agaping apes and fools, —
Ruling his world by riving his own rules!

A worthy way! Sure am I, if anon
Some mighty-mouthéd prodigy, — yon stone,
Say, — dumb as Pharaoh in his pyramid,
Should suddenly find tongue, and, speaking, bid
The hearers worship me, — or where, below
There, like a mangled serpent trailing slow,
The camel-path twists in and out the rocks,
Yon sandy fissure, which the sly bitch-fox
Would choose well for her yellow nursery,
Gave forth a voice, to every passer by
Proclaiming me the Appointed One, ... they all
Would straightway grovel at my feet, and call
Heaven to attest how they believed, — each thief
And liar vigorous in his vowed belief!
But 't will not be."

After a little pause,
"Why not?" said Amru.

"Why not, friend? Because,"
Mohammed answered, "Allah will not bring
His heaven and earth together, just to wring
Credence from creatures incapacious, slight,
And void, as these. Nor, though his own hand write
The wondrous warrant to this life of mine,
Dare I so much as publish the divine
Commission. Still the cautious earth and skies
Keep close the secret. Let who will be wise.
God shuts me in the hollow of his hand;
Though in my heart I hear his stern command,
'Go forth, and preach.'"

With petulant foot he spurned
The sandy pebbles from him.

Amru turned
His forehead, bright with sudden bravery, up;
And all his face flowed over, as a cup
Wherein wine mantles, with a noble thought.

"And God doth well!" he answered, "though by
naught,
Mohammed, proved a mightier miracle
(And, sure, God's gracious gift!) than is the spell
Thou hast to sway to thine my inmost heart,
Do I undoubtingly believe thou art
The Man Appointed, — yet, indeed, for such
As these, of whom thou speakest, needing much
More gross and vulgar warrant for belief, —
Incompetent to see in thee the Chief
Of Prophets, by the dominant pale brow
And eyes from which the sworded seraphs bow
Their foreheads abasht, — O wherefore need God
send
A miracle more mighty than — a Friend,
Who loves" . . . .

"A friend!"

"I say, what miracle
Diviner than the heart that loveth well?"

"So well?" Mohammed faltered.

"Even so,"
Said Amru, drooping faint his head, as though
The effort to uplift that heavy weight
Of his devoted passion proved too great,
And dragged him down to earth.

Mohammed sat
Gasping against the silence: staring at
The man before him, with a smould'ring eye:
Whilst his hand shut and opened silently,
As though the Fiend's black forelock, slipping through
His feverish clutch, just foiled him: and the hue
Waned into whiteness on his swarthy cheek.
Then Amru, when Mohammed would not speak,
Lifted his looks, and gazed, as though in doubt
Of what strange thing the silence was about.
And Amru said:

"Mohammed, let thy slave
Find favor in thy sight! — albeit, I have
No wit in counsel. Get thee privily
Again to Mecca. Leave this night to me.
To-morrow, stand up in the market-place
And plead against the people, face to face,
And call them hither; prophesying they
By sign and miracle along the way
Shall know The Man Appointed. I, meanwhile,
Will creep into yon crevice . . . . Ha! dost smile,
Mohammed? Dost approve the thing I mean? —
Will creep into yon crevice, and, unseen,
Await the multitude, — which must come by,
Thou guiding. Unto whom a voice shall cry,
'*This is Mohammed! I, the Lord of Heaven,*
Make known to all this people, I have given
To him to preach My Law, — that he may be
My Prophet to all nations under Me.' —
Smile! smile again, Mohammed! . . . . Only smile
Less terribly upon me! . . . . Of the vile

The vilest, — yet thy servant, Awful One!
Less terribly, Mohammed! . . . .

"Then, anon,
When all the place is silent, — the crowd far —
Far out of sight — and nothing but yon star
To witness, — I will steal out of the cave." . . . .

"Hah!" . . . .

"O Mohammed, am I not thy slave?
Look not so fiercely on me! . . . . And far off
Follow the silly people. Who will scoff?
Who will misdoubt thee then? . . . . Mohammed,
speak!"

Mohammed spake not.

All the Prophet's cheek
Was wan with whirling thoughts that o'er it cast
Their troubled shades, and left it calm at last,
As battle-fields, — when battles have been won
Or lost, and dawn breaks slowly.

"Be it, my son,
As thou hast spoken. This is God's command."
He wearily sighed, and laid a heavy hand
On Amru's shoulder. "I to Mecca go
This night. At dawn, as thou hast said, so do."

And all night long, over the silent sand,
Under the silent stars, across the land
Mohammed fled: as though he heard the feet
Of Iblis following, and a voice repeat
Close at his ear, monotonous and slow,

"Thou wouldst have had this man trust thee. But now,
Mohammed, thou thyself must trust to him."

And the voice ceased not; nor the feet; till, dim
At first, then flaring in a stormy sky,
The drear dawn lightened o'er him angrily.

That day he stood up in the market-place,
And pleaded with the people face to face;
Pouring from urns of solitary thought
A piercing eloquence upon them, brought,
Word after word, by wondrous Spirits from far,
Shrill with the music of the morning star,
Weighty with thunder. Some averred they saw
The light that lighted Moses, when the Law
On Sinai from God's finger he received,
Enhalo all his brow. The noon achieved
The dawn's desire. They followed him by flocks
Far through the Desert to the rifted rocks.
And, ever as they journeyed, in their van
A thunder-cloud, that, since the day began,
Had labored to demolish half the sky,
Travelled to reach Mount Hara, and there die.
And still the people followed; and, beside
The mountain halting, heard a voice which cried
(Out of a rocky fissure, the ground story
Of some wild coney's dismal dormitory):

"This is Mohammed! I, the Lord of Heaven,
Proclaim to all this people, I have given
To him to preach My Law, that he may be
My Prophet, to all nations under Me."

And, as the voice ceased, suddenly a streak
Of forked fire flickered from a riven creek
In the spent cloud, which, splitting overhead
Bellowed.
And all the people cried, and said
"The Voice of God!"
And then did each man fall
Flat at the Prophet's feet, and, grovelling, call
On Heaven's Appointed.

"Speak, Mohammed! speak!"

Mohammed spake not.

All the Prophet's cheek
Was white with pain, as warring angels passed
Across his trampled soul, — left bare at last
As battle-fields, when battles have been won,
Or lost, and dawn breaks slowly.

Blocks of stone,
Tumbled by ages in the rifted sand,
Burned white about the lion-colored land,
And, beaten by a blinding sunlight, made
Blots, in a level glare, of sprinkled shade.
Mohammed stretched his hand. Not Moses' rod
Won easier reverence.

"Ay! the Voice of God
Hath spoken, not to be misunderstood,
This day unto us. Wherefore, it seems good
To build, O friends, an altar to The Lord
Here on the spot from whence the wondrous Word
Hath issued. And see! Nature, warned before
Of this forecast event, hath furnished store

Of stone to build with. Never from this day
Be it averred that any beast of prey
Or reptile base hath been allowed to dwell
Where God first housed his Holy Oracle!
Cram every crevice of this mountain flaw:
Leave not a loophole for the leopard's paw,
A cranny that a mouse might wriggle through!
If anything unclean hath crept into
This Mouth of Earth where Heaven's high Voice
abode
Erewhile, O friends, — worm, adder, viper, toad,
There let it perish 'neath a costlier tomb
Than ever reptile owned! Seal up the womb
Of this dread prodigy. Hark! from yon cloud
Above us, Spirits of the thunder, bowed
To watch, grow wild, impatient to be gone.
Begin the work. Pile strong with ponderous
stone
The altar. Bear ye each his burden . . . . Nay,
None but myself the first firm stone shall lay
Unto this sacred fabric!" . . .

Then himself
Fiercely dislodging from its sandy shelf
A mighty mountain fragment, rolled, with might
And main, the rock-surrendered offering right
Against the cave. And turned himself about
And hid his face. In prayer, as who shall doubt?

And, when the people heard this, they were glad
Exceedingly: not only to have had
No heavier task enjoined them, but because
If any man profane had dared to pause
And doubt till then, he, certes, had no choice

But to believe henceforth. For, if the *voice*
Were nothing more than human, the *command*
Was something less. Could mere Ambition stand
Thus calmly contemplating, stone by stone,
The immurement of some creature of its own?
And so they heartened to the work, until
The rocky altar rose against the hill;
And then Mohammed blest it.

And that day,
Upon that altar, Providence, they say,
Founded a new Religion. Which, thus reared
In the lone Desert, spread, and soon ensphered
The quadripartite globe. But, from that day,
Mohammed went no more alone to pray
On Hara, as his wont had been before.

For him, the sweet of solitude was o'er.

THE ROSES OF SAADI.

I.

MOSES AND THE DERVISH.

OD, that heaven's seven climates hath spread forth,
To every creature, even as is the worth,
The lot apportions, and the use of things.
If to the creeping cat were given wings,
No sparrow's egg would ever be a bird.

Moses the Prophet, who with God conferred,
Beheld a Dervish, that, for dire distress
And lack of clothes to hide his nakedness,
Buried his body in the desert sand.
This Dervish cried:
"O Moses, whom the Hand
Of the Most High God favors! make thy prayer
That he may grant me food and clothes to wear
Who knows the misery of me, and the need."

Then Moses prayed to God, that he would feed
And clothe that Dervish.

Nine days after this,
Returning from Mount Sinai in bliss,

Having beheld God's face, the Prophet met
The Dervish in the hands of Justice, set
Between two officers ; and, all about,
The rabble followed him with hoot, and shout,
And jeer.
The Prophet asked of those that cried,
"What hath befallen this man ?"

And they replied,
"He hath drunk wine, and, having slain a man,
Is going to the death."

Moses began
To praise the Maker of the Universe,
Seeing that his prayer, though granted, proved perverse,
Since God to every living soul sets forth
The circumstance according to the worth.

II.

THE BOY AND THE RING.

FAIR chance, held fast, is merit. A certain king
Of Persia had a jewel in a ring.
He set it on the dome of Azud high;
And, when they saw it flashing in the sky,
Made proclamation to his royal troop,
That whoso sent an arrow through the hoop
That held the gem, should have the ring to wear.

It chanced there were four hundred archers near,
Of the king's company, about the king.

Each took his aim, and shot, and missed the ring.

A boy, at play upon the terraced roof
Of a near building, bent his bow aloof
At random, and behold! the morning breeze
His little arrow caught, and bore with ease
Right through the circlet of the gem. The king,
Well pleased, unto the boy assigned the ring.

Then the boy burnt his arrows and his bow.

The king, astonished, said, "Why dost thou so,
Seeing thy first shot hath had great success?"

He answered, "Lest my second make that less."

III.

THE EYES OF MAHMUD.

Sultàn Mahmùd, son of Sabaktogin,
Swept with his sceptre the hot sands of Zin,
Spread forth his mantle over Palestine,
And made the carpet of his glory shine
From Cufah to Cashmere; and, in his pride,
Said, "All these lands are mine."

At last he died.

Then his sons laid him with exceeding state
In a deep tomb. Upon the granite gate
Outside they graved in gold his titles all,
And all the names of kingdoms in his thrall,
And all his glory. And beside his head
They placed a bag of rice, a loaf of bread,
And water in a pitcher. This they did
In order that, if God should haply bid
His servant Death to let this sultan go
Because of his surpassing greatness, so
He might not come back hungry. But he lay
In his high marble coffin night and day
Motionless, without majesty or will.

Darkness sat down beside him, and was still.

Afterwards, when a hundred years had rolled,
A certain king, desiring to behold
This famous sultan, gave command to unlock

The granite gate of that sepulchral rock,
And, with a lamp, went down into the tomb,
And all his court.

Out of the nether gloom
There rose a loathsome stench intolerable.
Hard by the marble coffin, on a sill
Of mildewed stone the earthen pitcher stood,
Untouched, untasted. Rats, a ravenous brood,
Had scattered all the rice, and gnawed the bread.
All that was left upon his marble bed
Of the great Sultan was a little heap
Of yellow bones, and a dry skull, with deep
Eye-sockets. But in those eye-sockets, lo!
Two living eyes were rolling to and fro,
Now left, now right, with never any rest.

Then was the king amazed, and smote his breast,
And called on God for grace. But not the less
Those dismal eyes with dreadful restlessness
Continually in their socket-holes
Rolled right and left, like pained and wicked souls.
Then said the king, "Call here an Abid, wise
And righteous, to rebuke those wicked eyes
That will not rest."

And when the Abid came
The king said, "O mine Abid, in the name
Of the High God that judges quick and dead,
Speak to those eyes."

The Abid, trembling, said:
"Eyes of Mahmud, why is your rest denied
In death? What seek ye here?"

The eyes replied,
Still rolling in their withered sockets there:
"God's curse upon this darkness! Where, O where
Be my possessions? For with fierce endeavor
Ever we seek them, but can find them never."

THE APPLE OF LIFE.

FROM the river Euphrates, the river whose source is in Paradise, far
As red Egypt, — sole lord of the land and the sea,'twixt the eremite star
Of the orient desert's lone dawn, and the porch of the chambers of rest
Where the great sea is girded with fire, and Orion returns in the West,
And the ships come and go in grand silence, — King Solomon reigned. And behold,
In that time there was everywhere silver as common as stones be, and gold
That for plenty was 'counted as silver, and cedar as sycamore trees
That are found in the vale, for abundance. For GOD to the King gave all these,
With glory exceeding; moreover all kings of the earth to him came,
Because of his wisdom, to hear him. So great was King Solomon's fame.

And for all this the King's soul was sad. And his heart said within him, "Alas,
For man dies! if his glory abideth, himself from his glory shall pass.
And that which remaineth behind him, he seeth it not any more:
For how shall he know what comes after, who knoweth not what went before?

I have planted me gardens and vineyards, and gotten me silver and gold,
And my hand from whatever my heart hath desired I did not withhold:
And what profit have I in the works of my hands which I take not away?
I have searchéd out wisdom and knowledge: and what do they profit me, they?
As the fool dieth, so doth the wise. What is gathered is scattered again.
As the breath of the beasts, even so is the breath of the children of men:
And the same thing befalleth them both. And not any man's soul is his own."

This he thought, as he sat in his garden, and watched the great sun going down
In the glory thereof; and the earth and the sky, in that glory, became
Clothed clear with the gladness of color, and bathed in the beauty of flame.
And "Behold," said the King, "in a moment the glory shall vanish!" Even then,
While he spake, he was 'ware of a man drawing near him, who seemed to his ken
(By the hair in its blackness like flax that is burned in the hemp-dresser's shed,
And the brow's smoky hue, and the smouldering eyeball more livid than lead)
As the sons of the land that lies under the sword of the Cherub whose wing
Wraps in wrath the shut gateways of Paradise. He, being come to the King,
Seven times made obeisance before him. To whom, "What art thou," the King cried,

"That thus unannounced to King Solomon comest?" The man, spreading wide
The palm of his right hand, showed in it an apple yet bright from the Tree
In whose stem springs the life never-failing which Sin lost to Adam, when he,
Tasting knowledge forbidden, found death in the fruit of it . . . . So doth the Giver
Evil gifts to the evil apportion. And "Hail! let the King live forever!"
Bowing down at the feet of the monarch, and laughingly, even as one
Whose meaning, in joy or in jest, hovers hid 'twixt the word and the tone,
Said the stranger (as lightly the apple he dropped in the hand of the King),
"For lo ye! from 'twixt the four rivers of Eden, God gave me to bring
To his servant King Solomon, even to my lord that on Israel's throne
He hath 'stablisht, this fruit from the Tree in whose branch Life abideth; for none
Shall taste death, having tasted this apple."
And therewith he vanished.

Remained
In the hand of the King the life-apple: ambrosial of breath, golden-grained,
Rosy-bright as a star dipt in sunset. The King turned it o'er, and perused
The fruit, which, alluring his lip, in his hand lay untasted.

He mused,
"Life is good: but not life in itself. Life eternal, eternally young,

That were life to be lived, or desired! Well it
were if a man could prolong
The manhood that moves in the muscles, the rap-
ture that mounts in the brain
When life at the prime, in the pastime of living, led
on by the train
Of the jubilant senses, exulting goes forth, brave
of body and spirit,
To conquer, choose, claim, and enjoy what 't was
born to achieve or inherit.
The dance, and the festal procession! the pride in
the strenuous play
Of the sinews that, eager for service, the will,
though it wanton, obey!
When in veins lightly flowing, the fertile and boun-
tiful impulses beat,
When the dews of the dawn of Desire on the roses
of Beauty are sweet:
And the eye glows with glances that kindle, the lip
breathes the warmth that inspires,
And the hand hath yet vigor to seize the good
thing which the spirit desires!
O well for the foot that bounds forward! and ever
the wind it awakes
Lifts no lock from the forehead yet white, not a
leaf that is withered yet shakes
From the loose flowers wreathing young tresses!
and ever the earth and the skies
Abound in rich ardors, rejoicings, and raptures of
endless surprise!
Life is sweet to the young that yet know not what
life is. But life, after Youth,
The gay liar, leaves hold of the bawble, and Age,
with his terrible truth,

Picks it up, and perceives it is broken, and knows it unfit to engage
The care it yet craves. . . . Life eternal, eternally wedded to Age!
What gain were in that? Why should any man seek what he loathes to prolong?
The twilight that darkens the eyeball: the dull ear that 's deaf to the song,
When the maidens rejoice, and the bride to the bridegroom, with music, is led:
The palsy that shakes 'neath the blossoms that fall from the chill bridal bed.
When the hand saith, '*I did*,' not '*I will do*,' the heart saith '*It was*,' not ''*T will be*,'
Too late in man's life is Forever, — too late comes this apple to me!"
Then the King rose. And lo, it was evening. And leaning, because he was old,
On the sceptre that, curiously sculptured in ivory garnished with gold,
To others a rod of dominion, to him was a staff for support,
Slow paced he the murmurous pathways where myrtles, in court up to court,
Mixt with roses in garden on garden, were ranged around fountains that fed
With cool music green odorous twilights; and so, never lifting his head
To look up from the way he walked wearily, he to the House of his Pride
Reascended, and entered.

In cluster, high lamps, spices, odors, each side,

Burning inward and onward, from cinnamon ceilings, down distances vast
Of voluptuous vistas, illumined deep halls through whose silentness passed
King Solomon sighing; where columns colossal stood, gathered in groves
As the trees of the forest in Libanus, — there where the wind, as it moves,
Whispers, "I, too, am Solomon's servant!" — huge trunks hid in garlands of gold,
On whose tops the skilled sculptors of Sidon had granted men's gaze to behold
How the phœnix that sits on the cedar's lone summit 'mid fragrance and fire,
Ever dying and living, hath loaded with splendors her funeral pyre;
How the stork builds her nest on the pine-top; the date from the palm-branch depends;
And the shaft of the blossoming aloe soars crowning the life which it ends.
And from hall on to hall, in the doors, mute, magnificent slaves, watchful-eyed,
Bowed to earth as King Solomon passed them. And, passing, King Solomon sighed.
And, from hall on to hall pacing feebly, the King mused . . . . "O fair Shulamite!
Thy beauty is brighter than starlight on Hebron when Hebron is bright,
Thy sweetness is sweeter than Carmel. The King rules the nations; but thou,
Thou rulest the King, my Belovéd."

So murmured King Solomon low
To himself, as he passed through the portal of porphyry, that dripped, as he passed,

From the myrrh-sprinkled wreaths on the locks and the lintels; and entered at last,
Still sighing, the sweet cedarn chamber, contrived for repose and delight,
Where the beautiful Shulamite slumbered. And straightway, to left and to right,
Bowing down as he entered, the Spirits in bondage to Solomon, there
Keeping watch o'er his love, sank their swords, spread their wings, and evanished in air.
The King with a kiss woke the sleeper. And, showing the fruit in his hand,
"Behold! this was brought me erewhile by one coming," he said, "from the land
That lies under the sword of the Cherub. 'T was pluckt by strange hands from the Tree
Of whose fruit whoso tasteth shall die not. And therefore I bring it to thee,
My belovéd. For thou of the daughters of women art fairest. And lo,
I, the King, I that love thee, whom men of man's sons have called wisest, I know
That in knowledge is sorrow. Much thought is much care. In the beauty of youth,
Not the wisdom of age, is enjoyment. Nor spring, is it sweeter, in truth,
Than winter, to roses once withered. The garment, though broidered with gold,
Fades apace where the moth frets the fibres. So I, in my glory, grow old.
And this life maketh mine (save the bliss of my soul in the beauty of thee)
No sweetness so great now that greatly unsweet 't were to lose what to me

Life prolonged, at its utmost, can promise. But
 thine, O thou spirit of bliss,
Thine is all that the living desire, — youth, beauty,
 love, joy in all this!
And O, were it not well for the praise of the world
 to maintain evermore
This mould of a woman, God's masterwork, made
 for mankind to adore?
Wherefore keep thou the gift I resign. Live forever,
 rejoicing in life!
And of women unborn yet the fairest shall still be
 King Solomon's wife."
So he said, and so dropped in her bosom the apple.

But when he was gone,
And the beautiful Shulamite, eying the gift of the
 King, sat alone
With the thoughts the King's words had awakened,
 as ever she turned and perused
The fruit that, alluring her lip, in her hand lay
 untasted, — she mused:
"Life is good; but not life in itself. So is youth,
 so is beauty. Mere stuff
Are all these for Love's usance. To live, it is well;
 but it is not enough.
Well, too, to be fair, to be young; but what good
 is in beauty and youth
If the lovely and young are not surer than they
 that be neither, forsooth,
Young nor lovely, of being beloved? O my love,
 if thou lovest not me,
Shall I love my own life? Am I fair, if not fair,
 Azariah, to thee?"
Then she hid in her bosom the apple. And rose.

And, reversing the ring
That, inscribed with the word that works wonders,
and signed with the seal of the King,
Hath o'er spirits and demons dominion — (for she,
for a plaything, erewhile
From King Solomon's awful forefinger, had won it
away with a smile) —
The beautiful Shulamite folded her veil o'er her
forehead and eyes,
And, with footsteps that fleeted as silent and swift
as a bird's shadow flies,
Unseen from the palace, she passed, and passed
down to the city unseen,
Unseen passed the green garden wicket, the vine-
yard, the cypresses green,
And stood by the doors of the house of the Prince
Azariah. And cried,
In the darkness she cried, — "Azariah, awaken!
ope, ope to me wide!
Ope the door, ope the lattice! Arise! Let me
in, O my love! It is I.
Thee, the bride of King Solomon, loveth. Love,
tarry not. Love, shall I die
At thy doors? I am sick of desire. For my love
is more comely than gold.
More precious to me is my love than the throne of
a king that is old.
Behold, I have passed through the city, unseen of
the watchmen. I stand
By the doors of the house of my love, till my love
lead me in by the hand."
Azariah arose. And unbolted the door to the fair
Shulamite.
"O my queen, what dear folly is this, that hath led
thee alone, and by night,

To the house of King Solomon's servant? For lo you, the watchmen awake.
And much for my own, O my queen, must I fear, and much more for thy sake.
For at that which is done in the chamber the leek on the housetop shall peep:
And the hand of a king it is heavy: the eyes of a king never sleep:
But the bird of the air beareth news to the king, and the stars of the sky
Are as soldiers by night on the turrets. I fear, O my queen, lest we die."
"Fear thou not, O my love! Azariah, fear nothing. For lo, what I bring!
'T is the fruit of the Tree that in Paradise God hideth under the wing
Of the Cherub that chased away Adam. And whoso this apple doth eat
Shall live — live forever! And since unto me my own life is less sweet
Than thy love, Azariah, (sweet only thy love maketh life unto me!)
Therefore eat! Live, and love, for life's sake, still, the love that gives life unto thee!"
Then she held to his lips the life-apple, and kissed him.

But soon as alone,
Azariah leaned out from his lattice, he muttered, "'T is well! She is gone."
While the fruit in his hand lay untasted. "Such visits," he mused, "may cost dear.
In the love of the great is great danger, much trouble, and care more than cheer."

Then he laughed, and stretched forth his strong arms. For he heard from the streets of the city
The song of the women that sing in the doors after dark their love ditty.
And the clink of the wine-cup, the voice of the wanton, the tripping of feet,
And the laughter of youths running after, allured him. And "*Life, it is sweet*
While it lasts," sang the women, "*and sweeter the good minute, in that it goes,*
For who, if the rose bloomed forever, so greatly would care for the rose?
Wherefore haste! pluck the time in the blossom." The prince mused, "The counsel is well."
And the fruit to his lips he uplifted: yet paused. "Who is he that can tell
What his days shall bring forth? Life forever . . . . But what sort of life? Ah, the doubt!"
'Neath his cloak then he thrust back the apple. And opened the door and passed out
To the house of the harlot Egyptian. And mused, as he went, "Life is good:
But not life in itself. It is well while the wine-cup is hot in the blood,
And a man goeth whither he listeth, and doeth the thing that he will,
And liveth his life as he lusteth, and taketh in freedom his fill
Of the pleasure that pleaseth his humor, and feareth no snare by the way.
Shall I care to be loved by a queen, if my pride with my freedom I pay?
Better far is a handful in quiet than both hands, though filled to overflow

With pride, in vexation of spirit. And sweeter the roses that blow
From the wild seeds the wind, where he wanders, with heedless beneficence flings,
Than those that are guarded by dragons to brighten the gardens of kings.
Let a man take his chance, and be happy. The hart, though hard pressed by the hounds,
When the horn of the hunter hath scattered the herd from the hills where it sounds,
Is more to be envied, though Death with his dart follow fast to destroy,
Than the tame beast that, pent in the paddock, tastes neither the danger nor joy
Of the mountain, and all its surprises. The main thing is, not to live *long*,
But to *live*. Better moments of rapture soon ended than ages of wrong.
Life's feast is best spiced by the flavor of death in it. Just the one chance
To lose it to-morrow the life that a man lives to-day doth enhance.
The may-be for me, not the must-be! Best flourish while flourish the flowers,
And fall ere the frost falls. The dead, do they rest or arise with new powers?
Either way, well for them. Mine, meanwhile, be the cup of life's fulness to-night.
And to-morrow . . . . Well, time to consider" (he felt at the fruit). "What delight
Of his birthright had Esau, when hungry? To-day with its pottage is sweet.
For a man cannot feed and be full on the faith of to-morrow's baked meat.
Open! open, my dark-eyed beguiler of darkness!"

Up rose to his knock,
Light of foot, the lascivious Egyptian, and lifted the latch from the lock,
And opened. And led in the prince to her chamber, and shook out her hair,
Dark, heavy, and humid with odors; her bosom beneath it laid bare,
And sleek sallow shoulder; and sloped back her face, as, when falls the slant South
In wet whispers of rain, flowers bend back to catch it; so she, with shut mouth
Half unfolding for kisses; and sank, as they fell, 'twixt his knees, with a laugh,
On the floor, in a flood of deep hair flung behind her full throat; held him half
Aloof with one large languid arm, while the other up-propped, where she lay,
Limbs flowing in fulness and lucid in surface as waters at play,
Though in firmness as slippery marble. Anon she sprang loose from his clasp,
And whirled from the table a flagon of silver twined round by an asp
That glittered, — rough gold and red rubies; and poured him, and praised him, the wine
Wherewith she first brightened the moist lip that murmured, "Ha, fool! art thou mine?
I am thine. This will last for an hour." Then, humming strange words of a song,
Sung by maidens in Memphis the old, when they bore the Crowned Image along,
Apples yellow and red from a basket with vine-leaves o'erlaid she 'gan take,
And played with, peeled, tost them, and caught them, and bit them, for idleness' sake;

But the rinds on the floor she flung from her, and
laughed at the figures they made,
As her foot pusht them this way and that way together. And, "Look, fool," she said,
"It is all sour fruit, this! But those I fling from
me — see here by the stain! —
Shall carry the mark of my teeth in their flesh.
Could they feel but the pain,
O my soul, how these teeth should go through them!
Fool, fool, what good gift dost thou bring?
For thee have I sweetened with cassia my chambers." "A gift for a king,"
Azariah laughed loud; and tost to her the apple.
"This comes from the Tree
Of whose fruit whoso tastes lives forever. I care
not. I give it to thee.
Nay, witch! 't is worth more than the shekels of
gold thou hast charmed from my purse.
Take it. Eat. Life is sweeter than knowledge:
and Eve, thy sly mother, fared worse,
O thou white-toothed taster of apples!" "Thou
liest, fool?" "Taste, then, and try.
For the truth of the fruit's in the eating. 'T is thou
art the serpent, not I."
And the strong man laughed loud as he pushed at
her lip the life-apple. She caught
And held it away from her, musing; and muttered . . . . "Go to! It is naught.
Fool, why dost thou laugh?" And he answered,
"Because, witch, it tickles my brain
Intensely to think that all we, that be Something
while yet we remain,
We, the princes of people — ay, even the King's
self — shall die in our day,

And thou, that art Nothing, shall sit on our graves, with our grandsons, and play."
So he said, and laughed louder.

But when, in the gray of the dawn, he was gone,
And the wan light waxed large in the window, as she on her bed sat alone,
With the fruit that, alluring her lip, in her hand lay untasted, perusing,
Perplext, the gay gift of the Prince, the dark woman thereat fell a musing,
And she thought .... "What is Life without Honor? And what can the life that I live
Give to me, I shall care to continue, not caring for aught it can give?
I, despising the fools that despise me, — a plaything not pleasing myself, —
Whose life, for the pelf that maintains it, must sell what is paid not by pelf!
I? .... the man called me Nothing. He said well. 'The great in their glory must go.'
And why should I linger, whose life leadeth nowhere? — a life which I know
To name is to shame, — struck, unsexed, by the world from its list of the lives
Of the women whose womanhood, saved, gets them leave to be mothers and wives.
And the fancies of men change. And bitterly bought is the bread that I eat;
For, though purchased with body and spirit, when purchased 't is yet all unsweet."
Her tears fell: they fell on the apple. She sighed .... "Sour fruit, like the rest!
Let it go with the salt tears upon it. Yet life .... it were sweet if possessed

In the power thereof, and the beauty. 'A gift for a king' . . . . did he say?
Ay, a king's life is life as it should be, — a life like the light of the day,
Wherein all that liveth rejoiceth. For is not the King as the sun
That shineth in heaven and seemeth both heaven and itself all in one?
Then to whom may this fruit, the life-giver, be worthily given? Not me.
Nor the fool Azariah that sold it for folly. The King! only he, —
Only he hath the life that's worth living forever. Whose life, not alone
Is the life of the King, but the life of the many made mighty in one.
To the King will I carry this apple. And he (for the hand of a king
Is a fountain of hope) in his handmaid shall honor the gift that I bring.
And men for this deed shall esteem me, with Rahab by Israel praised,
As first among those who, though lowly, their shame into honor have raised:
Such honor as lasts when life goes, and, while life lasts, shall lift it above
What, if loved by the many I loathe, must be loathed by the few I could love."

So she rose, and went forth through the city. And with her the apple she bore
In her bosom: and stood 'mid the multitude, waiting therewith in the door
Of the hall where the King, to give judgment, ascended at morning his throne:

And kneeling there, cried, "Let the King live for-
ever! Behold, I am one
Whom the vile of themselves count the vilest.
But great is the grace of my lord.
And now let my lord on his handmaid look down,
and give ear to her word."
Thereat, in the witness of all, she drew forth, and
(uplifting her head)
Showed the Apple of Life, which who tastes, tastes
not death. "And this apple," she said,
"Last night was delivered to me, that thy servant
should eat, and not die.
But I said to the soul of thy servant, 'Not so.
For behold, what am I?
That the King, in his glory and gladness, should
cease from the light of the sun,
Whiles I, that am least of his slaves, in my shame
and abasement live on.'
For not sweet is the life of thy servant, unless to
thy servant my lord
Stretch his hand, and show favor. For surely the
frown of a king is a sword,
But the smile of the King is as honey that flows
from the clefts of the rock,
And his grace is as dew that from Horeb descends
on the heads of the flock:
In the King is the heart of a host: the King's
strength is an army of men:
And the wrath of the King is a lion that roareth
by night from his den:
But as grapes from the vines of En-Gedi are favors
that fall from his hands,
And as towers on the hill-tops of Shenir the throne
of King Solomon stands.

And for this, it were well that forever the King,
who is many in one,
Should sit, to be seen through all time, on a throne
'twixt the moon and the sun!
For how shall one lose what he hath not? Who
hath, let him keep what he hath.
Wherefore I to the King give this apple."

Then great was King Solomon's wrath.
And he rose, rent his garment, and cried, "Woman,
whence came this apple to thee?"
But when he was 'ware of the truth, then his heart
was awakened. And he
Knew at once that the man who, erewhile, unawares
coming to him, had brought
That Apple of Life was, indeed, GOD's good Angel
of Death. And he thought,
"In mercy, I doubt not, when man's eyes were
opened and made to see plain
All the wrong in himself, and the wretchedness,
GOD sent to close them again
For man's sake, his last friend upon earth, — Death,
the servant of GOD, who is just.
Let man's spirit to Him whence it cometh return,
and his dust to the dust!"

Then the Apple of Life did King Solomon seal in
an urn that was signed
With the seal of Oblivion: and summoned the
Spirits that walk in the wind
Unseen on the summits of mountains, where never
the eagle yet flew;
And these he commanded to bear far away, — out
of reach, out of view,

Out of hope, out of memory, — higher than Ararat
buildeth his throne,
In the Urn of Oblivion the Apple of Life.

But on green jasper-stone
Did the King write the story thereof for instruction.
And Enoch, the seer,
Coming afterward, searched out the meaning. And
he that hath ears, let him hear.

END OF BOOK V.

BOOK VI.

TWELFTH AND THIRTEENTH CENTURIES.

SIEGE OF CONSTANTINOPLE.

"Εἰ δὲ πεπόνθατε δεινὰ δι' ὑμετέρην κακότητα,
Μή τι Θεοῖς τούτων μοῖραν ἐπαμφέρετε.
Αὐτοὶ γὰρ τούτους ηὐξήσατε ῥύσια δόντες,
Καὶ διὰ ταῦτα κακὴν ἔσχετε δουλοσύνην."

NICETAS.

THE

SIEGE OF CONSTANTINOPLE.

A CHRONICLE OF THE FALL OF THE GREEK EMPIRE.

IN FOUR PARTS.

PART I.

"Lá vint al Comte, si comme dit
Vn Danziaus, ki ioenes estoit
A qui toute Gresse appendoit,
Par son Oncle ies deserités
Et de chastiaus & de cités.
Alexis ot nom, mult fu biaus,
Bien enseniés iere le Danziaus:
*   *   *   *   *
Conté li a tot son afaire,
Et li Quens ki bien li vot faire,
Li fist jurer le sairement,
Kil en iroit tout voirement
A quan qu'il poroit outremer
Auec lui s'il puet recouurer
Sa tierre, & tant faire li sache
Que couronne porter li face."

PHILIPPES MOUSKES.

I.

THE EMPEROR ISAAC.

IN gold Byzantium, girt with purple seas,
Isaac is Emperor, and reigns at ease.
For, if he smiles, a swarm of gilded slaves
Smiles also, grateful for the grace that saves
Their fortunes one day longer: if he frowns,
Spears sparkle on the walls of frightened towns,
And half the East is darkened: if he sleeps,
The soul of Music o'er his slumber keeps
Melodious vigil, and, down lucid floors
Of marble chambers vast, at sighing doors
Dusk faces watch, while long-haired large-eyed girls
Crouch at his pillow fringed with dropping pearls.
Proud to up-prop his throne, four lions — four
Large bulks of blazing gold — crook evermore
Their wrinkled backs. For him the murex dies
In Tyrrhene nets. For him, 'neath golden skies,
In gorgeous cluster, all those glittering isles
That circle Delos, where the sun first smiles,
Broider the sea's blue breast with beauty rare.
For him, through valleys cooled with shadowy air,
The Phrygian shepherd leads his numerous flocks.
His are the towers on Helespontine rocks,
And his the hill-built citadels that crown
Morean bays, by many a mountain town.
For him, from antique Thessaly's witch-lands
Sweet sorceries breathe. For him, the hardy bands
Of snowy Thrace, a multitude of spears,
March with the Macedonian mountaineers.
From strong Durazzo's battlemented steep

To sultry Tarsus, and Malmistra, sweep
His glowing realms; and to his sway respond
All Anatolia's tribes, from Trebezond
Far as the Syrian Gates. His standards float
And flash athwart Pamphylian shores remote,
Throng all Meander's many-winding stream,
And in blue Asian weather blaze supreme
From ancient cities, proud and populous,
O'ertopping temples white in Ephesus,
Sardes, and Smyrna, and among the groves
The swarthy-faced Laödicean loves,
Or where, in Philadelphia's teeming squares,
The turbaned trader spreads his silken wares.
The glories of old Rome, by all the line
Of Latin Cæsars left to Constantine,
Blaze in his eyes, to make him glad and great.
Red Asia doth green Europe emulate
Which with most lavish hand shall treasures heap
Within his palace gates. All sails, that sweep
The waters of the world and every shore,
Meet in his harbors. Princely Pages pour
For him the Chian and the Lesbian wine
In agate cups and vases crystalline,
Wrought first in Rome, when through the Triumph Gate
Pompeïus came from conquering Mithridate.
For him, on gems and jasper stones is writ
The Arab wisdom and the Persic wit.
For him, Greek Monks, in Thracian convents cold,
Guard Homer's songs on parchments graved with gold.
To nourish this one man a million starve:
And on his tables kingborn butlers carve
The quadripartite globe: earth, sea, and air

Are devastated for his daily fare.
To serve him, twice ten thousand eunuchs stand,
Who start if he but nod or wave his hand.
Daily, his Prophet, whom for smiling views
He pays with Patriarchal revenues,
Prophesies to him of ease, pleasantness,
And length of days, glory, and great success
And realms extended from Euphrates far
As where the Lebanonian cedars are.
The grandeur of the East and of the West
Glows in his galleries. He is potent, blest,
Supreme. He hath two bloodhounds in a leash,
Terror and Force: two slaves that serve his wish,
Pleasure and Pomp.

II.

IS SAD.

Yet, in despite of all,
The Emperor Isaac sits in his vast hall
An undelighted man. To him all meat
Is tasteless, and all sweetnesses unsweet:
To him all beauty is unbeautiful,
All pleasures without pleasantness, and dull
Each day's delights. His women and his wine
Nauseate the sense they sate not. His lamps shine
In cedarn chambers, ceiled with gold, as gleam
Corpse-lights in charnels. Music's strenuous stream
Of pining sounds makes passionatest pain
About his joyless heart and jaded brain.
So harsh an echo in the hollowness
Within him dwells, that echo to suppress

He, if he could, would make the whole world mute.
He curses both the flute-player and the flute:
He strikes both lyre and lyrist to the ground:
The silence is less tolerable than sound.
For men's praise undeserved, the pain assigned
To this praised man is scorn of all mankind.
To please him, Age its reverend form foregoes,
And wrinkled panders for his public shows
Invent new vices. At his least of looks
Manhood forsakes its manliness, and crooks
Beneath a truculent foot a slavish neck.
White-fronted Womanhood, if he but beck,
Wallows in shame, unshamed; while Youth, to
charm
His fancy all the Virtues doth disarm,
Disgracing all the Graces. And, for this,
He hates Man, Woman, Youth, and Age. No bliss
In youthfulness, no dignity in years,
Men to this man, by men adored, endears:
Because his greatness, being of a kind
That grows from all men's littleness combined,
Dwells self-condemned among the multitude
Of voices lifted to proclaim it good,
And tongues that lick the dust, and knees that fall,
And backs that cringe before its pedestal.
Him all these immense means to make him glad,
Misused immensely, make immensely sad.

III.

AND SO IS HIS BROTHER ALEXIUS: WHO PROPOSES

Beside the Emperor sits the Emperor's brother:
Companions, one as joyless as the other,

And soul-distempered both: — the first, with what
He hath; the second, that he hath it not.
So, turning to Alexius, with dull eyes
By dull eyes met, Isaac the Emperor sighs:
"How things desired, and had, desire destroy!
How hard it is, enjoyment to enjoy!
Advise us, Brother, how may Pleasure borrow
Some new disguise to fool the querulous Morrow
From his foreseen reproval of To-day?"
Whereto Alexius:

"I have oft heard say
That more wild beasts than men be left in Thrace,
Wherefore" . . . .
"The chase!" the Emperor cries, — "the chase!
A happy thought! Such sleep as nightly flies
The silken couch where Ease, uneasy, lies,
Perchance kind Nature charitably drops
On wearied limbs from perilous mountain-tops.
And ancient poets say that pure Content
Was never yet in crowded city pent.
She, with young Health, her hardy child, they say
After the shadows of the clouds doth stray,
Or near the nibbling flocks by grassy dells,
And, bee-like, feeds at eve in myrtle-bells
On little drops of dew, deliciously
As the fair Queen of Fays. I know not, I,
If that be true: but this I know full well,
That not in any palace where I dwell, —
Neither beneath Blachernæ's sculptured roofs,
Nor in Boucoleon, where my horses' hoofs,
Shod with red gold, strike echoes musical
From porphyry pavements in a silver stall, —
This Phantom hath her haunt. We'll try the woods,

Wild-watered glens, and savage solitudes;
And, if she hide with Echo in her cave,
We 'll rouse her; if with Naiads in the wave,
We 'll plunge to find her; though black Death should leap
From out the lair whence she may chance to peep.
The chase to-morrow morn!"

IV.

A PARTY OF PLEASURE.

The morrow morn
At sunrise, to the sound of fife and horn,
Byzantium's spacious marble wharves, from stair
To stair, with broidered cloths, and carpets rare
Of crimson seamed and rivelled rough with gold,
A train of swarthy servants spread and fold,
For the proud treading of Imperial feet,
Down to the granite pedestals; where meet
Thick myrtle boughs, and oleanders flush
The green-lit lymph. There, little galleys push
Their golden prows beneath the glossy dark
Of laurel leaves; and many a pleasure-bark
Lolls in the sun, with streaming bandrol bright,
And gorgeous canopies, that shut soft light
Under soft shadow. Suddenly, shrill sounds
The brazen music, and the baying hounds
Drag sideways at the hunter's hand. The drums
Throb to the screaming trumpet.

And forth comes
The Emperor.
Then his courtiers; then his slaves.

At sunset, to the wilds beyond the waves
They came: light revellers armed with bow and spear,
Cinct for the chase, and gay with hunting-gear.
With silk pavilions gleam the lonely glens,
Glad of their unaccustomed denizens
That shout across dark tracts of starry weather.
To grassy tufts young grooms, light-laughing, tether
Sleek-coated steeds. And, where the bubbled brooks
Leap under rushy brinks, white-turbaned cooks
In silver vessels plunge the purple wine.
Within the tents, the lucid tables shine
(Under soft lamps from burning odors lit)
With sumptuous viands; and young wassailers sit,
With heated faces femininely fair,
And holiday arms thick-sheathed with jewels rare,
Babbling of battles. Round the mountain lawn
The sportive court leans, propped on skins of fawn,
And quilts thick-velveted of foreign fur,
Marten, and zibeline, and miniver,
Brought by the barbarous fair-haired folk that come
Blithe from the north star, where they have their home
Among the basalt rocks, and starry caves
Stalactical, and walk upon the waves
Sandalled with steel. Low-sounding angelots
Sprinkle light music in among the knots
Of laughing boys that tinkle cups of gold
Round heaps of grapes, and rough-globed melons cold,
And purple figs. There, down the glimmering green
Half-naked dance, with tossing tambourine,

Greek girls, whose flusht and panting limbs flash
bare
Across the purple glooms.

At dawn, they dare
The distant crags, and storm the savage woods.
Then, all day long, through slumbrous solitudes
Flit the sweet ghosts of glad and healthful sounds
Scattered from fairy horns, and flying hounds:
And, in and out, among the thickets lone
The dazzling tumult darts; as, one by one,
Through bosk and brake, gay-gilded dragon-flies
Flash, and are gone. When mellow daylight
dies,
Well-pleased, they bear their shaggy burden back
To the silken camp, adown the mountain track,
And roast the bristly boar; and quaff and laugh,
And sing, and ring the goblets gay; till, half
Drowsed, and half roused again by rosy wine,
They drink, and wink, and sink at last supine
On the fresh herbage by their watchfires red;
While the wind wakes the gloomy woods o'erhead,
Unnoticed, and unnoticed, now and then,
Sound distant roarings from the rocky glen.
So pass the days, the nights; so pass the weeks,
The months.

V.

WHICH ENDS UNPLEASANTLY.

At length the Emperor upbreaks
His wandering camp. Of wood and mountain
tired,

Town life he deems once more to be desired.
Aye, from illusion to illusion tost,
Men seek new things, to prize things old the most.
Life wastes itself by wishing to be more,
And turns to froth and scum whilst bubbling o'er.
Thus, having all things, save the joy they give,
The Imperial pauper still is fain to live
For means of life (which nothing known supplies)
Dependent on the charity of surprise.
Sick as he went, he to Byzance returns.
There, from the warders on the walls he learns
That his bold brother, whom (while he the chase
Pursued) himself had charged to hold his place
Is pleased to keep it; which the soldiery, bought,
Are pleased to sanction; and the people, taught
That Power in Place is Power where it should be,
Pleased, or displeased, obedient bow the knee.
'T is idle knocking at your own house-door
When your own house-dog knows your voice no more.
Fly, or be bitten!

Flying all alone
(Friendless, being powerless), into Macedon, —
A fugitive from his own guards, the scorn
Of his tame creatures, turned on, hunted, torn
By his own bandogs, Isaac, — yesterday
Lord paramount of half a world, great, gay,
Glorious, and strong, — to-day, a something less
Than all earth's common kinds of wretchedness, —
Fled from the refuse of himself; but, caught,
And back a prisoner to Byzantium brought,
They dropped him down a donjeon.

VI.

OUT OF THE LIGHT, INTO THE DARK.

Four wet walls;
Round which the newt, his sickly housemate, crawls
To criticise, and, being abhorred, abhor
What men had crowned, and surnamed Emperor,
And tremblingly admired. A mouldy crust,
Some muddy water, once a day down thrust
Into this putrid pit, still keep aware
The nameless human thing forgotten there
That it is wretched, and alive in spite
Of wretchedness. In nothingness and night
This nothing lives: cast out of Life, flung back
By Death, unpitied. And, to make more black
The blackness that is there to blot it out,
The new-made Emperor beckoned from the rout
Of smiling and of crawling creatures, — things
That do ill-make, and are ill-made by, kings,
Feeders of infamy, and fed by it, —
One that most smiled, and lowest crawled, to fit
His master's humor: unto whom he said:
"Our Brother hath two eyes yet in his head,
Worth nothing now to him, worth much to me
Get them away from him, and thou shalt be
The gainer by his loss."
This deed was done.
They left him in the dark.

VII.

ALEXIUS THE YOUNGER FLIES FROM ALEXIUS THE ELDER.

He hath a son,
This miserable remnant of man's being

That lives and hath no life, — unseen, unseeing!
God gave him both a brother and a son,
And both men name Alexius. And the one
Is Emperor now, and reigns, where he once reigned,
In bright Byzance; and drains, as he once drained,
In agate cups, from vases crystalline,
Careless, the Chian and the Lesbian wine,
By princes poured: for him, the murex dies
In Tyrrhene nets: for him, green Europe vies
With tawny Asia to extol his state:
For him those twice ten thousand eunuchs wait
In whisperous halls: for him, the Thracian spears
March with the Macedonian mountaineers:
And him men praise.
Meanwhile, the other flees,
'Scaped from his clutch, across the great salt seas,
And thanks kind heaven's rough winds that blow so rude
Upon his cheek. Among the multitude,
In seaman's garb, he, gliding secret, found
A Venice galley for Sicilia bound:
And, thence, through many lands, for many years,
Wandering in search of succor from his peers,
The exiled Prince draws far in foreign climes
The breath of life; and broods upon the times.

VIII.

AND TRIES HIS FORTUNES AND HIS FRIENDS.

But Greatness, God keeps fast upon its throne,
Is ever prompt full greatly to disown
Greatness by God struck down.
The Pope is wise,
Humane, and just.

The Pope the Prince first plies
With the sad story of his sire's distress.
And "*Pax vobiscum!*" sighs His Holiness.
"*Leonem, Optime, mox conculcabis,*"
Urges the Prince, "*me quoque liberabis*
De laqueo venantium."
Whereunto
The Pontiff:
"*Cœlum dedit Domino,*
Hominum autem terram filiis.
Schismatics, also, are ye Greeks, I wis."
And still the Prince:
"O Holy Father, stay!
The Greek shall to the Latin rite give way,
If Latin arms the Grecian throne recover."

"Another time, my son, we'll talk this over.
Festina lente. Vale!" sighs the Pope,
And waves him off.
He nurses yet his hope,
And flees to Germany.

In Germany
Philip is Kaiser; and by craft holds high
A brow serene above the brawling crowd, —
Fine-balanced on Fate's pinnacle, and proud.
And Kaiser Philip hath, in summers fled,
Irene, sister to Alexius, wed:
And Kaiser Philip doth with deep concern
The fallen fortunes of his kinsman learn:
Concerned the more, that he just now can spare
Nor men, nor money; since his rival there,
The lynx-eyed Otho, lurking for a spring,
Crouches hard by, and troubles everything.
The times are wild.

Meanwhile, the Red Cross Lords
(Five hundred sail, and thrice ten thousand swords)
In Zara halt, the new Crusade to plan.
And thither wends the prince.

IX.

A GREAT MAN.

Venetian
Dandalo, Doge elect, and Amiral,
And Captain, sits in solemn council hall.
His long beard, lustrous with the spotless snows
Of more than fourscore winters, amply flows
To hide the angry jewel, clasped with gold,
That firmly doth his heavy mantle hold.
Covered he sits. Above his blind bald brow
The Ducal bonnet (Tintoret shows ye how)
Glows like a sunset glory on the scalp
Of some sublime and thunder-scathéd alp.
And the furred velvets o'er his breastplate fall
In folded masses, as majestical
As honors on the manhood of the man.
Soon may ye tell, if ye his posture scan,
By the grand careless calmness of the way
His mantle laps and hangs, that in the play
Of this world's business he hath ever been
Chief actor, chosen for each foreground scene;
Whence, living is to him a stately thing
Made easy by long wont of governing.
Those deep blind eyes for Venice' sake burned out!
Since he, whom Venice feared, most feared, no doubt,

Those eyes. The firm fine features of that face,
In strength so delicate, so strong in grace!
All those augustest opposites that mix
In some superlative character, to fix
With one strong soul, and grace with one fit frame,
Man's evanescent elements, became
Associate ministers to this man's will. —
The symbols of the valley and the hill:
The storm, the eagle, and the cataract, —
Passions, and powers that passionately act;
The streamlet, and the vineleaf in the sun, —
Graces that gracious influence acts upon;
Meet in the aspect of that bended head.
And the great Lion of St. Mark doth spread
His mighty wings above the baldachin
That decks the throne; mute 'mid the trumpet's din,
Claiming his own.
The smooth and spacious floors
Are open-porched. Through airy corridors
You mark the marshalled heralds, stationed calm
About the broad stone platform, bathed in balm
Of blissful weather, and the warm noon-light.
Down the sloped hill the streeted city, white,
Hums populous. The sea-breeze, blowing in,
Flutters gay flags in harbors Zaratin;
Heaving on balustraded ramparts wide,
And at high casements, thronged and balconied,
Thick streams of many-colored silken scarves.
And all about the warmèd quays and wharves,
The sea is strewn with snowy sails, by swarms
Of high-decked galleys, from whose prows the arms
Of heroes hang, and low-hulled palanders.

X.

AND SOME NOTABLE MEN.

Meanwhile, among his council-keeping Sers,
The great Doge greets from his unenvied throne
The Barons, striding inwards, one by one,
From that bright background, and the golden noon,
Like banded forms on Byzant frescos. Soon
The hall is crammed. Below the high daïs sit
Peers, princes, prelates, paladins.
To wit: —
The conqueror of Asti, Boniface,
Marquis of Montferrat; who with his mace
Can brain a bull. When Theöbald, their chief,
Count of Champagne, left Christendom in grief,
Dying untimely, and dispute arose
About the headship, him the Barons chose
(Favored by fame, though foreign to the Franks)
As Dux and Daysman of the Red Cross Ranks.
Baldwin; whose dreams are of a diadem,
Since last the Turks have tugged Jerusalem
From Lusignan; content to wait meanwhile
As Count of Flanders, till his fortunes smile:
Him, also, Hainault's hardy race respect,
Scion of Charlemagne by line direct,
And cousin to the Royalty of France.
Beside him, having broken his last lance
At Bruges, in that great tourney, where the twain
First crossed their shields, Count Henry, with his train
Of Flanders knights. Sir Guy, the Gascon; grim,
Gray, gaunt, as on the Pyrenean rim
His own three cloudy border castles are,

Held fast for his White Heiress of Navarre,
Daughter of good King Sance, surnamed The Wise,
Blanche with the golden hair and holy eyes.
Whose husband, Theöbald, last year expired
In the fond arms of Friar Fulk, admired
By weeping Barons; but bewailed the most
By that stout servant of the Red Cross Host,
Geoffroy of Ville-Hardouïn, Lord of Bar
And Arcis, and the hillside country far
As Troyes, and both the blossom-bearing banks
Of Aube; Ambassador of all the Franks,
And Marshal of Champagne. Miles, Lord of Brie.
Geoffroy de Joinville. And those Gautiers three
Of Vignory, Montbeliard, and Brienne.
Roger de Marche. Bernard de Somerghen.
William, surnamed The Red; Lord Advocate
Of Arras, Seignieur of Bethune; whose straight,
Strong amber locks, like haum, in heaps half smother
His heavy brow. And Conon, his boy-brother.
Renier de Trit. And Jaen, the Castelain
Of Bruges. And Dreux, the Seignieur of Beaurain.
Baldwin of Beauvoir. Anseau de Kaieu.
Huges de Belines. Eustache de Cantelieu.
With shields slung frontwise over chain habergeons,
Gautier de Stombe, and Renier de Monz.
Gray Gervais and young Heruë of Castèl,
Jakes of Avesnnes, Bernard of Monstrüel,
Robert of Malvoisin. And Nicolas
De Mailli. Guy de Coucy, he that was
The son of Adela. Those brothers two,
Stephen and Jeffry, offspring of Rotrou,

And Counts of Perche. St. Pol, to prove whose power
His daughter Elzabet had brought in dower
To Chatillon two counties. Mathieu, Lord
Of Montmorency. Trifling with the sword
He leans on, Piere, the new-made Cardinal
Of Capua; who was the first of all
To take the cross. And he of Trainel, learned
Bishop of Troyes, Garniers; who back returned
Anon from spoiled Byzance, "with nothing less"
(Quoth Alberic) "to grace his diocess
Than the true scull, from Grecian monks reclaimed,
Of Philip the Apostle. Near him (named
By Gunther *magnæ sanctitatis vir*)
Neuelon; "on whom the Pope was pleased confer
Thessalonica's new archbishopric
Some few years afterwards," writes Alberic;
Bishop, meanwhile, of Soissons; whose grandsire,
Gerard, the Frankish chroniclers admire
As "Castelain of Laon, and noble prince";
Returned from Rome, well pleased, a fortnight since
With absolution won from Innocent
For Zara captured, to the discontent
Of those that sought to break the Red Cross ranks,
This prelate sits, requited by the thanks
Of pious souls, in comfortable chat
With those of Bethlehem and Halberstadt,
Receiving praise of Fulk himself; the Monk
Of Neuilly; who, when English Richard shrunk,
And Frankish Philip, from his fierce appeal,
Stirred up their Barons to a proper zeal;
The Boänerges of the new crusade;
A lean sharp-faced enthusiast, with shorn head

And starry eyes, — no hawk's, from Norway brought,
More vivid, or more vigilant, — his thought
So flashes through them 'neath his cowl's gray serge.
De Montfort; whom the Pope proclaims "God's scourge,"
Though styled "Hell's Hangman" by the Albigeois,
And "Bloody Simon." Louis, Count of Blois
And Chartre; the crownless kinsman of the kings
Of France and England, whose high humor springs
From blood twice royal. Peter of Courtenay;
Whose sires upon the sons of kings, men say,
Imposed their name and arms, "*three torteaux, or,*"
Which Godfrey, Bouillon's famous chieftain bore
In Christ's first battle for His sepulchre.

Not the least warlike of these warriors were
Those Bishops four, of Soissons, Bethlehem,
And Halberstadt. In conference with them
That strong-limbed Legate, loved by Innocent,
And (thanks to skill in arms with learning blent)
Acre's Elect Archbishop, sits beside
Loces' stout Abbot. Ugo, the one-eyed,
The Lord of Forli, leaning on his spear
And whispering to the gray Gonfalonier
O' the Holy See. Pons of Sienna, lord
Of empty coffers and a hungry sword
At all men's service, trusting from the sack
Of pagan towns to take good fortune back.
John of Brienne; whose daughter Frederic
Made Queen of Naples later; Almeric,
His wife's grandfather, gave him from the grave

Jerusalem, still later; gray-haired, brave,
And, though untitled, honored, him men call
The noblest Christian warrior of them all.
Guy, Abbot of Sernay and Val; anon
Made by the Pope Bishop of Carcasson;
Suspected leader of the malcontents.
Henry of Orm; whose Brabant shield presents
Argent, three chevrons, gules. Roger de Cuick,
Lord only of a little bailiwick.
Garnier of Borland; whose assaults, when Hell
Stirred him against the Church, a miracle
Defeated; for the blood of God His Son,
To warn him back, did on the rood down-run,
Seen at St. Goar, of Treves, upon the Rhein;
Sister to Godfried, that of Eppestein
Was Baron (and good Bishop Siegfried's brother)
His mother was; his sister, too, was mother
O' the other Siegfried that of Ratisbon
Was Bishop. Ogier de Sancheron.
Jaen de Friaise. Gautier de Gadonville.
Guillaume de Sains, and Oris of the Isle,
With gray Menasses: and stout-limbed Machaire,
St. Menehould's Lord: and Renaud de Dampière.
Mathieu of Valincourt: and Eudes of Ham:
And Piere of Amiens, called The Wolf; whose dam
Was nameless Madge. Haimon of Pesmes, and
Guy;
Eudes of Champlite, and Hugues of Cormory.
Eustache le Marchis, with his helmet on,
And, undisguised, his quilted gamboison,
Fret by no hauberk, half-way to his knee.
Villers, and Aimory of Villerey,
Peter of Braiquel, Eudo of the Vale,
Rochfort, and Ardelliers, and Montmirail.

Pietro Alberti; who, as simple Ser
Of Venice, boasts his power to confer
Titles, he deems less grand because his sire
Helped Dominic, the Doge, to get back Tyre
(That famous town Agenor built, say some)
From those two former foes of Christendom,
The Egyptian Kailif, and that Soldan damned
Who in Damascus kept his dungeons crammed
With Christian souls: he fingers his gold chain,
And, with a smile of careless gay disdain,
Folds his patrician robe across his knees.
Less grave, and chatting too much at his ease,
Pataleone Barbo; whose renown,
Scarce older than his senatorial gown,
Folks yet dispute. Francesco Contarini:
And that famed Ser, Thomaso Morosini:
Lorenzo Gradenigo: Giammarìa
Francesco Gritti, famed in Apulìa:
Daniele Gozzi: Jacopo Pisani:
And Giambattista Ercole Grimani;
Noble Venetians.

Side by side they sit,
Gray faces in grave circle. Could I fit
This rough-edged rhyme-work into finer frames
For their smooth-vowelled, voluble, sweet names,
No wrong done, no wrench to them, bruise or wound, —
As when the torturer to his engine bound
The melting-limbed deliciousness of some
Dear lady, doomed to luckless martyrdom, —
Friends, you should know their noblenesses all
Henceforth forever, and to mind recall
By special name each serious face of them,

Pale, 'mid its pomp of purple robe and gem,
Forth peering over every fur-trimmed vest.
Search ye the Golden Volume for the rest,
You whom fate favors, whosoe'er ye be,
With leave, once lavished, long denied to me,
To walk, a living man, in Venice' streets,
Where ghost meets ghost, and spirit spirit greets,
Among the doves and bells, and bounteous things
Strewn 'twixt the sky that clings, the sea that clings
To the sweet city, — 'twixt gloom, glory, 'twixt
Life, death, in maze inextricably mixt
Of gorgeous labyrinth.

Leaning by the wall,
Near the great doorway, fair-haired, blue-eyed, tall,
Behind St. Pol (who tunes, to pass the time,
Humming unheard, an amorous Norman rhyme
To the slow music of a Latin hymn)
Bussy d'Herboise, the frank French knight, whose trim
And sober surcoat, of no special hue,
Attracts, by seeming to evade, the view.
Ulric of Thun : and Charles of Aquitaine :
Eberhard, Count of Traun, and castelain
Of the Imperial fortress of Pavìa :
Giàn the Unnamed ; for whom his mother Pia
Forgot to choose a father ere she died,
Being embarrassed by a choice too wide ;
Martin the fighting Abbot ; whose priest's gown
Scarce hides the corselet which in Basil town
He bought last month, to join the northern knights
From windy burgs sea-beat on Baltic heights,
Fair-meadowed manors, and gray castles cold,

'Mid blue Bohemian woods, on windy wold
In the dark Hartz, or Salzburg's mountains bleak.
Henry of Ofterdingen, who the week
Before, came bringing, for his part, indeed,
Only his lute, his lance, his squire, his steed.
Ludwig the Ironhead, of Falkenstein :
Ulric the Hawk ; whose mother Adeline
Priests say the Pope will canonize next year :
And Ottoker, men call the Blear-eyed Bear :
The Duke of Styria, leaning on his shield, —
A milk-white panther-rampant, on a field
Vert: Witikind, Carinthia's Duke, some say
The bastard son of Bilstein's Countess gay,
Who, helped by some sleek nameless Levantine,
Contrives to keep alive the ducal line.

Only the constellations and the suns
Are called by kingly names : the millions
Of lesser lights, in charts celestial,
Are noticed merely by a numeral.
These, but the special stars that strongest flame
In foremost firmament. No need to name
The many more, less noble, or less known,
All known, all noble ; all content to own
A greater than their greatest in that great
Gray-headed, blind, old man, who sits sedate
And serious in their midst ; the central soul
Of this brute power which he doth all control,
Shaping the many-minded multitude
To oneness ; both the worthless and the good,
The weak, the strong. For he is born of those
High seldom spirits that of all earth's shows
Suck out the substance, and make all men's wills
The agents of their own.

XI.

LE VALET DE CONSTANTINOPLE.

The trumpet shrills
Thrice in the outer porch, with brazen din,
Thrice in the vestibule, and thrice within
The vaulted aisles.
Then, through the clanging arch,
The gaunt, red-crossed, steel-shirted heralds march.
Then silence.
Then, a humming, and a sound
Of metal clinked upon the marble ground,
And in between those six that, either side
The columned entry, gleam in tabards pied,
Bare-headed, with no blazon on his breast,
Comes the discrownéd Heir of all the East,
Alexius Angelus, the last in line
Of those Greek heirs to Christian Constantine,
The Byzant Emperors.

Who seeks for aid
Must show how service sought can be repaid.
Therefore the Prince, as soon as on bent knee
He gave the Doge the Kaiser's letter, — free
To plead his cause before the assembled knights
Of Christendom, and urge his wrongs and rights, —
Pledges himself to pay, upon his crown,
Two hundred thousand marks of silver down:
To join the Egyptian Pilgrims: and make cease
The age-long schism dividing Rome and Greece:
To find and furnish at his proper cost,
For Christendom, and to the Red Cross Host,
For one whole year, ten thousand mounted men,

Soldier and horse: and, ever after then,
A company of fifty knights, — a Band
Vowed to the service of the Holy Land. —
"*Le Valet de Constantinople,*" states
The Frankish Chronicler, whose pen relates
What his eye witnessed, since himself was there,
"*Li cuers des genz esmeut, mainte lerme amere*
Moult durement plorant." Thus, with filial tears,
Comment and argument, to lay their fears
And lift their valors, — now, with poured appeal
To sacred Justice and the Public Weal,
Now, hinting novel outlets to be won
To teeming Trade, — until the set of sun,
Full passionately pleading, spake the Prince.

XII.

A BLIND MAN SEES FAR.

And all this time, Doge Dandalo, — for, since
His sight was saved from surfaces and shows
That grossly intercept the sight of those
'Vho, seeing many things, see nothing through,
.e with serene, unvext, internal view
.eheld all naked causes and effects
In that clear glass whereon the soul reflects,
Unshaked by Time's distraught and shifting glare,
Events and acts, — while passionately there
The Prince stood pleading, saw, as in a trance,
Constructed out of golden circumstance,
The steadfast image of a far-off thing
Glorious, and full of wonder . . . .

Clear upspring
Into the deep blue sky the golden spires

That top the milkwhite towers, like windless fires:
O'er gardened slopes, slant shafts of plumy palm
Lean seaward from hot hillsides breathing balm:
Green, azure, and vermilion, fret with gold,
Blaze the domed roofs in many a globéd fold
Of splendor, set with silver studs and disks:
And, underneath, the solemn obelisks
And sombre cypress stripe with blackest shade
Sea-terraces, by Summer overlaid
With such a lavish sunlight as o'erflows
And drops between thick clusters of wild rose
And clambering spurweed, down the sleepy walls
To the broad base of granite pedestals
That prop the gated ramparts, round about
The wave-girt city; whence flow in and out
The wealth and wonder of the Orient World:
And, high o'er all this populous pomp, unfurled
In the sublime dominions of the sun,
And fanned by floating Bosphorus breezes, won
To waft to Venice each triumphant bark,
The winged and warrior Lion of St. Mark!
All this he saw beforehand: so foreknew
What last great deed God kept for him to do:
Which, being apprehended, was half done
In his deep soul, though yet divined by none.
So when the Prince had ended, and the hall
Began to buzz, and those flusht faces all
To turn their glances on the Doge (because
He was the inventor of their wills) no pause
For further thought he needed: but smoothed down
Across his knee one crease of his calm gown,
And answered, very quietly, "It is good,"
And rose.

XIII.

QUOT HOMINES TOT SENTENTIÆ.

But then began that multitude
To murmur. And some said, "The thing is wild,
And not to be endeavored." Others smiled,
Played silent with the pommels of their swords,
And sided with the loudest. Many lords
And many princes drew themselves aside,
And, blaming all the rest, with ruffled pride,
Took ship and so departed home again,
Gnawing their beards and hinting high disdain.
So was there great division of men's minds,
And tempest worse than of the waves and winds
When tides are equinoctial. It appears
The priests first took each other by the ears,
Arguing if war be lawful, waged as well
On Christian sinner, as on infidel,
Bid text trip text, and learning learning trample.
The unlearnéd laics followed their example.
Those Abbots stout of Loces and of Val
With Latin curses evangelical
Denounced each other. Borland then took sail,
And left the camp, followed by Montmirail.
Froieville, and Belmont, and Vidame as well,
And with them the boy Henry of Castèl,
Went, swearing on the Holy Gospels Four
To come again, but never came they more;
Nor spared God's wrath the recreant fugitives,
Of whom five hundred Barons lost their lives,
Sunk in one ship, and hundreds more beside,
Slaughtered by peasants in Sclavonia, died.
And daily still, some brawling baron went,

Clinking his arms and clamoring discontent
Whereon he in his burgs and towers would brood.

The Doge said very quietly, "It is good."

Now, of the remnant of the Red Cross Ranks
The most part were Venetians, the rest Franks.

PART II.

"Li bruis fu mult granz par le dedenz, et le message s'en tornent, & vienent à la porte, et montent sur les chevaux. Quant ils furent de fors la porte, ni ot celui ne fust mult liez et ne fu mie granz mervoille, qui il erent mult di grant peril escampé : que mult se tint à pou, que il ne furent tuit mort, & pris."

GEOFFROY DE VILLE-HARDOUIN, c. 113, p. 86.

I.

THE EMPEROR MAKES A PROCLAMATION.

ON all the walls and gateways of the town
Of great Byzantium, passing up and down,
Men read this placard : —

"IN THE EMPEROR'S NAME,

"Great, gracious, just, and clement! let his fame
Endure, whom may God bless and keep! Amen.
People!

"It is notorious to all men
That one Alexius, son of Isaac (late
Emperor of the East; whom, by just fate
And the high hand of Heaven dethroned, our grace
And clemency, ill-merited, did place
In safety, suffering him to live) hath stirred
By treasonable act and traitrous word
Against our state a barbarous armament
Of Latins, chiefly out of Venice sent
And France; pretexting in the misused name

Of Christendom, by them deceived, the same
High cause which our own arms have heretofore
Not slightly served, in famous fields of yore.
Now therefore, having called about our throne
Our loyal liegemen, we to all make known
That we have set our price upon the head
(Six, if alive, three thousand, byzants, dead)
Of this Alexius Angelus, self-styled
Prince and Augustus, falsely, since exiled
And forfeit of his life, and titles all.
"By order of our Lord Imperial
and Paramount, his servant,
"MUZUFER."

And after this, the city was astir
With rumors; and, from ramparts, wharves, and streets
Wild whisperers watched the coming of the fleets.

II.

AND RECEIVES THE AMBASSADORS.

When the Ambassadors of Venice, France,
And the Allied Crusade, bearing the lance
And lion of St. Mark, the gonfalon
O' the Holy See, the sword, and habergeon,
And mace of Charlemagne, with heralds came
Before the Emperor, and the amber flame
Of the great Oriental sunlight flowed
Through the long-galleried hall, and hotly glowed
About the pillared walls with purple bright,
They were at first as men whom too much light
Staggers, and blinds; so much the inopinate
Magnificence and splendor of his state
Amazed them.

At the Emperor's right hand,
Tracing upon the floor with snaky wand
Strange shapes, was standing his astrologer
And mystic, Ishmael the son of Shur,
A swarthy, lean, and melancholy man,
With eyes in caverns, an Arabian.
Who seemed to notice nothing, save his own
Strange writing on the floor before the throne.
At the Emperor's feet, half-naked, and half-robed
With rivulets of emeroldes, that throbbed
Green fire as her rich breathings billowed all
Their thrilled and glittering drops, crouched Jezraäl,
The fair Egyptian, with strange-colored eyes
Full of fierce change and somnolent surprise.
She, with upslanted shoulder leaning couched
On one smooth elbow, sphinx-like, calm, and crouched,
Though motionless, yet seemed to move, — its slim
Fine slope so glidingly each glossy limb
Curved on the marble, melting out and in
Her gemmy tunic, downward to her thin
Clear ankles, ankleted with dull pale gold.
Thick gushing through a jewelled hoop, down rolled,
All round her, rivers of dark slumbrous hair,
Sweeping her burnisht breast, sharp-slanted, bare,
And sallow shoulder. This was the last slave
The Emperor loved. No sea-nymph in a cave
Ever more indolently dreaming lay,
Lulled by low surges, on a summer's day.
The midnight theft of some Bohemian witch,
Stol'n from a Moslem mother, when the rich

Turk camps in Carmel fled before the cross
That lured the remnant left by Barbaross
To Suabia's Duke, was Jezraäl. Four black
dwarves
Like toads, green-turbaned, and in scarlet scarves,
The four familiars of the fair witch-queen,
With fans of ostrich feathers, dipt in sheen
Arabian dyes and reddened at the rims,
Stood round her, winnowing cool her coilèd limbs.
And, behind these, on either side the throne,
Stand two tame jackals to Apollyon:
One, in his right, across his shoulder props
An axe, and from his left a loose cord drops,
And he is nameless, and his trade is death.
The other, whose silk vest flows loose beneath
The small enamelled dagger at his hip,
Smiles, with a restless finger at the lip;
Sleek, subtle, beauteous, bloodless minister
Of evil; and men call him Muzufer;
And when he smiles the people are afraid,
And hide themselves. And smiling is his trade.

The Ambassadors of the Red-crossed Allies
Spake to the Emperor upon this wise:
"The supreme Pontiff of the Holy See
Of Rome, in concert with the sovereign, free
Republic of St. Mark, the Chevisance,
And gentlemen of Germany and France
In arms, — by us, Charles, Count of Aquitaine,
Eberhard, lord of Traun, and Castelain
Of the Imperial fortress of Pavìa,
Lorenzo Gradenigo, Giammarìa
Francisco Gritti, Jacopo Pisani,
And Giambattista Ercole Grimani,

Noble Venetians, — to Alexius, styled
And titled, falsely, Emperor, who despoiled
His brother of the purple and high place
Of power, to him allotted by God's grace : —
Render to Cæsar what is Cæsar's own,
And unto God good deeds : restore the throne,
By thee usurped with sacrilegious sword,
To Isaac, thine hereditary lord
And master : and so live, forgiven of men
And God. But if thou dost not this, know then
Thou art accurst, and anathematized."
The Egyptian lifted her large eyes, surprised,
And laughed. The scarlet-clad huge-handed man
That stood behind, with axe and cord, began,
Under a snarling lip, to gnash white teeth
The other monster half out of its sheath
Lifted his dagger, with the self-same smile
Wherewith he had been listening all this while.
The Emperor glanced at Jezraäl, and said,
" Yon young French Envoy hath a comely head.
Answer him, girl."

The glittering witch leaped up
With a shrill laugh, and seized a golden cup,
And shook her sparkling tunic to green flame,
And, hand on haunch, made answer :
" In the name
Of Satan, and the Powers that be ! Who saith
To Life, 'Live not : give up thy place to Death' ?
Who calleth to the Sun, 'Come down : make way
For Darkness' ? Who demandeth of the Day
To give his golden palace to the Night ?
Life answers, 'Fool ! I live.' And, saith the Light,
'Thou fool ! I shine.' Who cannot keep his throne

May lose it: whiles he hath it, 't is his own.
And, were I Emperor, I would answer, 'Lo!
Upon all hills that rise, all waves that flow,
And on the lives and souls of men, is cast
The shadow of my purple. Heaven is vast,
And Hell is deep. And God, if God there be,
Doth hide himself to leave this world to me.
Mankind is my tame dog; and, knowing it,
Fawns on me; on whose collar there is writ,
Sum Cæsaris. The world is but a wheel
That draws my chariot. I hold fast my heel
Upon the neck of my cringed vassal, Time.
Fear is my slave: my household creature, Crime.
The Lords of Hell are my retainers. When
I frown or smile, all Valor dies in men,
Virtue in women: men and women are mine,
Body and soul: their blood is in my wine,
The lion croucheth on my palace floors;
And Life and Death are suppliants in my doors.
The bolted thunder hangeth on my walls,
And, lo ye, when I nod the thunder falls!'"

"The thunder hangeth in the hand of God,"
Lorenzo cried; "and falleth at his nod.
See ye, from yonder golden pole, that props
The baldachin his burnisht barb o'ertops,
The many-colored silken streamers fall?
The same hand, from the same silk, fashioned all,
Nor hath the stuff with purple tinct imprest
Essential value more than all the rest.
Great Cæsar with his fortunes to admit
Death opes his doors no wider by a whit
Than for the beggar buried in a ditch.
The dust is brother to the dust. Seeing which,

And that alone the actions of the just
Are lords forever, and defy the dust,
Repent! spread sackcloth on thy former sin.
For, by the Living Lord that listeneth in
The everlasting silences on high,
I swear — beneath the patience of the sky,
Beneath yon gorgeous canopy, beneath
Yon golden roof, though incensed by the breath
Of prostituted slaves like this, and throned
In pomp, and girt with power, and crowned, and zoned
With the imperial purple of the East,
Alexius is a miscreant, and a beast.
And God shall say to him, as to that other
Whom he resembles, 'Cain, where is thy brother?'
But thou, dread degradation of the form
Of woman, — what art thou, strange glittering worm?
What public mother, to what sire unknown,
Spawned thee, shamed creature of a shameless throne,
That dost with insult answer Christendom?"

The Egyptian sprang, then stood death-white. A hum
As of a hornet's nest, all round the hall,
Responded to her gesture, augural
Of wrath. She stood, a sorceress brewing storm:
The jewels crackled on her stiffening form:
Her wild unholy eyes flashed hate: the breath,
Drawn sharply in, hissed through her sparkling teeth
Close clenched. But her rude lord, with laughter rough,

Waved to her a careless hand, and called, "Enough!
Crouch." And she crouched: then, like a beaten
child,
Whimpered upon the marble. Dryly smiled
The Emperor; and to Muzufer he said,
"The old Venice Envoy hath a reverend head,
Answer thou him." But he, "Great Lord, I have
Not any knowledge nor experience, save
(What much, I doubt, delights not these grave
Sers)
A little, of the various characters
Of wines and women. Nor indeed have I
Enough of Latinized theology
To answer, text for text, this reverend man."

The Emperor laughed. "Speak thou, Arabian,
That knowest all things." Then the Arab said:

"Nebuchadnezzar reigned: and he is dead.
When Babylon was mistress of the world,
He was the lord of Babylon. Death furled
His face in dark: and him the world forgot.
Greek Alexander reigned: his bones do rot.
This little earth was smaller than his state,
He held it in his hand. Men called him Great.
At last God blew his life out like a spark,
And he became a darkness in the dark.
To Alaric the eagle gave his wing,
His claw the lion, and the snake her sting.
His clarions, blown upon the seven hill-tops,
Shook the round globe. Grasses the wild goats
crops
Grow over him. A little sickness made
Of all he was nothing but dust and shade.

Attila reigned. The strong Huns worshipped him.
All mankind feared him. He was great and grim.
Rome grovelled at his feet. One night he ceased.
The worms upon his flesh have held high feast.
Behind the hosts of suns and stars, behind
The rushing of the chariots of the wind,
Behind all noises and all shapes of things,
And men, and deeds, behind the blaze of kings,
Princes and paladins and potentates,
An immense solitary Spectre waits.
It has no shape: it has no sound: it has
No place: it has no time: it is, and was,
And will be: it is never more, nor less,
Nor glad, nor sad. Its name is Nothingness.
Power walketh high: and Misery doth crawl:
And the clepsydra drips: and the sands fall
Down in the hourglass: and the shadows sweep
Around the dial: and men wake, and sleep,
Live, strive, regret, forget, and love, and hate,
And know it not. This spectre saith, 'I wait.'
And at the last it beckons, and they pass.
And still the red sands fall within the glass:
And still the shades around the dial sweep:
And still the water-clock doth drip and weep:
And this is all."

"Yea," said the Emperor, "then
If thus it fare with the world's mighty men,
And there be no more greatness in the dust,
How fares it with the men the world calls just,
Who lived not for the body but the mind,
Augustin, Plato, Socrates?"

"Behind
The mingled multitude of mortal deeds

Called good or ill, behind all codes and creeds,
All terrors, all desires, all hopes, all fears,
Behind all laughter, and behind all tears,"
The Arabian said, "this shapeless Spectre waits.
And no man knoweth what it meditates."

Frowning, he turned, and fashioned as before,
With snaky wand, upon the porphyry floor
Strange figures, cube, and pentagram, and sphere.
The Emperor mused; then murmured in the ear
Of Muzufer some word whereto replied
That minister: "Let your Majesty decide.
Yet I have heard what Emperors decree
Heaven doth approve; whereby it seems to me
This maxim may be broadly understood,
That for the good o' the state all means are good."

Thereat the Emperor rose; and from his face
Suddenly all its smiling ceased, — gave place
Forthwith to hate too deadly for disguise;
As when through sultry, seeming-empty skies
Suddenly rushes, wrapt in glare and gloom,
The blood-red darkness of the strong simoom.
With lips that labored 'neath the weight and strain
Of wrath, he cried:
"You — Sir of Aquitaine,
You — Sir of Traun — whose title we ignore,
Whose master styles himself an Emperor,
And is . . . . a puny Suabian Duke! You — all,
Of Venice — whose nobility we call,
Like its new banner and filched patron both,
Of doubtful origin, and upstart growth!
This is our answer to your host, and you: —
Come ye as peaceful pilgrims, to pursue

A pious journey to Jerusalem?
Then, nor your course we check, nor zeal condemn;
Then, market free, and passage fair, expect;
Our wealth shall aid you, and our power protect.
But come ye here, in hostile arms arrayed,
The sanctuary of Empire to invade?
Then, — mark me! as I live . . . . as I that speak
Am Emperor both of Roman and of Greek,
(Mark me!) I swear, — and swear it by the line
Of godlike Cæsars all since Constantine, —
Your myriads, were they ten times what they be,
Our scorn shall sweep from land, and sweep from sea,
As easily as yon light fan could sweep
A swarm of midges from the unvext sleep
Of our dark-eyelashed leman. And, in pledge
Of power to smite, — not less than we allege,
Our answer prompt to your barbarian crew
Shall be your heads . . . . the head of each of you!
Yours — Sir of Aquitaine! yours — Sir of Traun!
Fresh trophies for each gate of yonder town!
And yours — Venetian! . . . . yours! and yours! and yours!
Ho, in the gallery, there! Bar all the doors.
No foot budge hence till we be satisfied!"

"Disloyal lord! . . . . Enough!" Lorenzo cried.
"For us, — our response shall, in thunder-falls,
Be heard anon round yonder doomèd walls,
And rained in blood — less innocent than ours,
Ay, and less pure! — round yonder traitorous towers.
For thee, — mock emperor, true barbarian!
Whose image, stamped in the alloy of man,

Sullies the wealth that buys obedience base
To Treason trembling on a throne, — disgrace
Would be grace wasted. But hark . . . . ye, his slaves!
Who falls on us must fall on iron staves.
'Ware, the first traitor here, that lifts his hand!
Christ and his cause about this banner stand.
For every hair upon our heads, a host
In arms, for Justice wronged, shall claim the cost.
'Ware, the first slave that stands across our path
To yonder door! This wingéd lion hath
(For God, the giver of all strength to men,
Shall smite the smiter now, who smote him then)
The self-same strength between the wings of him
That once, between the wingéd Cherubim,
In Ashdod smote usurping Dagon down,
And shattered in the dust his idol crown,
Before the captived but triumphant Ark.
Now — God defend the Right, and good St. Mark!"

Forthwith outfurled, in resonant circle shone
Round those eight knights the rustling gonfalon.
And, through a hundred hands with hired swords
To murder purchased, marched the Red Cross Lords
Majestic, unmolested, down the hall,
Strode through the startled Guards Imperial,
And from the treacherous threshold passed in scorn.
Alexius, with white lips, and garment torn,
Screamed, "Cowards! slaves! Is Cæsar disobeyed?
Traitors! a hundred byzants for each head
Of those eight churls! Up, bloodhounds! or the whip
Shall mend the mongrel valor that lets slip
An Emperor's quarry!"

But the Eight meanwhile,
Spurring full speed, had passed the embattled pile
Of the great gate. Foiled, as they forward sprang,
Down in the gap the shrill portcullis rang.

PART III.

"ὧν μὲν γὰρ χεῖρας ἀπέτεμεν, ὧν δὲ δακτύλους ὡς ἀμπέλων περιέκειρε κλάδους, τινῶν δὲ πόδας ἀφήρηκε, πολλοὶ δὲ χειρῶν καὶ ὀφθαλμῶν ὑπέστησαν στέρησιν. ἦσαν δ' οἳ καὶ ὀφθαλμὸν δεξιὸν καὶ πόδα εὐώνυμον ἐζημίωντο, καὶ αὖ τοὐναντίον ἐπεπόνθεισαν ἕτεροι."—*Nicetas Chon.* de And. Comn. lib. i. p. 374.

I.

HOW THE EMPEROR PICKED UP WHAT THE DEVIL LET FALL.

Thereafter, met for mischief and debate
Morose, within a certain intricate
Small chamber, planned for plotting, with slant glooms
In glooms, beyond a maze of banquet-rooms,
Muzufer and his liege lord up and down
Were pacing leopard-like. Meanwhile, the town
Muttered outside the porphyry porches all
Like souls perturbed in Purgatorial
Abysses paced by lamentable throngs;
As to and fro i' the streets with surly songs
Among his myrmidons the headsman strode,
Beckoning in turn from each condemned abode
(So to appease the Emperor's discontent
Of his own creatures for that morn's event)
Some terror-stricken wretch whose mangled limb —
Lopped foot or hand — must serve ere dark to trim
Arch, column, obelisk, and cornice, where
Already sallow-visaged slaves prepare
The midnight banquet, o'er great gardens gay

With placid statues, and the luminous play
Of perfumed waters, leaping pure upon
Lipped lavers large of black obsidian,
Or alabaster filled with filmy light.
For 'mid his Court the Emperor sups to-night.
And in that chamber dim where these debate,
O'er the low bronzen door elaborate,
Some old Greek sculptor (dead an age ago
Ere Pisa yet brought forth her wondrous Two,
For Florence' sake, and all the world's, to impart
New sweetness to his barbarous Christian art)
Had wrought in monstrous imagery, bold,
Uncouth, and drear despite of paint and gold,
Christ tempted of the Devil upon the Mount:
Varying the tale the Evangelists recount
After the manner of the artist's mind.
Colossal forms! the Saviour of mankind,
And Tempter, — not alluring he, but grim
As the grim Middle Age imagined him;
Satan; that ancient hodman of the souls
That God forgets; in corners, dens, and holes
Where'er Sin squats, taking what he can find,
He rakes earth's offal for that hod behind
His hateful back; God's scavenger is he;
Who here, with obscene gesture, coarse and free,
Hell's twy-prong in his claw-bunch-fingers clutched,
Picks from the rubbish at his shoulder hutched,
And proffers to the Son of Man, a crown.

Now, while these two were pacing up and down
In moody talk, and Muzufer began
To praise and pity much that day's marred plan,
As being shrewdly plotted, — righteous, too,

If rightly looked at . . . . "For, Sir Emperor, who
Disputes the right of Christian Emperors
To slay the infidel ambassadors
Of Moslem monarchs, that by nature stand
Outside the law of every Christian land?
Yet Christians that, unchristianly, oppose
Your Christian Majesty, are, certes, foes
More formidable, therefore worse by far,
Than merely Ottoman and Moslem are.
Meanwhile, they have escaped us. We have failed.
Which is a pity. Fifty slaves impaled
Will poorly, poorly at the best, replace
Those eight Frank heads which we had hoped should grace
This evening's banquet. For although we preach
Thereby a wholesome homily to each
Incipient traitor, and although, indeed,
These cravens merit death, methinks you feed
On your own limbs thus, — prey on your own power,
Devoured the more, the more that you devour."
He speaking thus, against the bronzen door
Alexius struck his fist fierce-clenched, and swore
An angry oath that neither Heaven nor Hell
Should mar that evening's merriment.

Then there fell
With clink and clatter, by that blow shaked down,
Out of the Devil's claw the Devil's crown,
Striking the Emperor's foot.

The two stood still,
And stared upon each other.

"Omen ill!"
Mused Muzufer. "Hell's Monarch's clutch is not
So sure but it lets go what it hath got."
Alexius, laughing, answered quick, "Not so.
Nor is it the first time I have stooped as low
To get, — nor, gotten, thanked the Devil for
This glittering hoop." And, "Ay, Sir Emperor!"
With mimic mirth laughed Muzufer. Within
His dusky niche a sympathetic grin
The wrinkled visage of the Father Fiend
Emitted, till his coarse brows seemed thick-veined,
And dull eye seemed to wink with dismal glee.
So all together laughed that Wicked Three,
While Day, to reach the West's red innermost,
With lurid foot the lucid pavement crost.

Then at the casement Muzufer cried, "Hark!
The butchery has begun before 't is dark.
One . . . . two . . . . three . . . . four . . . . five wretches? how they twist
On those spiked staves! Sure, that 's a woman's wrist
And hand there, with the fluttering fingers? Phew!
We must not sup to windward of this stew,
Or you will find the hippocrass smell strong.
Burn, burn benzoin! How heavily hums along
Yon beetle, caring nothing for it all, —
Fool, and it sets me talking!"

"The shades fall
Fast," cried Alexius. "Come! the Banquet waits."

II.

AND HOW HE AFTERWARDS GAVE AWAY WHAT HE NO LONGER POSSESSED.

And while he spake, Byzantium's golden gates
From silver clarions to the setting sun
Breathed farewells musical; and, Day being done,
Night entered swift to meet the Sons of Night.

Not black however, but in blaze of light
Luxurious.
Gardens. Galleries. Walls o'erlaid
With marvellous, many-colored marbles, made
By multitudes of fragrant flames, that pant
From flashing silver lampads, fulgurant;
Cornelian, agate, jasper, Istrian stone
And Carian mixed, to shame the glories gone
From Roman streets since first Mamurra had
His own house-walls with milk-white marble clad.
And down deep lengths of glowing colonnades
The dim lamps twinkle soft through slumbrous shades
Around rich-foliaged frieze, and capitals
Of columns opening into halls, and halls
Warm with sweet air, and wondrous color rolled
From rare mosaics, — azure dasht with gold;
'Neath domes of purple populous with star
On star of silver, coved o'er circular
Vermiculated pavements interlaid
With wreaths of flowers and intricatest braid
Of delicate device, about the base
Of granite basins broad, which all the race
Of sea-gods and sea-horses linger round,

In love forever with the long cool sound
Of lucent waters that low-laughing fall
And fall from pedestal to pedestal
Among those curling nymphs and tritons bold
That bridle restive dolphins reined with gold.
Beyond, 'twixt pillared range and statued plinth,
The lustrous maze of marble labyrinth
Unfolds ; and, disentangling from itself
Its luminous spaces, spreads into a shelf
Of shining floorage carpeted with deep
Thick-tufted crimsons, soft as summer sleep
Under the footsteps of delicious dreams.
O'er which, through dark arcades, steal airy gleams
And sumptuous odors, and mellifluous waves
Of music that with swimming languor laves
Dim gardens green and deep, and flowery plots
Where minstrels strike their golden angelots,
And sing, — now, Cæsar's splendor, Cæsar's state,
That doth Olympian glories emulate, —
And now, lascivious songs, the wanton loves
Of Mars and Venus, — till the lemon groves
Are loud with lyric rapture.

Piled and built
On glowing tables, garlanded and gilt,
Of Mauritanian tree, the Banquet shines, —
Bright-beaming vessels brimmed with costly wines,
And savorous fruits on golden salvers heaped,
And smoking meats in misty spices steeped, —
All round the terraced porch. In plenitude
Of power, here, midmost of his multitude
Of Greek Patricians robed in purple pomp
Alexius sits. Meanwhile the bronzen tromp,
Blown from dim-gaping galleries far behind,

Strives, with the clang of sudden cymbals joined,
To crush all feebler sound out of each dull
Low wail, or intense shriek, that in the lull
Of that loud music ever and anon
Some wind, from outer darkness poured upon
The palace thresholds, pulsing passionate,
Contrives to filter through the golden grate.

Along a brilliant frieze of burnished wall
That beams behind the throne Imperial,
In rangéd groups embossed and painted, blaze
Byzantine sculptures that perpetuate praise
Of Trajan's Justice, and the Sages Seven
Of Antique Greece: between whose tablets driven
Great cedarn beams, that prop the deep pavilion,
Drop cataracts down of silken streams vermilion.
Beneath, in bronze, Alcides with his club,
And that she-wolf that had for sucking cub
Rome's founder. But before the Emperor gleam
High argent censers, whence thick odors stream
From left to right in vast voluptuous clouds
Of incense that with floating mist enshrouds
His glory like a God's. And by his side,
At his left hand, dark-haired, delicious-eyed
Egyptian Jezraäl leans. Around her twine
The curling odors, and the fragrant wine
Is lucent on her humid lip: and he,
Beneath the loaded board, with amorous knee
Frets her lascivious tunic's light-spun folds,
And in hot palm her languid finger holds.
Anon, with heated eyes, turning from her
(All glitter and all glare) to Muzufer
(All gravity, all gloom) that sits meanwhile
On his lord's right, — forgetting even to smile,

So much his mind is busy at the task
Of plotting how to slip from life's main mask
Silently, unperceived, by some side-way
Into safe darkness, ere God's Judgment lay
Pride's revel all in ruins . . . . for he read
Strange writing on the walls, — Alexius said:
"What wise and weighty matter is astir
Behind those knitted brows?"

Then Muzufer,
Like one surprised without his armor on,
Caught up his smile in haste, and answered: "None,
Great Master, weigh more anxiously than I
The mighty interests of your Majesty;
Whose greatness needs must oft oppress the brain,
Compelled its utmost faculty to strain
In contemplating the august extent
Of power that doth, as doth heaven's firmament,
Invest the world with glory. Who oppose
Your Majesty, oppose mankind, which owes
From realms unnumbered homage to your rule.
Who doubts this is a miscreant and a fool:
Whoe'er your Majesty's most sacred, high,
And solemn rights dare question or deny
Is a vile traitor and an arrant knave:
But they that now in arms presume to brave
Your power supreme are sinners more accurst
Than any, save (if such there be) that worst
Of wicked men that, being Grecian born,
This barbarous rabble doth not loathe and scorn
More than Turk, Jew, or Saracenic scum
Of nameless nations scorned by Christendom.
If such there be, were he my father's son,
Myself would hold, to hang that caitiff on,
No gibbet high enough. My thoughts are these."

"Paul's body!" quoth Alexius, "well they please
Our passing humor. Wherefore we assign
Hereby, from this time forth to thee and thine
In title principal, and lordship free,
Our palace of Chalcedon by the sea."

And while he spake thus, echoed by the shout,
"Long live Alexius!" from the gates without
Hoarse hubbub streamed, and up the revelling hall,
Bearing the bannered bird imperial,
A legionary captain, pale with fear,
Made way towards the throne.

To whom, "What cheer?"
With husky wine-quenched voice the Emperor cried,
And to the Emperor, rueful, he replied:
"Ill cheer, Sir Emperor! The Latin Host
Hath fallen upon Chalcedon. We have lost
Many brave men, and one fair palace you."
"Pish!" cried the Emperor. "The Franks are few.
What's lost to-night may be to-morrow won,
Palaces be there many a fairer one
For us to feast in, you to fight for, still.
Begone!"

III.

WHAT WAS SHOWN TO THEOCRITE, THE MONK.

So feasted they. No bird of ill
With boding note around the rooftree croaked,
Nor bearded star the masoned turrets stroked,
Nor howled the hoarse wolf near the revelling town.

Only, that night a marvellous thing was shown
To Theocrite the Monk, when he in prayer,
After long fast went forth to breathe the air
What time the air was stillest. For to him
Appeared in heaven, above the city dim,
The helmeted Arch-Angel of high God,
That in his right hand held a measuring-rod,
Stretched over all the East. To whom God gave
Command to measure out a mighty grave
Wherein to bury and hide from human eye
The body of a world about to die.
This thing in vision at the mid of night,
'Twixt heaven and earth, was shown to Theocrite.

PART IV.

"Ὦ πόλις πόλις, πόλεων πασῶν ὀφθαλμὲ, ἄκουσμα παγκόσμιον, θέαμα ὑπερκόσμιον, ἐκκλησιῶν γαλουχὲ, πίστεως ἀρχηγὲ, ὀρθοδοξίας ποδηγὲ, λόγων μέλημα, καλοῦ παντὸς ἐνδιαίτημα! ὢ ἡ ἐκ χειρὸς κυρίου τὸ τοῦ θυμοῦ πιοῦσα ποτήριον, ὢ ἡ γενομένη πυρὸς μερὶς πολλῷ δραστικωτέρου τοῦ καταιβασίου πάλαι πυρὸς πενταπόλεως, τί μαρτυρήσω σοι;" —*Nicetas*, Alexius Ducas, p. 763, c. 5.

I.

JUSTICE

"*Te lucis ante terminum*" . . . . and lo,
One half of heaven is wrapt in rosy glow!
"*Rerum creator poscimus*" . . . . the hymn
Sweet-heaving swells o'er solemn air and dim.
Sunset. A few large stars. The sea-wind vents
Among the narrow-streeted silken tents,
From Chalcedonian palace chambers calm,
The lofty, pure, sonorous Latin psalm
Forth-poured by sworded priests athwart the tramp
And hoarse buzz humming deep from camp to camp
Of those six battles, ranged and bannered all
Under the Counts of Flanders, of St. Paul,
Of Montmorency, of Blois, and Montferrat
Who, with his Lombards, holds the rear, stretched flat
Behind the city, lengthening many a mile
Into the midnight toward St. Stephen's pile.

And all athwart this rustling region far,
Buzzed over by the sounding wings of War
(That frets and flutters, bound in brazen chain,
And breasts his iron cage), from brain to brain
One passionate purpose seethes.

For now those eight
Ambassadors, returned, with wrath relate
In clamorous conclave their scorned embassage:
Whose high compeers consult how best to wage
Now-imminent conflict with self-confident Crime,
And wield the weighty instrument of Time,
Ready to smite.
So, after lowly prayer,
Each Knight upon his naked sword doth swear
A solemn oath to see dread justice done,
And rouse the slumbering war at rise of sun.
Therefore, all night, the humming tents about,
By twos and threes conversing, in and out,
'Twixt mighty mangonel, and wheeléd tower
Armed with spring-shouldered arbalists of power,
The great chiefs stride indignant.

II.

ARMED

At sunrise
The six-times-folded Battle, serpent-wise,
Slid past Blachernæ, and with steely fold
At sunset wrapt gray Boemond's castle hold.
There, by long laboring in the dark, was made
All round the camps deep trench and palisade;
'Gainst which the war for many a night and day
Flared, rocked, and roared.

Full hard it were to say
What multitudes of mighty deeds were done,
Since first Lascaris by the Bourgignon
Was captived, till the Danish curtle-axe
Dropped on the walls, before those fierce attacks
Which, all unarmed, Eustache Le Marchis led,
Only an iron cap upon his head.

III.

BY SEA AND LAND,

Meanwhile, at sea, the white Fleet, following,
Hovered hard by; and crept with cautious wing
Under the wave-girt city; planting there
A formidable grove.

Not anywhere
Through seas and skies were ever sailed or rowed
Ships huge as these. The Paradiso proud,
Like a broad mountain, monarch of the morn,
By the mad clutch of tumbling Titans torn
Down from the windy ruins of the sky,
With Jove's chained thunders throbbing silently
In his strong pines, adown the displaced deep
Shoulders the Pelegrino, — half asleep,
With wavy fins each side a scarlet breast
Slanted. Hard by, more huge than all the rest, —
Air's highest, water's deepest, denizen,
A citadel of ocean, thronged with men
That tramp in silk and steel round battlements
Of windy wooden streets, 'mid terraced tents
And turrets, under shoals of sails unfurled, —
That vaunting monster, Venice calls "The World."

And now is passed each purple promontory
Of Sestos and Abydos, famed in story,
And now all round the deep blue bay uprise
Into the deep blue air, o'er galleries
Of marble, marble galleries; and lids
O'er lids of shining streets; dusk pyramids
O'er pyramids; and temple walls o'er walls
Of glowing gardens, whence white sunlight falls
From sleepy palm to palm; and palace tops
O'ertopped by palaces. Naught ever stops
The struggling Glory, from the time he leaves
His myrtle-muffled base, and higher heaves
His mountain march from golden-grated bower
To bronzen-gated wall, — and on, from tower
To tower, — until at last deliciously
All melts in azure summer and sweet sky.
Then, after anthem sung, sonorous all
The bronzen trumpets to the trumpets call;
Sounding across the sea from bark to bark,
Where floats the wingéd Lion of St. Mark,
The mighty signal for assault.
A shout
Shakes heaven. And swift from underneath up-spout
Thick showers of hissing arrows that down-rain
Their rattling drops upon the walls, and stain
The blood-streaked bay. The floating forest groans,
And creaks, and reels, and cracks. The rampart-stones
Clatter and shriek beneath the driven darts.
And on the shores, and at the gates, upstarts,
One after one, each misshaped monster fell
Of creaking ram, and cumbrous mangonel,

Great stones, down-jumping, chop, and split, and crush
The rocking towers; wherefrom the spearmen rush.
The morning star of battle, marshalling all
That movement massive and majestical,
Gay through the tumult which it guides doth go
The grand gray head of gallant Dandalo.
With what a full heart following that fine head, —
Thine, noble Venice, by thy noblest led!
In his blithe-dancing turret o'er the sea,
Glad as the gray sea-eagle, hovers he
Through sails in flocks and masts in avenues.

Elsewhere, the inland battle, broken, strews
With flying horse the hollows; while but ill
The heavy-harnessed Frankish Knighthood still
Strains, staggering as each Flanders stallion falls,
In the rear region, round the city walls,
Against those silken turms and squadrons light,
That follow and fly, scatter and reunite,
Tormenting their full balked too-cumbrous foe;
Like swarms of golden bees that come and go
About the bear whose paw is on their hive
Patient and pertinacious, though they drive
Their stings into his eyes, settle and swarm,
Disperse and close again, to do him harm,
Unharmed. For there in splendor eminent
Is pitched the purple-topt Imperial tent,
And domes of crimson glow i' the azure sky,
Girt by Byzantium's gorgeous chivalry.

So to the kindling of the Even Star
The groaning-hearted battle greatens.

IV.

IS TRIUMPHANT.

Far
And near the strong siege tugs by sea and land
The storm-struck city, — hugged on either hand
By heavy ruin, — till from mast to wall,
From sea to shore, the high drawbridges fall,
And in mid-air the armed men march, and drop
On battlemented roof and turret top.
The deadly Greek fire dips, and drips, and crawls,
And twists, and runs about the ruining walls,
And all is blaze and blackness, glare and gloom.
Pietro Alberti, the Venetian, whom
His sword lights, shining naked 'twixt his teeth
Sharp-gripped, through rushing arrows, wrapt with death,
Leaps from his ship into the waves: now stands
On the soaked shore: now climbs with bleeding hands
And knees the wall: now left, now right, swift, bright,
Wild weapons round him whirl and sing: now right,
Now left, he smites, fights, shakes, breaks, all things down.

The Standard of St. Mark is on the town!

André d' Herboise, the gallant gay French knight,
Fast following him, hath gained the other height.
Prompt as a plunging meteor, that strikes straight
And instantaneous through the intricate
Thick-crowded stars its keen aim, flitting through

The choked breach, flashes dauntless Dandalo.
In rush the rest. In clattering cataract
The invading host rolls down. Disrupt, distract,
The invaded break and fly. The great church bells
Toll madly, and the battering mangonels
Bellow. The priests in long procession plant
The cross before them, passing suppliant
To meet the marching conquest. With fierce cries
Against the throne the rabble people rise,
And slaves cast off their fetters, and set free
Their hidden hates. For aye the craven knee
That meekest crooks, adoring present power,
Before the little idol of the hour,
Is cousin to the craven hand that smites
Most fiercely down the image it delights
To insult and shame when greater gods wax wroth.

V.

SICUT FUMUS.

Now, therefore, when Alexius saw that both
The creatures and destroyers of his power
Were on him, to his soul he said: "The Hour
Is mine no more. Soul, we have lived our day."
Then, waiting for the night, he fled away
Into the night. Night took him by the hand
And led him silently into the land
Of darkness. Darkness o'er his forehead cast
Her mighty mantle, murmuring, "Mine, at last!"

In the great audience chamber at Byzance
A Latin soldier, leaning on his lance

Fatigued with slaughter, on the marble ground
Blood-bathed an empty purple garment found.
And then, for the first time, immersed in thought,
The Latin soldier muttered, "I have fought
Against an Emperor!"
Jewels in her head
And serpents in her hand, — smiling, and dead,
And beautiful in death, — each glorious globe
(Loosed from the glittering murrey satin robe)
Of her upturned defiant bosom, bare,
Save for the few locks of delicious hair
That swept them — saved by scornful death from
scorn —
Only the beauty left of her — at morn
They found the Egyptian Jezraäl.
So fades
Star after star along the cypress glades,
Face after face from the rose-bowers: so song
After song dies the lonesome lawns along.
Each to his time! The revel and the rout,
Lamp after lamp, mask after mask, go out;
Still for new singers the old songs to sing
In the same place to the same lute-playing:
Still for new dancers, to new tunes the same
Dance dancing ever, to take up the game
All lose in turn.
Another time begins.
New passions, and new pleasures, and new sins,
Forever the old failure in new forms;
To fashion a metropolis for worms,
And write in dust man's moral!

Meanwhile, where
Hides Muzufer? what doth he? how doth fare?

How fares the small sunshiny insect thing
That feeds on death and in the beam doth sing,
When quenched the beam, and stopped the moment's play?
Nature both brings to birth and sweeps away
Myriads of minims such: whose souls minute
For loss or gain doth Heaven or Hell compute?
Please they, or tease they, how shall Fate devise
Fit retribution for dead butterflies?

Then, Power being changed, the changeful people went,
And from the noisome pit where he was pent
Drew forth blind Isaac.
Seven black years of night
Clung to him, and kept him cold in the sun's light.
For he had grown to hold familiar talk
With newts and creeping things, — long wont to walk
About him in the silent dark down there,
Which he would miss henceforth. He was aware
Of little else. And it was hard to him
To understand (so very faint and dim
To his dull memory were the former times)
Why the great world, intent upon its crimes
And pleasures, was at pains to take him back,
Unto itself, from that oblivion black,
Where he, the loveless man of long ago,
Had learned to love, what men abhor, — the slow,
Soft-footed dwellers of the dark. He had
So lost the habitude of being glad,
And all the strength of it, that, though thrice o'er
New friends explained to him his joy, no more
Than one born deaf and dumb he seemed to find

A meaning to the matter in his mind.
So, passively, he yielded to the crowd
That robed him, crowned him, and proclaimed
aloud
Him only the true Cæsar.

VI.

TWO BLIND MEN.

Now once more
Proud to up-prop all Power, those lions four,
Subservient, their broad blazing backs upon
The bright floor crouch, beneath the throne whereon
Blind Isaac sits; with fumbling hand, in dull
Delaying doubt, to affix the golden bull
And great sign manual, by the Barons claimed,
To that high treaty with Alexius framed
In Zara.
Which to place in those weak hands,
Blind Dandalo before blind Isaac stands.
Two gray old men, and sightless each. The one
Sits robed in royal state on sumptuous throne,
Distinguisht by the imperial diadem
And purple mantle proud with many a gem;
And sees them not: but, in himself, doth gaze
On darkness, gloomy death, and guilty days.
The other, by long noble labors marred,
With august brows by battle thunder scarred,
Stands, — marked to sight by honorable soils
Of his yet recent self-regardless toils;
And sees them not: but, in himself, doth see
The bright beginnings of great days to be,
And glory never dying.

VII.

THE DOGE IS OBSTINATE.

After this,
In the Cathedral (as old custom is)
On battle shield, in purple buskins, borne,
And vermeil robe, by new made Cæsars worn,
The young Alexius, in full pomp and state
Of sovran power, supreme beneath the great
Imperial ensign's eagle wings unfurled,
Receives high homage of one half a world.

Which things accomplisht; and a month or more
Of pageant and carousal being o'er
(Whose swiftly sliding and soft-footed hours
Slipped unsuspected by, 'mid myrtle bowers,
From porphyry palaces), the Red Cross lords,
Yawning, with listless looks down their long swords,
As banquet after banquet palled on them,
Cry . . . . "Now for Joppa and Jerusalem!"

The new-made Emperor still their presence prays
And added aid, with promised guerdon: says
Need yet remains to heal by wholesome arts
The much-hurt empire, — all the popular parts
Bind up in single, and compact the state;
Which tasks more time: hints vaguely hindrance great;
Claims to appease, and scruples nice to weigh;
Funds hard to find; grave causes for delay;
With promise fair of further profit still,
Thereby implied.
"The Treaty, signed, fulfil
First, Emperor of the East," said Dandalo.

VIII.

VERTIGO.

Alas, that in this world 't is ever so!
For men might be as gods, if it were not
That greed of power goes mad from power got.
Who stands upon the pinnacle, as 't were,
Of Greatness, — seeing, hearing, everywhere
About himself the dazzling orb spin round,
Turns dizzy at the sight and at the sound,
And tumbles from the top to the abyss.
Of all high places this the danger is; —
That those who stand there needs must gaze beneath,
Till they wax desperate; being wooed to death
By depth; from whose black clutch some point of sight
Above them seen, if such there were, — some height
Higher than theirs, — whereon to fix their eyes,
Might haply save them. But this Heaven denies.
And, seeing that, of Emperors and Kings,
The Scribe of Judgment (who plucks out his wings
To write their histories o'er and o'er again,
Leaving meanwhile the lives of meaner men
To kind oblivion) doth record to us
So many monsters, so few virtuous,
What wonder if some weary souls suppose
That 't is perchance *the thing itself* (who knows?)
Time cannot cure: the nature of the *thing*,
Not of the *man:* the *kingship*, not the *king?*

Howe'er that be, Alexius, now made strong
By rights restored, forthwith waxed weak by wrong

Renewed: and paltered both with his allies
And with his people; teasing each with lies,
And fronting bothways with a double face.
Thus, since, with reason shrewd, the populace
Looked coldly, and askance, on power restored
By foreign arms, the frightened Prince ignored
Those foreign friends to whom he owed his throne:
Carped at their claims, and did his oath disown.
For heedless Hope in misery oft is fain
To mortgage more of gratitude for gain
Than, in possession, frugal Memory yields
Her clamorous claimant, from full harvest fields.
But since, withal, he feared the people too,
He plotted still, and still desired (untrue
To all alike), by foreign arms kept still,
Still, too, to keep in check the people's will.
Till foes, thus finding friends in friends turned foes,
Said, "Power is powerless."

IX.

A DARK DEED.

Then one night uprose
Myrtillus, the one-eyebrowed, in the dark
(Marked out for mischief by the Devil's mark
Across his squinting, double-minded eyes),
And seized on the Boy-Emperor, by surprise
And treason foul, in unsuspecting sleep;
Whom, having plunged him down a dungeon deep,
Six times with hell-brewed hebanon he tried
To poison. But the Prince, because he died
That way too slowly, being young and hard
Of life, 't is said, was strangled afterward.

No need to strangle Isaac. Soon as told
Of what was done, he did his mantle fold
Across his brows, and said, "This was to be
Because of my great sins that follow me."
And that same night he died.
The morrow morn,
On battle shield, in purple buskins, borne,
Myrtillus men crowned Emperor.

X.

THE FULNESS OF TIME.

Dandalo
Said then . . . . "The time is come, which long ago
I saw in Zara. Who eschew the good
Must choose the evil. Drunk with brawl and blood,
This Empire reels upon her downward road;
Corrupt at home, contemptible abroad.
Devilish, she would be godlike without God:
Godless, would rule, who needs, herself, the rod:
And deems, not being good, she can be great: —
Great, without one great man, i' the face of Fate!
The singular tyrant breeds the general slave,
And shameless citizens shamed cities have.
The time is now, and ours the hands, O friends,
To sweep this rubbish hence, and make amends
To earth, too long encumbered with the same. —
To arms, for all men's sake, and in God's name!"

So, down before the iron Occident
The guilty golden-crownèd Orient went.

Because those Powers that make, and break, and
keep,
And cast away — Spirits that in the deep
And toilful stithy of that underground
Gray miner, Nature, with unheeded sound
Monotonously hammer, heave, and beat,
And bend with blow on blow, and heat on heat,
The pliant world to every shape it wears,
Upon the stubborn anvils of the years —
Said to each other, "Break we up this Past!'
And suddenly one half a world was cast
Into the furnace, to be forged anew.

XI.

THE HORSES OF LYSIPPUS.

At midnight, in the murtherous streets, the dew
Was blood-red, and the heavens were hurt with
sound
Of shriek and wail the ransacked region round.
So that men heard not, in the Hippodrome,
Those Four Bronze Horses, that had come from
Rome,
In conference, talking each to each.
One said
"Our purple-mantled master, Power, is fled.
And how shall We Four fare? Let us away
Through the thick night! For ever since the day
We followed that great Western Cæsar home
To grace the glories of Augustine Rome,
We Four have felt no hand upon our manes
Less great than theirs, who grasp the golden reins
Of Empire; they behind whose chariot wheel

Yet-burning ruts their fervid course reveal,
Who rode the rolling world. We also, when
Power passed from Rome, his car drew here again,
And carried Conquest in his course divine
From West to East, to dwell with Constantine.
But now is Power departed, who knows where?
Out of the East!"
So spake that voice in air.
The others answered: "Whither shall we go?
Our master being gone? For who doth know
Where we may find him?"

XII.

AND THE LION OF ST. MARK.

Listening in the dark,
To these replied the Lion of St. Mark:
"Power rideth on my wings. Come also ye
Whither I go, across the vassal sea.
And let us bear with us, to please him well,
Beauty, the spouse of Power. And we will dwell
Together."
Then they answered, "Even so,
Lion! and where thou goest we will go."

So those Five Beasts went forth. And took with them
Power and Beauty. For whose diadem
They also brought great store of precious things,
And gathered graven gems in golden rings,
And carved and colored stones, to be the dower
Of Beauty and the heritage of Power:
Clear agate cups and vases crystalline,

Porphyry, and syenite, and serpentine,
Obsidian, alabaster: statues fair
Of lucid gods: garments of richness rare:
And gold, and bronze, and silver: turkis blue
As Venus' veins: and rubies red in hue
As Adon's lips: and jasper, onyx, opal.

In this way Venice took Constantinople.

NOTES TO THE SIEGE OF CONSTANTINOPLE.

Page 260. *Isaac is Emperor, and reigns at ease*, &c.

"ἦν οὖν τὰ περὶ τὴν δίαιταν ὁ βασιλεὺς οὗτος πολυτελέστατος καὶ διαδοτικὸς βρωμάτων τοῖς παρεστῶσιν. εἶχεν οὖν ἀτεχνῶς τὴν τράπεζαν Σολομώντειον, καὶ τὰς ἐσθῆτας ὡς ἐκεῖνος καινοφανεῖς περιέκειτο, βουνίζων μὲν τοὺς ἄρτους, λόχμην δὲ κνωδάλων ἰχθύων τε διάπλευσιν καὶ πόντον οἴνοπα δεικνὺς τὴν ἑστίασιν. καὶ μὴν ἑτερημέροις ἐνηυπάθει λουτροῖς, ὠσφραίνετό τε μυρεψουμένων εὐωδιῶν, καὶ ταῖς στακταῖς ἐρραντιζετο, ὡς ὁμοίωμά τε ναοῦ στολαῖς ἐξάλλοις ἐκέκαστο βοστρυχίζόμενος· ἐπιδεικτικός τε ἦν ὡς ταὼς ὁ φιλόκοσμος καὶ μὴ δὶς τὸν αὐτὸν χιτῶνα ἐνδιδυσκόμενος ὥσπερ ἐκ παστοῦ νυμφίος καὶ ὡς ἐκ λίμνης περικαλλοῦς ἥλιος προῄει καθ' ἑκάστην τῶν ἀνακτόρων· χαίρων δὲ ταῖς εὐτραπελίαις καὶ τοῖς ἐκ τῆς ἁπαλῆς Μούσης ᾄσμασιν ἁλισκόμενος, ἐγερσιγέλωσί τε ἀνθρωπίσκοις συμπαραθύρων, οὐκ ἐπεζύγου Κέρκωψί τε καὶ μίμοις καὶ παρασίτοις καὶ ἀοιδοῖς τὰ βασίλεια." — κ. τ. λ.

Nicetæ Choniatæ, de Isaacio Angelo, lib. iii. p. 579. 2.
(The Bonn edition, edited by Bekker.)

Page 261. *In agate cups, and vases crystalline*, &c.

"Vasi d'oro, d'argento d'agata, sorprendenti per la loro grandezza, i quali erano stati portati in trionfo da Gneo Pompeo dopo la sua vittoria su i re Tigrane e Mitridate."

Origine delle Feste Veneziane, di Guistina Renier Michiel. Venice, 1817. Vol. 2, p. 163.

Page 262. *And realms extended from Euphrates far*, &c.

See Nicet. Chon. de Isaac. Ang. lib. iii. p. 565, 566.

Page 264. *The chase! the Emperor cries,—the chase!* &c.

See Nicet. Chon. de Isaac. Ang. lib. iii. p. 593.

Page 266. ***Marten, and zibeline, and miniver,*** &c.

"De samiz, et de dras de soie, & de robes Vaires & Grises, & Hermines, & toz les chiers auoirs qui onques furent trouué en terre."

Ville-Hardouin, p. 102, cap. 132. Paris, 1557, folio.

Page 269. ***Our Brother hath two eyes yet in his head,*** &c.

See Nicet. Chon. de Isaac. Ang. lib. iii. p. 595. 3. This punishment was special to the usage of the Greeks of the Lower Empire, and adopted from them by other nations. There were two ways of inflicting it. The first, by means of a bull's pizzle so applied as to force, by extreme pressure, the eyeballs out of their sockets: the second, and least painful, by pouring boiling vinegar into the eyes. See *Procopius Hist. Arcana.* There is also a curious account (which is probably false) in Egantius, lib. ix. c. 12 *de exempl. illustr. Viror. Venet. Civit.*, of the manner in which (according to this writer) the eyes of Henry Dandalo were destroyed by the Emperor Manuel, — "*candente laminâ æreâ ejus oculis objectâ, quam ille intueri continuo cogeretur.*"

Page 270. ***Meanwhile the other flees,*** &c.

"Et ejus filium Alexium interfici jusserat; sed per quemdam Senescaldum manus ejus evadens Alexius, ad Suevorum ducem Philippum regem Alemaniæ confugit."

Alberic. Ann. MCCII.

Page 271. ***The Pope the Prince first plies,*** &c.

See Gest. Innocent. III. p. 71, 72.

Page 271. ***Irene, sister to Alexius wed,*** &c.

She was widow of Roger, King of Sicily (the son of Tancred), and espoused Philip, the Suabian Kaiser, after the death of her first husband. In Germany she seems to have been best known under the name of Maria. Witness her epitaph in the monastery of Lorch: —

"Nobilis atque pia hic cineratur graeca Maria
Philippi regis conjux. Hanc atria regis
fac intrare pia semita virgo Maria."

Page 272. *Meanwhile the Red Cross Lords*, &c.

> " Et li Quens & tous ses Barnés
> S'en fu droit à Gadres alés,
> V li Duc de Venise l'ot
> Menet, car el faire n'en pot."
> Philippes Mouskes.

Page 272. *Venetian Dandalo*, &c.

He was eighty years old when elected to the Dukedom, and died thirteen years afterwards at Constantinople, where his tomb in St. Sophia (*see Ville-Hardouin*) existed till that city was taken by the Turks (*see Rhamusius*). Most authors attribute the loss of the Doge's eyesight to Manuel Comnenus; and in the present poem I have adopted this supposition, although I think the truth of it extremely doubtful. Godefroy, a monk of S. Pantaleone, writes of him that "*ad expugnandam quandam civitatem Regis Vngariæ nomine Sadram çæcatus fuit*"; and Philippes Mouskes also asserts that the Doge lost his sight at the siege of Zara. This is obviously a mistake, or perhaps even a wilful misstatement, designed to imply a Divine judgment on an undertaking condemned by the Pope. But it is highly probable that his blindness was from accidental or natural causes. Sabellicus, indeed, avers that the Doge was not entirely blind, and this opinion is supported by a passage in Sanutus.

Page 273. *From whose prows the arms*
Of heroes hang, and low-hulled palanders.

Ville-Hardouin (c. 14) makes the Doge say in his reply to the embassy from the Barons, "*Nos ferons Vuissiers à passer quatre milles cinq cens chevaux, et neuf mille Escuyers.*" This indicates clearly enough the character of these vessels; which were built flat for carrying horses. The etymology of the word itself also (Huissiers — *Galies Huissieres* — from *huis*, or doors) implies that they were made with doors to open and shut for the entry and issue of the horses, — probably much after the same fashion as the flying bridges now common in Germany and America. Huges,

Count of S. Pol, in an epistle describing the first siege of Constantinople, calls them *naves usariæ*, and the Greeks, *Hippegi*, *Hippagogi*, *Hippagones*, &c. The Sire de Joinville (Hist. of S. Louis) describes the usage of them very distinctly: "*Nous entrasmes au mois d'Aoust celuy an en la nef à la Roche de Marseille, & fut ouuerte la porte de la nef pour faire entrer nos cheuaux, ceux que deuions mener outremer. Et quant tous furent entrez, la porte fut reclouse, & estouppée, ainsi comme l'on voudrait faire un tonnel de vin: parce que quand la nef est en la grant mer, toute la porte est en eau.*"

It was the custom of this time for the knights to hang their shields over and along the decks of the galleys, so as to form a sort of shelter from the arrows of the enemy. This was also done for show in naval parade. Guillaume Guiart sings of the naval armament under Grimaldi: —

"*Où tant ot bannieres inclines*
Dras enarmés à euures fines,
Enuiron les bors espandus,
Lances droites, escus pandus,
Blans haubers," &c.

And again:

"*Et au desous des creneleures*
De riches dras à enarmures,
Atachiés comme à bastonceaus,
Targes, banières, penonceaus," &c.

Page 274. *And some notable men.*

In Ville-Hardouin the Doge says to the embassy from the Barons, "*Vostres Seignors sont li plus hauts homes qui soient sans corone.*" Some few of these names will be familiar to every reader, but the greater number of them is unnoticed by either Gibbon or Voltaire, or any modern historian that I know of. They will be found, however, in Ville-Hardouin, Alberic, and other of the early chroniclers. The reader can, of course, if he pleases, skip the list of these Notables, which, following the fashion of the old rhymers, I have furnished for the satisfaction of a curiosity which is not likely to be felt by many.

Page 275. ***With shields slung frontwise over chain habergeons.***

These shields, or scutcheons, were blazoned with the arms of those who wore them, and usually slung under the neck. "Is scutum simul colloque pependit." Abbo de Bel. Par. lib. ii. So also the Sire de Joinville, "Et s'en alla à eux l'escu au coul," p. 61.

Page 278. ***Garnier of Borland, whose assaults when Hell,*** &c.

"*Eodem anno contigit in Diœcesi Treverensi supra Renum apud S. Goaris oppidum, cum Garnerus de Borlande, qui erat in parte Regis de Suevia, obsideret Ecclesiam in ipso castro sitam et munitam Clericis deintus Crucifixum locantibus in fenestra, unus de forinsecus diabolico spiritu repletus querelam repente traxit contra Crucifixum, et ecce de Crucifixo infixo sanguis fluxit largissime cunctis et foris et intus qui aderant cernentibus, et ipse Garnerus territus obsidionem dimisit, et ab eo loco aufugit.*" Alberic, Ann. 1201.

Page 278. ***Whose dam***
Was nameless Madge.

The surname and family of Marguerite his mother is not known. His father was Dreux of Amiens.

Page 278. . . . . ***his quilted gamboison.***

"*Tot ferri sua membra plicis, tot quisque patenis*
Pectora tot coriis, tot Gambesonibus armat."

Guillaume le Breton, lib. xi. Philipp.

So also the Sire de Joinville, in his History of S. Louis, "*Je trouué illec prés un Gaubisson d'estouppes,*" &c., and Guillaume de Guigneville, in the Soul's Pilgrimage.

"*Car dessous va la Gamboison*
Qui le veut armer par raison."

It was a quilted garment of thick stuff, which went under the hauberk and reached over the thighs. That it was sometimes worn in war without armor of any kind would appear from a passage in Ville-Hardouin, as well as from the following, in which Nicetas, speaking of Conrad of Montferrat, describes his gamboison. . . . . "*αὐτὸς μέντοι ἄνευ θυρεοῦ τηνικαῦτα διηγωνίζετο, ἐκ δὲ λίνου πεποιημένον ὕφασμα οἴνῳ αὐστηρῷ ἱκανῶς ἡλισμένῳ διάβροχον πολλάκις περιπτυχθὲν δίκην θώρακος ἐνεδύετο· ἐς τοσοῦτον δ᾽ἦν ἀντιτυπὲς ἁλσὶ καὶ οἴνῳ συμπιληθὲν ὡς καὶ βέλους εἶναι παντὸς στεγανώτερον· ἠριθμοῦντο δ᾽ εἰς ὀκτωκαίδεκα καὶ πλείω τὰ τοῦ ὑφάσματος συμπτύγματα.*" From which it would seem to have been prepared with wine and salt, and doubled eighteen times.

Page 280. ***Bussy d'Herboise, the frank French knight.***

Brother of André d'Herboise, who distinguished himself (together with Pietro Alberti the Venetian) at Constantinople.

Page 281. *Henry of Ofterdingen*, &c.

Mythical.

Page 281. ***A milk-white panther rampant, on a field Vert.***

"***Panthera alba in campo, ut vocant, viridi splendebat.***"
Wolfg. Lazü de Gent. migr. p. 223.

Page 282. ***Le Valet de Constantinople.***

So King Pepin, in the Roman des Loherancs, says of himself:

Iceste guerre commant à maufez vis,
Quant commença Vallez ere & meschins.

That is to say, that, when the war began, he was still valet, and young prince. In France, at this time, the Nobility consisted of Three Orders. The First, composed of all who were entitled to carry their own banner in war (hence knights Banaret — the lowest of this order): the Second, Chevaliers (simple) or knights, whose fiefs were not large enough to furnish the contingent entitled to carry a banner, and who therefore fought under the banner of some more powerful chief: these were called Bachelors (Bacheliers — Bas Chevaliers): the Third, Esquires (Escuyers), sons of nobles of all ranks, to whose youth the genius of Chivalry assigned the grace and dignity of a noble servitude (*Ich dien*), and who carried (as a privilege) the shields (*Escus*) of their patrons in war. Camden derives the term "Esquire" (scutcheon-bearer) from the right to bear arms. But it is more probable that the term represents the "*devoir*" to bear the shield of another, — not the right to blazon one's own. To be Chevalier or Baron, it was necessary to have risen, as it were, from the ranks in the service of chivalry, to have been Valet before being Lord, Soldier before being Captain, Esquire before being Knight. Our playing-cards record the tradition, which our usage dishonors. The Valets, although they have become knaves, still retain the noble names of Launcelot du Lac, and Huon of Bordeaux, &c.

Page 285. *Borland then took sail.*

"En cel termine se trauailla tant un halz hom de l'ost qui ére d'Alemaigne Carniers de Borlãde que el s'en alla en une nef de mercheans."

Ville-Hardouin, 51.

Page 285. . . . . *but never came they more.*

"Et li sairemenz que il firent ne furent mie bien tenu, que il ne reparérent pas en l'ost."

Id. id.

Page 285. *Of whom five hundred Barons lost their lives.*

"En une nef s'en emblérent bien cinq cens, si noiérent tuit, & furent perdu. Vne altre compagnie s'en embla par terre, & s'en cuida aller par Esclavonie : & li paisant de la terre les assaillierent, & en occistrent assez."

Id. id.

Page 288. *When the Ambassadors of Venice, France*, &c.

"Giunti nella sala del trono, i loro occhi furono abbagliati dallo splendore dell' oro e delle gemme, solita sostituzione al poter vero, e alla vera virtù."

Origine delle Feste Veneziane, vol. 2, p. 153.

Page 291. *Render to Cæsar what is Cæsar's own*, &c.

"Quar il le tint à tort, & à perchié contre Dieu, & contre raison. Ainz est son neuvu qui çi siet entre nos . . . . fil de son frere l'Empereor Sursac. Més s'il voloit à la merci son neuou venir, & li rendoit la corone, & l'empire, nos li proieriens que il li pardonast," &c.

Ville-Hardouin, c. 73, p. 55.

Page 296. *Come ye as peaceful pilgrims, to pursue*, &c.

" Se vos vos i estes poure, ne disetels, il vou donnera volentiers de ses viande & de son auoir, and vos li vindiez sa terre. . . . . Car se vos estiez vint tant de gent, ne vos en porroiz vos aller, se il mal vos voloit faire, que vos ne fussiez morz & desconfiz."

Id., c. 72, p. 54.

Page 297. *Our answer prompt to your barbarian crew*
Shall be your heads, &c.

" Prima però di nulla intraprendere si deliberò di spedere Ambasciatori all' usurpatore Alessio, intimandagli di remettere la città e lo scettro a Isaaco ed al giovane Alessio, che n'erano i padroni legitimi. Il tiranno non solo recusè di arrendersi, ma minacciò persin della vita gli stessi Ambasciatori."

Feste Veneziane, vol. 2, p. 152.

This, however, is not true. The Embassage was sent, not by the Barons to Alexius, but by the Emperor to them ; and the only menace put forth on that occasion was what I have cited above, from Ville-Hardouin. The author or authoress of the Feste has evidently confounded the event here referred to with what Ville-Hardouin describes as having afterwards taken place between the deputies of the Barons and the younger Alexius, in reference to which that pious chronicler thanks God that the Ambassadors escaped with their lives. Justification for the episode, as I have related it, exists nevertheless in the universal custom of the time to address in the first instance, by embassage, a summons to the sovereign against whom war was to be declared, and the fact, which is sufficiently attested by Ville-Hardouin, that on these occasions the Ambassadors were sometimes placed in no small peril of their lives.

Page 312. *Meanwhile, at sea*, &c.

For obvious reasons, justifiable, I trust, by the purposes and privileges of art, the principal details of the two sieges have been thrown together, so as to present only a single picture.

Page 322. *Myrtillus, the one-eyebrowed*, &c.

For the sake of euphony, the Italian orthography of Murzoufle has been adopted. The name, I believe, implies the peculiar feature of its owner's physiognomy. He is said to have had but a single eyebrow, extending over both eyes, without interruption at the nose. Some say that he also squinted.

END OF BOOK VI.

BOOK VII.

ELEVENTH TO FIFTEENTH CENTURY.

LEGENDS, BALLADS, AND ROMANCES.

"Uns ist in alten mœren
Wunders vil geseit,
Von helden lobebœren,
Von grôzer kuonheit."
Der Nibelunge Noth.

FAREWELL TO THE HOLY LANDS.

(ELEVENTH CENTURY.)

1.

HRICE, ho trumpeter, sound!
And around, and around
With the merry red wine once more, friends!
Then to stirrup and selle,
And away, — fare ye well, —
For my ship is at hand on the shore, friends!

2.

Shout! for Baldwin hath ta'en
All his own back again,
And O well for the brave right hands
That have won by the rood,
From the Infidel brood,
God his ground in the Holy Lands!

3.

Here 's, from each and from all,
To the old Amirál!
Fair weather to him and his bark!
For a King among kings
Is the Lion with wings;
The strong lion of stout Saint Mark!

4.

And here 's now to the worth
Of the West and the North,
The hearts of the North and the West!
And the eyes and the lips
Of those sweet she-slips
Of the East, that we each loved best!

5.

Friend, praise me the dame,
Whose so soft southern name
I never could learn how to say,
Though I well know the bliss
Of her soft southern kiss
That hath kissed better knowledge away:

6.

And I 'll pledge you that Greek
Learnéd Lady's loved cheek,
And the depth of her dark eye-glance,
All whose praises you sung
In the great Latin tongue
Through the gardens of golden Byzance.

7.

Prithee shine out afar,
Thou red-eyed Even Star,
Shine over the seas and the sands!
And so light me again
To the wood, hill, and plain
Where mine own pleasant castle stands.

8.

Far in Thüringenwald,
Far in Thüringenwald,
There the nightingale calls for me
Through the dewy spring night,
When the walls glimmer white
To the moon on the long dark lea.

9.

Farther still, o'er the Baltic,
Old friend, black, basaltic,
With the whirlwind grim in his grip,
There your castle awaits,
Behind close-cullised gates,
The sound of that horn at your hip

10.

Like a snowdrop, so white,
Shy, tender, and slight,
In the window your little daughter
Is at watch for a sail,
When the twilight is pale
O'er the vast Suevonian water.

11.

But in Thüringenwald,
O in Thüringenwald,
My good wife is waiting me,
While the nightingale sings
To her marvellous things
Of the deeds done over the sea.

12.

Western star, merry star,
Glitter fair, glitter far
To the silvery northern climes !
Blow ye sea-breezes sweet,
Blowing homeward, and greet
My lady ten million times !

13.

Fare thee well, friend, and leader !
And farewell to thee, Cedar
On Lebanon ! Fare ye well, too,
Sweet Cyprus and Sicily !
Ah, beck not so busily,
We shall not weigh anchor for you.

14.

Ye soft-eyed siren maids,
In the rich-scented shades
Of your rose-bearing gardens yonder !
We have wives over there
Of our own, all as fair, —
Far more fair, as I think, — and fonder.

15.

For the rest of my life,
Save my old hunting-knife,
Not a weapon will I wear now :
And your bow and seal-spear,
Friend of mine, you shall bear
Henceforth but in sport, or for show.

16.

We will hang up our mail
On a great golden nail,
And dispute which is bruised the sorest.
In a doublet of green
I will follow my Queen
Through the old Thuringian Forest!

DOGE ORSO'S NIGHT'S WORK.

(ELEVENTH CENTURY.)

1.

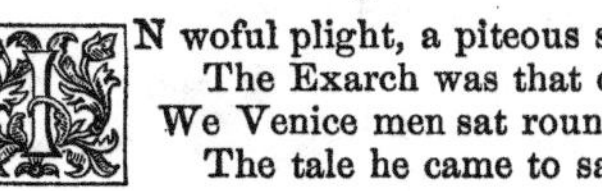

IN woful plight, a piteous sight,
The Exarch was that day
We Venice men sat round to hear
The tale he came to say.

2.

"The Greek hath lost, with little cost,
The Lombard he hath won
To the iron crown, the stoutest town
That stands beneath the sun:

3.

"For, while the old wolf Luitprand
Was fighting for the Franks,
His wily nephew Hildebrand,
Among whose robber ranks

4.

"Vicenza's Duke rode unabashed,
Hath seized Ravenna town,
And from the Imperial city dashed
The Imperial standard down."

5.

A joyful man the Exarch was
The morrow of that day

We Venice men set sail again
  To seize the Lombard's prey.

6.

At close of day Ravenna lay
  Before us on the height:
We dropped adown beneath the town
  After the fall of night:

7.

At fall of night there was no light,
  There was no noise of bells:
Without a sound we ran aground,
  And fixed our mangonels:

8.

At mid of night was sound and light
  Through all Ravenna town:
Loud rang the bells above the yells
  Of thousands trampled down:

9.

At ope of day in fetters lay
  The Lombard Hildebrand:
The town was ours: about the towers
  We roamed, a merry band.

10.

The fight, God wot, was short and
  "Bear Hildebrand aboard.
Renew your oath," Doge Orso quoth,
  "And take your lawful lord.

11.

"The Duke is dead," he laughed, and said,
  "The city is all our own.
Stand forth Exarch! To thee Saint Mark
  Gives back Ravenna town."

12.

Then all outright for great delight
  The Exarch wept, I trow.
As he had woful been before,
  So was he joyful now.

13.

By that night's cost the Lombard lost,
  What our Duke Orso won
With great renown, the stoutest town
  That stands beneath the sun.

SALZBURGENSIS VAGABUNDUS.

(THIRTEENTH CENTURY.)

AX DEI VOBISCUM! We are, by your leave, friends,
Three poor travelling scholars. All the more we grieve, friends,
That now-a-days good wine 's so dear, and learning still so cheap, alas!
O ghost of good Archbishop Reinhold, you for us would weep Alas!
But you have left this wicked world, and you are gone to glory.
Mihi est propositum in tabernâ mori!
All the way from Salzburg here, in this season blowy,
Bitter blue the hill-tops were, bleak the roads and snowy.
Sure, a man must warm his wits when the weather pinches,
And the snow 's above his boots some half-dozen inches!
We from hostle on to hostle, thirsting to replenish
Empty bellies and dry throttles with a flask of Rhenish,
Set the Muses up for sale, — liquor begged for learning,
Not a doit for all our pains from the numskulls earning.
Little favor didst thou get, great Horatius Flaccus,

Of our thick-skulled Thaliarchs swilling German
Bacchus!
Folly's citadel resists each classic catapulta,
Penitus inutilis, penitusque stulta!
Lord! you should have seen the looks of those unlatined laics,
Hailed in choice hexameters, and sued to in alcaics!
Hairy Jews with money-bags: troopers from Pavía:
Hamburgers, and Bambergers . . . . Herr Josef!
Frau Maria!
Zum Teuffel! groans my yellow Jew; the trooper
growls *va via!*
Zounds! I wish those Jews, with all my heart, into
. . . . Judæa!
Barefoot trots the begging Muse among this harum-scarum.
Loca vitant publica quidam poetarum.
Snug as hedgehog hid in hedge, most comfortably curled up,
And looking not a whit less proud than if it
wrapped the world up,
Safe upon the mountain-side, secured from all infraction,
And reckless how the plain may fare, in high self-satisfaction
Smiled this blessèd burg; — resolved we three
should make a climb of it,
And cool as Lot's small city when the rest had a
hot time of it.
"*Vides*," then "*ut altâ*" . . . . there . . . . "*stet
nive*" . . . . shouted Hax to us,
And Fritz . . . . "'T is not good wine, I trust, the
little city lacks!" to us.

"*Deprome*," then, "*quadrimum*," I . . . . so here we
are among you,
Praying the Lord, good gentlefolks, your good
lives to prolong you!
There 's in us a thirsty devil raging to consume
us.
Salutemus igitur bibuli qui sumus!
Sure, you have n't heard the news? The Hohen-
staufen . . . . Zooks there!
Is that mine host's fair daughter? 'Faith, I knew
her by her looks there.
Illa formosissimis tam nota virgo brachiis!
The brute that 's not in love with her no better
than a lackey is!
What 's the little lady's name? To *Lina* rhymes
divina.
Dear demozel, if I were *Rex*, I know who 'd be
Regina.
See her foot and ankle fine! if you 'd a soul for
beauty
You 'd fit me with the proper phrase . . . . *egregia
juventute!*
Sir, will you buy an epitaph for your now-sainted
lady?
Something pious, chaste, and sweet, to suit the
yew-trees shady?
Hax, here, with his lantern jaws . . . . Beseech you
only try Hax!
He 'll turn you off in half a trice a score of elegiacs.
Sic solamine non carebis for the dear departed.
Or you, young lord, a love-song fierce, impassioned,
fiery-hearted,
For your heart's queen with strong black eyes
. . . . or blue? It matters little.

Fritz there, with his woman's face, will paint her to a tittle.
Fritz knows all the pretty things in Ovid and Tibullus,
For all his looks demure . . . . *non facit monachum cucullus.*
Whate'er you want we'll furnish you, *cantandum aut scribendum,*
But if you want a drink-song, come to me for *Nunc bibendum!*

A KING AND A QUEEN.

WILLIAM OF LORIS TO THE LADY OF THE ROSE.

1.

ISE, my Queen, and away with me!
From the kingdoms where I am King
Two Spirits to lead me to thee
Have outspeeded the wild-bird's wing.

2.

For the sake of thy dear dark eyes
My soul have I given this Twain;
Who are pledged to win me the prize
I die if I do not obtain:

3.

Yet they are not Spirits accurst,
But each is a delicate Sprite;
And Sleep is the name of the first,
The name of the second is Night.

4.

O hearken! O hearken! Our horses
Are waiting for thee and for me.
More fleet than the wind in his courses,
More strong than the hurricanes be,

5.

They shall bear us, nor ever tire,
Over hollow, and hill, and stream:

The name of the one is Desire,
  The name of the other is Dream.

6.

Away! I am thine, thou art mine:
  One body, and spirit, and heart!
Stoop! midsummer leaps in the wine
  I pour to thee, ere we depart.

7.

List! midsummer melodies stray
  From the strings of my throbbing lute,
With music to lead us away
  Through the dim world starry and mute!

8.

The lute is of fanciful fashion,
  The wine strong, and tender, and bright:
And the name of the wine is Passion,
  The name of the lute is Delight.

9.

On the strand is anchored my boat:
  It is built to live in all seas:
We have but to set it afloat,
  It will bear us far as we please:

10.

For it is so light that, in sooth,
  'T will sink not, though loaded with treasures:
The name of the helmsman is Youth,
  The crew that he pilots are Pleasures.

11.

But linger not now, for 't is late,
And we have the world to go through.
Poor world ! 't is in such a sad state,
It surely hath need of us two ;

12.

So much that needs setting to rights !
Hate, massacre, murder, and war . . . .
But . . . . how sweet are these midsummer nights !
Shall we let things rest as they are ?

13.

At least we must travel in state,
Since a king and a queen are we :
And scatter our largesse, elate
And lavish as monarchs should be.

14.

Before us our herald shall go :
And their gates all cities shall ope,
When his clarion he doth blow,
For our herald his name is Hope :

15.

Our almoner cometh behind,
And he singeth a saintly hymn :
He is wealthy, and wise, and kind,
Gentle Memory men call him.

16.

To the sweet, the afar, the unseen,
Fair, joyous, majestic, and free,

Lead by Sleep and by Night, my Queen,
   Away, through the world, now, with me!

17.

And the world shall do us sweet duty,
   As royally through it we move:
For thou art a queen — thou art Beauty!
   And I am a king — I am Love!

FAIR YOLAND WITH THE YELLOW HAIR.

I.

KNIGHT that wears no lady's sleeve
Upon his helm from dawn to eve,
And all night long beneath the throng
Of throbbing stars, without reprieve
My moan I make, as on I ride
Along waste lands and waters wide,
The haunts of bitterns; smoky strips
Of sea-coast where there come no ships;
Or over brambly humpbacked downs,
And under walls of hilly towns,
And out again across the plain,
Oft borne beneath a hissing rain
Within the murmurs of the wind,
That doth at nightfall leave his lair
To follow and vex me; till I find
Fair Yoland with the yellow hair.

II.

On a field azure, all pure or,
A fountain springing evermore
To reach one star that, just too far
For its endeavor, trembles o'er
The topmost spray its strength will yield,
For my device upon my shield
Long since I wrought; and under it
Along a scroll of flame is writ

The legend, thus . . . . "I SHALL ATTAIN."
In letters large: albeit "In vain!"
My heart replies to mock mine eyes;
For where that fountain seems to rise
Its highest, it is back consigned
To earth, and falls in void despair,
Like my sad seven-years' hope to find
Fair Yoland with the yellow hair.

III.

Seven years ago (how long it seems
Since then!) as free as summer streams
My fancy played with sun and shade,
And all my days were dim with dreams.
One day — I wot not whence nor how
It flashed upon me, even now
I marvel at the change it wrought! —
My whole life leapt into one thought,
Which thought was made my lifelong act;
As, dashed in dazzling cataract,
From its long sleeps, at last outleaps
Some lazy ooze, which henceforth keeps
One steadfast way; so all my mind
Was in that moment made aware
That henceforth I must die, or find
Fair Yoland with the yellow hair.

IV.

Since then, how many lands and climes
Have I ransacked — how many times
Been bruised with blows — how many foes
Have dealt to death — how many crimes
Avenged — how many maidens freed!

And yet I seem to be, indeed,
No nearer to the endless quest.
Neither by night nor day I rest:
My heart burns in me like a fire:
My soul is parched with long desire:
Ghostlike I grow: and where I go,
I hear men mock and mutter low,
And feel men's fingers point behind, —
"The moon-struck knight that talks to air!
Lord help the fool who hopes to find
Fair Yoland with the yellow hair!"

V.

At times, in truth, I start, and shake
Myself from thought, as one men wake
From some long trance to hard mischance,
Who knows not yet what choice to make
'Twixt false and true, since all things seem
Mere fragments of his broken dream,
When I recall what men aver,
That all my lifelong quest of her
Is vain and void; since thrice (say they)
Three hundred years are rolled away,
And knights forgot, whose bones now rot,
And their good deeds remembered not,
Failed one by one, long ere I pined
For this strange quest; whence they declare
No living wight may hope to find
Fair Yoland with the yellow hair.

VI.

Ah me! . . . . For Launcelot maketh cheer
With great-eyed, glorious Guinevere;

In glad green wood; with Queen Isoud
Tristram of Lyones hunts the deer;
In cool of bloomy trellises
Sir Gareth and Sir Gaheris,
After long labors brought to end,
With their two dames in joyance spend
The blue June hours; Sir Agravaine
With Dame Laurell along the main
Seeks his new home; and Pelleas
Sits smiling calm in halls of glass
At Nimuë's knees. Good knights be these
Because they have their hearts at ease,
Because their lives and loves are joined:
O if two hearts in one life were,
What life were that! . . . . God, let me find
Fair Yoland with the yellow hair!

VII.

Mere life is vile. I may have done
Deeds not unworthy, and have won
Unwilling fame; though all men blame
This heart's unrest which makes me shun
The calm content that good men take
From good deeds done for good deeds' sake,
Deeds that in doing of the deed
Do bless the doer, who should need
No bliss beyond: but what to me
Is this, — that over land and sea
My name should fly? Or what care I,
For the mere sake of climbing high,
To climb forever steps that wind
Up empty towers? I only wear
Life hollow thus, unless I find
Fair Yoland with the yellow hair.

VIII.

Sometimes, whom I to free from wrong
Have dragons fought, strange folk do throng
About my steed, and lightly lead
My horse and me, with shout and song,
In bannered castle-courts ; and there
From chambers cool come dames most fair,
Whose forms as through a cloud I see ;
Whose voices seem far off to be ;
Though near they stand, and bid me rest
Awhile within, where, richly drest,
In order stored, with goblets poured,
I see the sparkling banquet-board ;
But far from these is all my mind,
For . . . . " What if foes, whom I must scare,
In noisome den now seek to bind
Fair Yoland with the yellow hair ? "

IX.

In deepest dark, when no moon shines
Through the blind night on the black pines
With bony boughs, if I, to drowse
(As sometimes mere despair inclines
A frame outworn), should slip from horse,
And lay me down along the gorse,
In some cold hollow far away
A little while, — albeit I pray
Ere I lie down, — my dreams are drear :
First comes a slowly creeping fear,
Like icy dew, that seems to glue
My limbs to earth, and freeze them through ;
Then a long shriek on a wild wind,
And " O," I think, " if hers it were,

And I a murdered corpse should find
Fair Yoland with the yellow hair!"

X.

Sometimes 'neath dropping white rose-leaves
I ride, and under gilded eaves
Of garden bowers where, plucking flowers,
With scarlet skirts and stiff gold sleeves,
Between green walls, and two by two,
Kings' daughters walk, whilst just a few
Faint harps make music mild, that falls
Like mist from off the ivied walls
Along the sultry corn, and stirs
The hearts of far-off harvesters;
Then, on the brink of hope, I shrink
With shuddering strange, the while I think,
"O, what if, after body and mind
Consumed in toil, and all my care,
Not a corpse, but a bride, I find
Fair Yoland with the yellow hair?"

XI.

But when at night's most lonely noon,
The ghost of an ill-buried moon
Frets in the shroud of a cold cloud,
And, like the echo of a tune,
Within mine ear the silence makes
A yearning sound that throbs and aches,
A whisper sighs . . . . "The grave is deep,
There is no better thing than sleep.
Life's fever speeds its own decease,
Let the mole work: be thou at peace."
Yet why should this fair earth, which is

So fair, so fit to furnish bliss,
Prove a mere failure, — stuff designed
By Hope to clothe her foe Despair?
And whence, if vain, this need to find
Fair Yoland with the yellow hair?

XII.

This grieving after unknown good,
Though but a sickness in the blood,
Cries from the dust. And God is just.
No rock denies the raven food.
For who would torture, night by night,
Some starving creature with the sight
Of banquets fair with plenty spread,
Then mock . . . . "crawl empty thou to bed,
And dream of viands not for thée!"
Yet night by night, dear God, to me,
In wake or sleep, such visions creep
To gnaw my heart with hunger deep.
How can I meet dull death, resigned
To die the fool of dreams so fair?
Nay, love hath seen, and life shall find,
Fair Yoland with the yellow hair!

XIII.

Good Pilgrim, to whatever shrine,
With whatsoever vows of thine,
Thou wendest, stay! I charge thee, pray
That God may bless this quest of mine.
Sweet maidens, whom from losel hands
Mine own have freed — in many lands,
I bid you each, when ye shall be
With your good knights, remember me!

And wish me well, — that some day I
May find fair Yoland; else I die
In love's defeat. To die were sweet,
If, dying, I might clasp her feet.
Death comes at last to all mankind;
Yet ere I die, I know not where,
I know not how, but I must find
Fair Yoland with the yellow hair.

TRIAL BY COMBAT.

HE doleful wind around around
The turret, trying to enter here,
Whines low, while down in the court-yard drear
The great bloodhound, to the flint fast bound,
Is baying the moon. The moon is clear
And dismal-cold: because a Fear,
Whose cat's-foot falls with no more sound
Than an eyelid that sinks on a sick man's swound,
Is lord of her light; whereby to-night
He walketh alone on the frozen mere
From the wood whence he cometh anear, — anear!
Ever, about the setting in
Of the darkness, now for a month or more,
The things on the gusty arras 'gin
To rustle and creep and mope and grin
At me, still sitting as heretofore
This last sad night (no whit less calm
Than when first he accused me a month before),
With elbow based on knee, and palm
Upslanted, propping a moody chin;
The better to watch with a glassy eye
The dull red embers drop, and lie
Forlorn of a lurid inner light,
Like days burned out by a deadly sin.
I marvel much if my mind be right,
All seems so wondrous calm within
This long o'er-labored heart, in spite
Of the howling wind and the hideous night,

And to-morrow that bringeth the final fight
When all is to lose or win.

What matter the end, so it be near ?
I can only think of how last year
We rode together, she and I :
She in scarlet and I in green,
Across the oak-wood dark and high,
Whose wicked leaves shut out the sky ;
Which, had I seen, that had not been,
I think, which makes me fear to die
And meet her there. I could not bear
Her dead face e'en. Who else, I ween,
Should hardly shrink from Conrad's eye,
For all his vaunting, not so keen,
The too-soon boasting braggart, (ay,
Even when he strode before the Queen,
And three times charged me with the lie !)
As my keen axe. More glad that day
She was, sure, than 't is good to be,
Lest some, that cannot be so glad
As she was then, should chance go mad,
Trying to laugh. O, all the way
She laughed so loud that even the wood
Laughed too. She seemed so sure, that day,
That life is sweet and God is good.
I could not laugh ; because her hood
Had fallen back, and so let stray
Of all her long hair's loveliness
A single shining yellow tress
Across her shoulder ; which made me
(That could not choose, poor fool ! but see)
More sad, I think, than men should be
When women laugh. The wood, I say,
Laughed with her, at me, all the way.

Once, too, her palfrey, while we rode,
Started aside, and in alarm
She leaned her hand upon my arm;
Whose light touch did so overload
My heavy heart, that, I believe,
Had she a moment longer so
Leaned on me, from my saddle-bow
I must have dropped down dead.

Near eve
We came out on the other land.
And I remember that I said,
"How still and lone the land is here!"
She only looked, and shook her head,
And, looking, laughed still louder, and
Said, laughing loudly, "What 's to fear?"
The accursèd echo, that low lay
Under that lonesome land, I knew,
For want of aught more wise to say,
Shrieked, "Fear!" and fell a-laughing too.
Deep melancholy meadow-grass,
Which never any man had mown,
So long our horses scarce could pass
Through the thick-heaped unheaving mass
Of heavy stalks, by no breath blown
Of any wind, all round was grown,
For some bad purpose of its own,
Up to the edge of the gray sky.
And underneath a stream ran by:
A little stream that made great moan,
Half mad with pain, the Fiend knows why:
'Twixt stupid heaps of helpless stone,
That chose upon its path to lie
Unreasonably, purpose none

Subserving (there resolved to stay
For spite's sake, with nor use nor grace),
It pushed and dashed at desperate pace,
In extreme haste to get away.
The owls might fly about by day,
For all the sky, there, had to say;
Which took no care to change its face
To any other hue but gray,
Having to light up such a place.
But for the moan of that mad stream
All things were dumb, resigned, and still,
And strange, as things are in a dream.
The whole land self-surrendered lay,
And let harsh Nature work her will,
For lack of strength to answer nay
To any sort of wrong or ill
That chose to vex it. Laughing gay
Into that lonesome land rode she.
The grass above her palfrey's knee
Was long and green as green could be.
She, laughing as she rode, 'gan trill
Some canzonet or virelay;
It mattered little, good or ill,
Whate'er the song, if any way
It eased her heart of laughter shrill.
Of trees were only blackthorns three,
Low-clumped upon the ugly hill,
Like witches when, to watch the weather,
They crook their backs and squat together.

We 'lighted down beneath those trees
Whereto did I our horses tether;
And on a bough I hung my shield.
She went up higher in the field,

And down her long limbs laid at ease
In the deep grass; which up and down,
Wave after wave of green, heaved over
Her bright gold-bordered scarlet gown;
And all but her small face did cover.
For now, out of some land unshorn
Behind the grassy upland, low,
A little wind began to blow
Faintly, and the dull air was strown
With a moist sickly scent of clover.

She, slanted o'er her propping arm,
Looked smiling sideways with a charm
To catch me; while, now forwards, now
Backwards, she swung with saucy brow
Her gold curls, like a gorgeous snake
That lifts and leans on lolling fold
A lustrous head, but half awake
From winter dreams when, coy and cold,
Spring stirs about the rustling brake.
She called me to her through the grass:
She called me "Friend": she said I was
Her Ritter of the rueful face:
"But I," she said, "am never sad."
Therewith she laughed. The hateful place
Laughed too: resolved to make me mad.
I went, and sat beside her there,
And gazed upon her glittering hair.
Musing, I said: "'T will soon be night;
Night must be very lonely here."
She looked at me, and laughed outright,
And, laughing, answered, "What's to fear?"
But "Fear!" the echo, laughing light,
Still added. It was hard to bear.

Long sat I silent in her sight,
Much musing. When I spoke at last
It may have been that all I said
Marred all I meant, — for there was passed,
Like burning lead, about my head
And on my brain, a heavy pain,
And, "Oh," I cried, "if it would rain,
And bring some change!" — Yet this I know,
That, soon as I had ended, she
Looked through her glittering hair at me,
Full in my face, and laughed again,
And answered, "Never! let this be
A thing forgot between us twain."
So, back beneath the blackthorn-tree,
Where my shield hung, I went away
A little while, and sat apart.
I could not speak: I could not pray:
I thought it was because my heart
Was in my throat, — it choked me so!
But now the devil's claw, I know,
It was, that would not let me go;
Me by the throat so fast he had.
Enough! You think that I went mad?
By no means. I grew strong and wise,
Went back, looked boldly in her eyes,
And stopped her laughing. It was she,
Not I, that trembled. I could see
The woman was afraid of me.
What wonder? I myself had been
Already, such a woful long
Wild while (even ere he waxed thus strong,
And let his wicked face be seen)
Afraid, too, of the fiend within
My heart; whereof she was the Queen,

Feeding him with the food of sin,
Forbidden beauty. Then I knew
That she was all mine through and through,
Whatever I might choose to do.
Mine, from the white brow's hiding-place
Under the roots of golden hair
That glittered round her frightened face;
Mine, from the warmth and odor there
Down to the tender feet that were
Mine too to guess in each great fold
Of scarlet bound about with gold.
So I grew dainty with my pleasure;
And, as a miser counts the treasure
His heart is loath to spend too fast,
So did mine eye take note and measure
Of all my new-gained wealth. At last
The Fiend, impatient to be gone,
Brought this to end.

When all was done,
I seemed to know what was to be,
And how 't would fare henceforth with me,
Who must ride home now all alone:
I knew that I should never see
The face of God, nor ever hear
Her laugh again. And so it was.
Yet 't was not mine, that blow, I swear.
Nor did I know it, till the grass
Was red and wet. When Conrad tries
To charge me with that deed, he lies!
And lies! and lies! Who could have guessed
That she had hidden in her breast,
Or in her girdle, (what know I?)
A dagger? Did she mean to die

Always, — even when she seemed so proud,
So sure of life? Ay, when so loud
She laughed that day? I only know
I would have given these two hands,
The moment I beheld her so,
Ay, all my lordships, all my lands,
If but on me had fallen that blow,
Not her. O what were Hell's worst pain
If I might hear her laugh again?

It must have been an hour or more
I think (it seemed long years) before
I, sitting there beside her still,
And listening, heard a sound of rain
In the three blackthorns on the hill.
"Too late it comes," I thought, "and vain,
For nothing here will change now." Chill
The evening grew. A wet wind blew
About the billowy grass. A few
Large drops fell sullenly. I thought,
"How cold she will be here all night
In this wet meadow!" Then I caught
(For by this time her lips were white,
Not red; nor warm, but rigid quite)
At the tall grass, and heaped and massed
Great handfuls of it, which I cast
Over her feet, and on her face;
But first drew down her scarlet gown
Over her limbs composed and meek
In great calm folds; and, o'er her cheek,
Smoothed the bright hair; and all the place
Where the black redness oozed, I hid
With heaps of grass. All this I did
Quite quietly, as a mother might

Put her sick child to sleep. 'T was night
Ere I had ended. A dull moon
Across the smearing rain revealed
A melancholy light, and soon
Began to peer about the field
To find what still the fresh grass kept
Well hidden. Then I think I crept
Down to the little stream; and stood
A long while looking at the wood,
Wondering what ever I should do.
There was a spot of blood I knew
Upon my hand. I did not dare
To wash it, lest the water there
Too far away the stain should bear,
And so make all the world aware
Of what was done.

The cock crows — hark!
Before his time, sure. Deep in dark
The drowsy land is lying yet.
Yon frosty cloud hides up the moon,
But I am sure she is not set.
To-morrow? Is it come so soon?
Well, let it come! A hundred eyes
Can make no worse the eyes I scorn.
For in his throat Count Conrad lies,
And on his body am I sworn
To prove the same this very morn.
Let Kaiser Henry range his state;
To mark the issue of my fate,
The lords of every Landgravate
From Rhine to Rhone, with looks elate,
Like gods between the earth and sky,
May crowd each golden balcony.

Come, Kaiser, call the fight!
Let the great trumpet blare on high
As though the Judgment Angel blew
The blast that bids the wicked rue;
Now, Conrad, to the lists, and smite
Thy very worst! I reck not, I,
Not though the dead should come to sight,
Nor though a hundred heralds cry,
"On! God maintain the right!"

RABBI BEN EPHRAIM'S TREASURE.

PERSECUTION OF THE JEWS IN SPAIN.

(FIFTEENTH CENTURY.)

I.

THE days of Rabbi Ben Ephraim
Were twoscore years and ten, the day
The hangman called at last for him,
And he privily fled from Cordova.
Drop by drop, he had watched the cup
Of the wine of bitterness filled to the brim;
Drop by drop, he had drained it up;
And the time was an evil time for him.
An evil time! For Jehovah's face
Was turned in wrath from his chosen race,
And the daughter of Judah must mourn,
Whom his anger had left, in evil case,
To be dogged by death from place to place,
With garments bloody and torn.
The time of the heavy years, from of old
By the mouth of his servant the Prophet foretold,
In the days of Josiah the king,
When the Lord upon Jacob his load should bring,
And the hand of Heaven, in the day of his ire,
Be heavy and hot upon son and sire,
Till from out of the holes into which they were driven
Their bones should be strewn to the host of Heaven
Whose bodies were burned in the fire.

Rabbi Ben Ephraim, day by day
(As the hangman, beating up his bounds
Through the stifled Ghetto's sinks and stews,
Or the Arch Inquisitor, going his rounds,
Was pleased to pause, and pick, and choose,—
Too sure of his game, which could not stray,
To miss the luxury of delay)
Had marked with a moody indignation
The abomination of desolation,
With the world to witness, and none to gainsay,
Set up in the midst of the Holy Nation,
And the havoc, which Heaven refused to stay,
In the course of his horrible curse move on,
Where, sometimes driven in trembling crews,
Sometimes singly, one by one,
Israel's elders were beckoned away
To the place where the Christians burn the Jews:
Till he, because that his wealth was known,
And because the king had debts to pay,
Was left, at the last, almost alone
Of all his people in Cordova,
A living man picked out by fate
To bear, and beware of, the daily jibe,
And add the same to the sum of the hate,
Made his on behalf of a slaughtered tribe.

II.

In the gloomy Ghetto's gloomiest spot,
A certain patch of putrid ground,
There is a place of tombs: Moors rot,
Rats revel there, and devils abound
By night, no cross being there to keep
The evil things in awe: the dead

That house there, sleep no Christian sleep, —
They do not sleep at all, it is said ;
Though how they fare, the Fiend best knows,
Who never vouchsafes to them any repose,
For their worm is awake in the narrow bed,
And the fire that will never be quenched is fed
On the night that will never close.
There did Rabbi Ben Ephraim
(When he saw, at length, the appointed measure
Of misery meted out to him)
Bury his books, and all his treasure.
Books of wisdom many a one, —
All the teaching of all the ages,
All the learning under the sun,
Learned by all the Hebrew sages
To Eliphaz from Solomon ;
Not to mention the mystic pages
Of Nathan the son of Shimeon
The Seer, which treat of the sacred use
Of the number Seven (quoth the Jews,
" A secret sometime filched from us
By one called Apollonius "),
The science of the even and odd,
The signs of the letters Aleph and Jod,
And the seven magical names of God.

Furthermore, he laid in store
Many a vessel of beaten ore,
Pure, massy, rich with rare device
Of Florence-work wrought under and o'er,
Shekels of silver, and stones of price,
Sardius, sapphire, topaz, more
In number than may well be told,
Milan stuffs, and merchandise

Of Venice, the many times bought and sold.
He buried them deep where none might mark,—
Hid them from sight of the hated race,
Gave them in guard of the Powers of the Dark.
And solemnly set his curse on the place.
Then he saddled his mule, and with him took
Zillah his wife, and Rachel his daughter,
And Manassah his son; and turned and shook
The dust from his foot on the place of slaughter,
And crossed the night, and fled away
(Balking the hangman of his prey)
From out of the city of Cordova.

III.

Rabbi Ben Ephraim nevermore
Saw Cordova. For the Lord had willed
That the dust should be dropped on his eyes before
The curse upon Israel was fulfilled.
Therefore he ended the days of his life
In evil times; and by the hand
Of Rachel his daughter, and Zillah his wife,
Was laid to rest in another land.
But, before his face to the wall he turned,
As the eyes of the women about his bed
Grew hungry and hard with a hope unfed,
And the misty lamp more misty burned,
To Zillah and Rachel the Rabbi said
Where they might find, if fate turned kind,
And the fires in Cordova, grown slack,
Should ever suffer their footsteps back,
The tomb where by stealth he had buried his wealth
In the evil place, when in dearth and lack
He fled from the foe, and the stake, and the rack;

IV.

" A strand of colors, clear to be seen
By the main black cord of it twined between
The scarlet, the golden, and the green:
All the length of the Moorish wall the line
Runs low with his mystic serpent-twine,
Until he is broken against the angle
Where thin grizzled grasses dangle,
Like dead men's hairs, from the weeds that clot
The scurfy side of a splintered pot,
Upon the crumbled cornice squat,
Gaping, long-eared, in his hue and shape
Like a Moor's head cut off at the nape.
The line, till it touches the angle, follow,
Take pebbles then in the hand and drop
Stone after stone till the ground sounds hollow.
Thence walk left, till there starts, to stop
Your steps, a thorn-tree with an arm
Stretched out as though some mad alarm
Had seized upon it from behind.
It points the way until you find
A flat square stone, with letters cut.
Stoop down to lift it, 't will not move,
More than you move a mountain, but
Upon the letter which is third
Of seven in the seventh word
Press with a finger, and you shove
Its weight back softly, as the South
Turns a dead rose lightly over:
Back falls it, and there yawns earth's mouth,
Wherein the treasure is yet to discover,
By means of a spiral cut down the abyss
To the dead men."

V.

When he had uttered this,
Rabbi Ben Ephraim turned his face,
And slept.

VI.

The years went on apace.
Manassah his son, his youngest born,
Trading the isleted sea for corn,
Was wrecked and picked up by the smuggler boat
Of a certain prowling Candiote;
And, being young and hale, was sold
By the Greek a bondsman to the Turk.
Zillah, his wife, waxed white and old.
Rachel, his daughter, loved not work,
But walked by the light of her own dark eyes
In wicked ways for the sake of gain.
Meanwhile, Israel's destinies
Survived the scorching stake, and Spain
At length grew weary of burning men;
When hungered, and haggard, and gaunt, these two
Forlorn Jew women crept again
Into Cordova; because they knew
Where Rabbi Ben Ephraim by stealth,
When he turned his back on his own house-door,
Had buried the whole of his wondrous wealth
In the evil place; and they two were poor.

VII.

So poor indeed, they had been constrained
To filch from the refuse flung out to the streets
('Mid the rags and onion-peelings rained

Where the town's worst gutter's worst filth greets
With his strongest gust and most savory sweets
Those blots and failures of Human Nature,
Refused a name in her nomenclature,
That spawn themselves toward night, and bend
To finger the husks and shucks heaped there)
The wretched, rat-bitten candle-end
Which, found by good luck, they had treasured
with care
Not a whit less solemn than though it were
That famous work of the son of Uri,
The candlestick of candlesticks, —
He the long-lost light of Jewry,
Whose almond bowls and scented wicks
Were the boast of the desert, and Salem's glory
Of the knops and flowers, with his branches six!
For this impov'rished, curtailed, flawed,
Maltreated, worried, gnawed, and clawed
Remnant of what perchance made bright
Once, for laughter and delight,
Some chamber gay, with arras hung,
Whose marbles, mirrors, and flowers among
A lover, his lady's lute above,
To a dear dark-eyelashed listener sung
Of the flame of a never-dying love, —
Little heeding, meanwhile, the fitful spite
Of the night-wind's mad and mocking sprite,
Which stealthily in at the lattice sprung,
And was wrying the taper's neck apace, —
Must now, with its hungry half-starved light,
Make bold the shuddering flesh to face
The sepulchre's supernatural night,
And the Powers of the Dark keeping guard on the
place.

VIII.

And when to the place of tombs they came,
The spotted moon sunk. Night stood bare
In the waste unlighted air,
Wide-armed, waiting, and aware,
To horribly hem them in. The flame
The little candle feebly gave,
As it winked and winced from grave to grave,
Went fast to furious waste; the same
As a fever-famisht human hope
That is doomed, from grief to grief, to grope
On darkness blind to a doubtful goal,
And, swayed by passion here and there
In conflict with some vast despair,
Consumes the substance of the soul
In wavering ways about the world.
The deep enormous night unfurled
Her bannered blackness left and right,
Fold heaped on fold, to mock such light
With wild defiance; no star pearled
The heavy pall, but horror hurled
Shadow on shadow; while for spite
The very graves kept out of sight,
And heaven's sworn hatred, winning might
From earth's ill-will, with darkness curled
Darkness, all space confounding quite,
So to engender night on night.

IX.

"Rachel Rachel, for ye are tall,
Lift the light along the wall."

"Mother, mother, give me the hand,
And follow!"

"What see ye, Rachel?"

X.

A strand
Of chorded colors, clear to be seen
By the main black dominant, twined between
The scarlet, the golden, and the green.

XI.

"Rachel, Rachel, ye walk so fast!"

"Mother, the light will barely last."

"What see ye, Rachel?"

XII.

Things that dangle
Hairy and gray o'er the wall's choked angle
From something dull, in hue and shape
Like a Moor's head cut off at the nape.

XIII.

"Once! twice! thrice! . . . . the earth sounds hollow.
Mother, give me the hand, and follow."

"Rachel, the flame is backward blowing,
Pusht by the darkness. Where are we going?
The ground is agroan with catacombs!
What see ye, Rachel?"

XIV.

Yonder comes
A thorn-tree, with a desperate arm
Flung out fierce in wild alarm
Of something which, it madly feels,
The night to plague it yet conceals.
No help it gets though! An owl dashed out
Of the darkness, steering his ghostliness thither,
Pried in at the boughs, and passed on with a shout
From who-knows-whence to who-knows-whither;
The unquiet Spirit abroad on the air
Moved with a moan that way, and spent
A moment or more in the effort to vent
On the tortured tree which he came to scare
The sullen fit of his discontent;
But, laughing low as he grew aware
Of the long-already-imposed despair
Of the terrified thing he had paused to torment,
He passed, pursuing his purpose elsewhere,
And followed the whim of his wicked bent:
A rheumy glow-worm, come to peer
Into the hollow trunk, crawled near,
And glimmered awhile, but intense fear,
Or tame connivance with something wrong
Which the night was intending, quenched erelong
His lantern. Therefore the tree remains,
For all its gestures void and vain,
Which still at their utmost fail to explain
Any natural cause for the terror that strains
Each desperate limb to be freed and away,
In sheer paralysis of dismay
Struck stark, — and so, night's abject, stands.

XV.

"Mother, the candle is cowering low
Beneath the night-gust: hoop both hands
About the light, and stoop over, so
The wind from the buffeted flame to shut,
Lest at once in our eyes the darkness blow."

"What see ye, Rachel?"

XVI.

A square stone cut
With letters. Thick the moss is driven
Through the graver's work now blunt and blurred:
There be seven words with letters seven:
A finger-touch on the letter third
Of seven in the seventh word,
And the stone is heaved back: earth yawns and gapes:
A cold strikes up the clammy dark,
And clings: a spawn of vaporous shapes
Floats out in films: a sanguine spark
The taper spits: the snaky stair
Gleams, curling down the abyss laid bare,
Where Rabbi Ben Ephraim's treasure is laid.

XVII.

There they sat them down awhile,
With that terrible joy which cannot smile
Because the heart of it is staid
And stunned, as it were, by a too-swift pace.
And the wicked Presence abroad on the place
So took them with awe that they rested afraid
Almost to look into each other's face.

Moreover, the nearness of what should change,
Like a change in a dream, their lives forever
Into something suddenly bright and strange,
Paused upon them, and made them shiver.
The old woman mumbled at length: "I am old:
I have no sight the treasure to find;
I have no strength to rake the red gold;
My hand is palsied, mine eye is blind,
Child of my bosom, I dare not descend
To the horrible pit!"

And Rachel said:
"I fear the darkness, I fear the dead;
But the candle is burning fast to the end:
We waste the time with words. Look here!
There rests between us and the dark
A few short inches. . . . . Mother, mark
The wasting taper! . . . . I should not fear
Either the darkness or the dead,
But for certain memories in my head
Which daunt me. . . . . We will go, we twain,
Together."

The old woman cried again:
"Child of my bosom, I will not descend
To the horrible pit, — and the candle-end
Is burning down, God curse the same!
I am old, and cannot help myself.
Young are ye! What your beauty brings
Who knows? I think ye keep the pelf.
Ye will let me starve. So the serpent stings
The bosom it lay in! Are ye so tame
Of spirit? I marvel why we came.
Poverty is the worst of things!"

Rachel looked at the dwindling flame,
And frowned, and muttered, "Mother, shame!
I fear the darkness, because there clings
To my heart a thought, I cannot smother,
Of certain things which, whatever the blame,
Thou wottest of, and I will not name;
For my sins are many and heavy, mother.
Yet because I hunger, and still would save
Some years from sin, and because of my brother
Whom the Greek man sold to be slave to a slave,
(May the Lord requite the lying knave!)
I will go down alone to the pit.
Thou, therefore, mother, watch, and sit
In prayer for me, by the mouth of the grave.
The light will hardly last me, I fear.
And what is to do must be quickly done. —
Mercy on us, mother! . . . . Look here;
Three inches more, and the light will be gone!
Quick, mother, the candle — quick! I fear
To be left in the darkness alone."

XVIII.

The mother sat by the grave, and listened.
She waited: she heard the footsteps go
Under the earth, wandering, slow.
She looked: deep down the taper glistened.
Then, the voice of Rachel from below:

"Mother, mother, stoop and hold!"

And she flung up four ouches of gold.
The old woman counted them, ouches four,
Beaten out of the massy ore.

"Child of my bosom, blessèd art thou!
The hand of the Lord be yet with thee!
As thou art strong in thy spirit now,
Many and pleasant thy days shall be.
As a vine in a garden, fair to behold,
Green in her branches, shalt thou grow,
And so have gladness when thou art old.
Rachel, Rachel, be thou bold!
More gold yet, and still more gold!"

"Mother, mother, the light burns low.
The candle is one inch shorter now,
And I dare not be left in the darkness alone."

"Rachel, Rachel, go on! go on!
Of thee have I said, She shall not shrink!
Thy brother is yet a bondsman, — think!
Yet once more, — and he is free.
And whom shall he praise for this but thee?
Rachel, Rachel, be thou bold!
Manassah is groaning over the sea.
More gold yet, and still more gold!"

"Mother, mother, stoop and hold!"

And she flung up from below again
Cups of the carven silver twain.
Solid silver was each great cup.
The old woman caught them as they came up.
"Rachel, Rachel, well hast thou done!
Manassah is free. Go on! go on!
Royal dainties forever be thine!
Rachel's eyes shall be red with wine,
Rachel's mouth shall with milk be filled,

And her bread be fat. I praise thee, my child,
For surely thou hast freed thy brother.
The deed was good, but there resteth another,
And art thou not the child of thy mother?
Once more, Rachel, yet once more!
Thy mother is very poor and old.
Must she close her eyes before
They see the thing she would behold?
More gold yet, and still more gold!"

"Mother, the light is very low.
The candle is wellnigh wasted now,
And I dare not be left in the darkness alone."

"Rachel, Rachel, go on! go on!
Much is done, but there resteth more.
Ye are young, Rachel, shall it be told
That my bones were laid at my children's door?
More gold yet, and still more gold!"

"Mother, mother, stoop and hold!"

The voice came fainter from beneath;
And she flung up a jewelled sheath.
The sheath was thick with many a gem;
The old woman carefully counted them.
"Rachel, Rachel, thee must I praise,
Who makest pleasant thy mother's days.
Blessèd be thou in all thy ways!
Surely for this must I praise thee, my daughter,
And therefore in fulness shalt thou dwell
As a fruitful fig-tree beside the water
That layeth her green leaves over the well.
More gold, Rachel, yet again!

And we shall have houses and servants in Spain,
And thou shalt walk with the wealthiest ladies,
And fairest, in Cordova, Seville, or Cadiz,
And thou shalt be wooed as a Queen should be,
And tended upon as the proud are tended,
And the algazuls shall doff to thee,
For thy face shall be brightened, thy raiment be
splendid,
And no man shall call thee an evil name,
And thou shalt no longer remember thy shame,
And thy mother's eyes, as she waxes old,
Shall see the thing she would behold —
More gold yet, and still more gold ! "

" Mother, the light is very low —
Out ! out ! . . . . Ah God, they are on me now !
Mother " (the old woman hears with a groan),
" Leave me not here in the darkness alone ! "

The mother sits by the grave, and listens.
She waits : she hears the footsteps go
Far under the earth — bewildered — slow.
She looks : the light no longer glistens.
Still the voice of Rachel from below,

" Mother, mother, they have me, and hold !
Mother, there is a curse on thy gold !
Mercy ! mercy ! The light is gone, —
Leave me not here in the darkness alone, —
Mother, mother, help me and save ! "

Still Rachel's voice from the grave doth moan.
Still Rachel's mother sits by the grave.

CATTERINA CORNARO.

(A PICTURE. — A. D. 1470.)

I.

N Cyprus, where 'live Summer never dies,
Love's native land is. There the seas, the skies,
Are blue and lucid as the looks, the air
Fervid and fragrant as the breath and hair
Of Beauty's Queen; whose gracious godship dwells
In that dear island of delicious dells,
'Mid lavish lights and languid glooms divine.
There doth she her sly dainty sceptre twine
With seabank myrtle spray, and roses sweet
And full as, when the lips of lovers meet
The first strange time, their sudden kisses be :
There doth she lightly reign : there holdeth she
Her laughing court in gleam of lemon groves :
The wanton mother of unnumbered Loves !

What earthly creature hath Dame Venus' grace
Dowered so divinely sweet of form and face
As that she may, unshamed in Cupid's smile,
Be sovereign lady of this lovely isle ?
Sure, Venus, not so blind as some aver
Was thy bold boy, what time, in search of her
Thou bad'st him seek, he roamed the seas all round,
And barbarous lands beyond ; since he hath found

This wonder out; whose perfect sweetness seems
The fair fulfilment of his own fond dreams:
And Kate Cornaro is the Island Queen.

II.

A Queen: a child: fair: happy: scarce nineteen!
In whose white hands her little sceptre lies,
Like a new-gathered floweret, in surprise
At being there. To keep her what she is, —
A thing too rare for the familiar kiss
Of household loves, — wifehood and motherhood, —
Fit only to be delicately wooed
With wooings fine and frolicsome as those
Wherewith the sweet West woos a small blush-rose,
Her husband first, and then her babe, away
Slipped from her sight, each on a summer day,
Ere she could miss them, into the soft shade
Of flowery graves. She doth not feel afraid
To be alone. Because she hath her toy,
Her pretty kingdom. And it is her joy
To dandle the doll-people, and be kind
And careful to it, as a child. Each wind
O' the world on her smooth eyelids lightly breathes,
As morn upon a lily whence frail wreaths
Of little dew-drops hang, easily troubled,
As such things are. The June sun's joy is doubled,
Shining through shadow in her golden hair.
Light-wedded, and light-widowed, and unaware
Of any sort of sorrow doth she seem;
Albeit the times are stormy, and do teem
With tumult round her tiny throne. Primrose,

Pert violet, hardy vetch, — no blossom blows
In March less conscious of a cloudy sky,
More sweet in sullen season. Days go by
Daintily round her. If her crown's light weight
Upon her forehead fair and delicate
Leave the least violet stain, when laid away
At close of some great summer holiday,
Her lovers kiss the sweet mark smooth and white
Ere it can pain her. She hath great delight
In little things: and of great things small care.
The people love her; though the nobles are
Wayward and wild. Yet fears she not, nor shrinks
To show she fears not. "For in truth," she thinks,
"My Uncle Andrew, and my Uncle Mark,
Have care of me." And, truly, dawn or dark,
These Uncles Mark and Andrew, busiest two
In Cyprus, find no lack of work to do:
Go up and down the noisy little state,
Silent all day: and, when the night is late,
Write letters, which she does not care to read,
(The Ten, she knows, will ponder them with heed)
To Venice — not so far from Cyprus' shore,
But what the shadow of St. Mark goes o'er
The narrow sea to touch her island throne.

III.

She is herself a dove from Venice flown
Not so long since but what her snowy breast
Is yet scarce warm within its new-found nest. —
Whence sings she o'er the grave of Giacomo
Songs taught her by St. Mark.

Cristofero
(He of the four stone shields which you may spy,
Thrice striped, thrice spotted with the mulberry,
In the great sunlight o'er that famous stair
Whose marble white is warmed with rose-hues, where
The crownings were once) wore the ducal horn
In Venice, on that joyous July morn
When all along the liquid streets, paved red
With rich reflections of clear crimson spread,
Or gorgeous orange gay with glowing fringe,
From bustling balconies above, to tinge
The lucid highways with new lustres, best
Befitting that day's pride, the blithe folk pressed
About St. Paul's, beneath the palace door
Of Mark Cornaro; where the Bucentor
Was waiting with the Doge; to see Queen Kate
Come smiling in her robes of marriage state
Through the crammed causeway, glimmering down between
The sloped bright-banded poles, beneath the green
Sea-weeded walls; content to catch quick gleams
Of her robe's tissue stiff with strong gold seams
From throat to foot, or mantle's sweeping shine
Of murrey satin lined with ermine fine.
Flushing the white warmth it encircled glad,
A sparkling karkanet of gems she had
About her fair throat. Such strong splendors piled
So heavily upon so slight a child
Made Venice proud: because in little things
Her greatness thus seemed greatest.

His white wings
The galley put forth from the blue lagoon.

The mellow disk of a mild daylight moon
Was hanging wan in the warm azure air,
When the great clarions all began to blare
Farewell. And, underneath a cloudless sky
Over a calméd sea, with minstrelsy,
The baby Queen to Cyprus sailed. . . . .

JACQUELINE.

COUNTESS OF HOLLAND AND HAINAULT.*

(1436.)

IS it the twilight, or my fading sight,
Makes all so dim around me? No, the night
Is come already. See! through yonder pane,
Alone in the gray air, that star again —
Which shines so wan, I used to call it mine
For its pale face; like Countess Jacqueline
Who reigned in Brabant once . . . . that's years ago.
I called so much mine, then: so much seemed so!
And see, my own! — of all those things, my star
(Because God hung it there, in heaven, so far
Above the reach and want of those hard men)
Is all they have not taken from me. Then
I call it still My Star. Why not? The dust
Hath claimed the dust: no more. And moth and rust
May rot the throne, the kingly purple fray: —
What then? Yon star saw kingdoms rolled away
Ere mine was taken from me. It survives.
But think, beloved, — in that high life of lives,
When our souls see the suns themselves burn low
Before that Sun of Righteousness, — and know

* This poem has been already printed in the "Wanderer," but is more properly placed here.

What is, and was, before the suns were lit, —
How Love is all in all . . . . Look, look at it,
My Star — God's star — for being God's 't is mine:
Had it been man's . . . . no matter . . . . see it
shine —
The old wan beam, which I have watched erenow
So many a wretched night, when this poor brow
Ached 'neath the sorrows of its thorny crown.
Its crown! . . . . ah, droop not, dear, those fond
eyes down.
No gem in all that shattered coronet
Was half so precious as the tear which wet
Just now this pale sick forehead. O my own,
My husband, need was that I should have known
Much sorrow, — more than most Queens, — all
know some, —
Ere, dying, I could bless thee for the home
Far dearer than the palace, — call thy tear
The costliest gem that ever sparkled here.

Enfold me, my belovéd. One more kiss.
O, I must go! 'T was willed I should not miss
Life's secret, ere I left it. And now see —
My lips touch thine — thine arm encircles me —
The secret 's found — God beckons — I must go.
Earth's best is given. — Heaven's turn is come to
show
How much its best earth's best may yet exceed,
Lest earth's should seem the very best indeed.
So we must part a little; but not long.
I seem to see it all. My lands belong
To Philip still; but thine will be my grave,
(The only strip of land which I could save!)
Not much, but wide enough for some few flowers,

Thou 'lt plant there, by and by, in later hours:
Duke Humphry, when they tell him I am dead
(And so young too), will sigh, and shake his head,
And, if his wife should chide, "Poor Jacqueline,"
He 'll add, "you know she never could be mine."
And men will say, when some one speaks of me,
"Alas, it was a piteous history,
The life of that poor Countess!" For the rest
Will never know, my love, how I was blest.
Some few of my poor Zealanders, perchance,
Will keep kind memories of me; and in France
Some minstrel sing my story. Pitiless John
Will prosper still, no doubt, as he has done,
And still praise God with blood upon the Rood.
Philip will, doubtless, still be called "The Good."
And men will curse and kill: and the old game
Will weary out new hands: the love of fame
Will sow new sins: thou wilt not be renowned:
And I shall lie quite quiet under ground.
My life is a torn book. But at the end
A little page, quite fair, is saved, my friend,
Where thou didst write thy name. No stain is there,
No blot, — from marge to marge all pure, — no tear; —
The last page, saved from all, and writ by thee,
Which I shall take safe up to Heaven with me.
All 's not in vain, since this be so. Dost grieve?
Belovéd, I beseech thee to believe,
Although this be the last page of my life,
It is my heart's first, only one. Thy wife,
Poor though she be, O thou sole wealth of mine,
Is happier than the Countess Jacqueline!

And since my heart owns thine, say — am I not
A Queen, my chosen, though by all forgot?
Though all forsake, yet is not this thy hand?
I, a lone wanderer in a darkened land,
I, a poor pilgrim with no staff of hope,
I, a late traveller down the evening slope,
Where any spark, the glow-worm's, by the way,
Had been a light to bless . . . . have I, O say,
Not found, belovéd, in thy tender eyes,
A light more sweet than morning's? As there dies
Some day of storm all glorious in its even,
My life grows loveliest as it fades in Heaven.

This earthly house breaks up. This flesh must fade.
So many shocks of grief slow breach have made
In the poor frame. Wrongs, insults, treacheries,
Hopes broken down, and memory which sighs
In, like a night wind! Life was never meant
To bear so much in such frail tenement.
Why should we seek to patch and plaster o'er
This shattered roof, crusht windows, broken door,
The light already shines through? Let them break!

Yet would I gladly live for thy dear sake,
O my heart's first and last, if that could be!
In vain! . . . . yet grieve not thou. I shall not see
England again, and those white cliffs; nor ever
Again those four gray towers beside the river,
And London's roaring bridges: nevermore
Those windows with the market-stalls before,
Where the red-kirtled market-girls went by
In the great square, beneath the great gray sky,

In Brussels: nor in Holland, night or day,
Watch those long lines of siege, and fight at bay
Among my broken army, in default
Of Gloucester's failing forces from Hainault:
Nor shall I pace again those gardens green,
With their clipt alleys, where they called me Queen,
In Brabant once. For all these things are gone.
But thee I shall behold, my chosen one,
Though we should seem whole worlds on worlds apart,
Because thou wilt be ever in my heart.
Nor shall I leave thee wholly. I shall be
An evening thought, — a morning dream to thee, —
A silence in thy life when, through the night,
The bell strikes, or the sun, with sinking light,
Smites all the empty windows. As there sprout
Daisies, and dimpling tufts of violets, out
Among the grass where some corpse lies asleep,
So round thy life, where I lie buried deep,
A thousand little tender thoughts shall spring,
A thousand gentle memories wind, and cling.
O, promise me, my own, before my soul
Is houseless, — let the great world turn and roll
Upon its way, unvext . . . . Its pomps, its powers!
The dust saith to the dust . . . . "the earth is ours."
I would not, if I could, be Queen again,
For all the walls of the wide world contain.
Be thou content with silence. Who would raise
A little dust and noise of human praise,
If he could see, in yonder distance dim,
The silent eye of God that watches him?
O, couldst thou see all that I see to-night
Upon the brinks of the great Infinite!

"Come out of her, my people, lest ye be
Partakers of her sins!" . . . . My love, but we
Our treasure where no thieves break in and steal
Have stored, I trust. Earth's weal is not our weal.
Let the world mind its business — peace or war;
Ours is elsewhere. Look, look, — my star, my star!
It grows, it glows, it spreads in light unfurled; —
Said I, "my star?" No star — a world — God's
world!
What hymns adown the jasper sea are rolled?
Even to these sick-pillows! Who infold
White wings about me? Rest, rest, rest I
come!
O love, I think that I am near my home.
Whence was that music? Was it Heaven's I heard?
"Write 'Blessèd are the dead that die i' the Lord,
Because they rest,'" . . . . because their toil is o'er.
The voice of weeping shall be heard no more
In the Eternal City. Neither dying
Nor sickness, pain nor sorrow, neither crying,
For God shall wipe away all tears. Rest, rest . . . .
Thy hand, my husband, — so — upon thy breast!

THE DIRGE.

Pluck the pale sky-colored periwinkle,
That haunts in dewy courts, and shuns the light:
Gather dim violets and the wild eyebright,
That green old ruined walls doth oversprinkle:
And cull, to keep her company
In death, rue, sage, and rosemary,
And flowery thyme from the faint bed o' the bee;
For they, when Summer's o'er, make savor sweet
To cherish Winter: strew black-spikèd clove,

And mint, and marjoram, to make my love
A misty fragrance for her winding-sheet.
But pull not up red tulips, nor the rose,
For these be flaunting flowers that live i' the world's
gay shows.

END OF BOOK VII.

BOOK VIII.

FROM 1525 TO 1789.

NARRATIVE, DRAMATIC, AND LYRICAL.

"Semper enim, ubi de spe æternitatis agitur, omnia alia contemnere non solum licet, sed etiam expedit."
Cardan Proxeneta., cxii. 666, Elzevir edit.

THE DEAD POPE.

[Possibly, one of those numerous *facezie*, common about Rome during the "Ages of Faith." Thence, after the Reformation, it may have found its way into Germany; being there caught up, and used as a weapon of offence by the zeal of the Reformed Pulpits; which, in the vehement and clumsy handling of it, contrived (as it would seem) to convert the fool's feather into the leaden sword. Thus it reaches us at last distorted and transformed. Hence the serio-comic, half grotesque, and altogether incongruous character of it.]

I.

HE whole day long had been wild and warm,
With a heavy forewarning of what was to come.
There had been, indeed, no such horrible storm
For many a year, men say, in Rome.
I remember it burst just after the close
Of the day when the dead Pope was laid in the Dome
Of St. Peter; taking his last repose,
To the grief of all good Christendom.

Here, before I am further gone with his story,
It is fit I should mention that, when he died,
He was of a good old age; grown hoary
In wearing the white robe, well descried

By sinner and saint and catechumen,
Judex gentium, mundi lumen!
Of a truth, he had sat so long in Rome,
Sat so long in Peter's chair,
Ruling the world, that he was come
To keep his power apart from care.
His hairs were few, and white
With the hoar of many years:
His eyes were filmy, and weak,
And humid, and heavy, and wan:
And all the look of the man
Was as dull, and feeble, and bleak
As the watery blunt starlight,
And thin snow, of a north March night,
When its wearied face appears
Bathed cold in a clammy gray,
Before the sluggish season clears
Earth's winter rubbish away.
Yet Winter's wine-cup cheers
The dull heart of his discontent,
While the joy of his jolly hearth endears
His home in the frosty element:
And, whatever the fretful folk may say,
This Pope was a pleasant Pope, and a gay,
For what should trouble his merriment?
There 's many a text, ... and this comes pat,
"*Dominus me lætificat,*"
And, "*Filii hominum usquequo*
Gravi corde?" David, too,
Sayeth in the psalm, "*In Deo*
Exultabo," also, "*meo*
In corde tu lætitiam
Dedisti." Saith he, "*Dormiam*
In pace." Where 's the harm of that?

So (since it is better to laugh than weep)
Leaving the wolf to look after the sheep,
Whilst ever the stormy nobles raved,
And the wickedness ran over in Rome,
And sinners, grown stout, refused to be saved,
Save now and then by a martyrdom,
He smiled, and, warming his heart with wine,
Daily, gayly quaffed the cup.
Albeit there were some who seemed to opine,
By their sullen faces and doggerel verses,
That the cup so quaffed was filled with curses,
Averring, as their spleen dictated,
That, to claim the price of its filling up
With the much-wronged blood of His bruiséd
Vine
The dreadful unseen Vintager waited
Aware at the gate. But we all of us know
The Devil is apt to quote Scripture so:
And what harm if still, as those famous keys
Of the double world's appointed porter,
From the good man's girdle hung at their ease,
While the days grew chillier, darker, shorter,
The cellar key in the cellar door
(More nimble than each of those rusty twins)
Daily, gayly, all the more
Made music among the vaults and bins?

II.

For O, what a paradise was there,
Set open by that kindly key!
Joyous, gentle, debonair,
The soul of every grape that dwells
By Tuscan slopes, o'er Umbrian dells,

Or else, where, oft, in azure air,
Round serene Parthenope
Witless wandering everywhere,
Drunken sings the sultry bee,
Or where, purpling tombs of kings,
Castel d' Aso's violet springs:
Montepulciano, the master-vine;
Chiante, that comforts the Florentine;
With many a merry-hearted wine
From Dante's own delicious vale,
Whose sweetness hangs, in odors frail
Of woods and flowers, round many a tale
Of tears, along the lordly line
Of the scornful Ghibeline, —
Dante's vale, and Love's, and mine,
The pleasant vale of the Casentine!
Nor lacked there many and many a train
Of kingly gifts, — the choicest gain
Of terraced cities over the sea:
The fiery essence of fierce Spain,
The soul of sunburnt Sicily,
The Frankish, Rhenish, vintage, all
The purple pride of Portugal, —
Whole troops of powers celestial,
The slayers of sullen Pain!
O what spirits strong and subtle!
Whether to quicken the pulses' play,
And dance the world, like a weaver's shuttle
To and fro in the dazzling loom
Where Fancy weaves her wardrobe gay;
Or soften to faintness, sweet as the fume
From silver censers swung alway
To music, making a mellow gloom,
The too intrusive light of the day.

Some that bathe the wearied brain,
And untie the knotted hair
On the puckered brows of Care;
Soothe from heavy eyes the stain
Of tears too long represt; make fair
With their transcendent influence
Fate's frown; or feed with nectar-food
The lips of Longing, and dispense
To the tired soul despaired-of good:
Others that stir in the startled blood
Like tingling trumpet notes intense,
To waken the martial mood.
By the mere faint thought of it, well I wis
Such a heaven on earth were hardly amiss;
And I hold it no crime to set it in rhyme
That I think a man might pass his time
In company worse than this.

III.

But, however we pass Time, he passes still,
Passing away whatever the pastime,
And, whether we use him well or ill,
Some day he gives us the slip for the last time.
Even a Pope must finish his fill,
And follow his time, be it feast time or fast time.
As it happened with this same Pope. No doubt
What sleep was his after that last bout,
When he could not wake! so they laid him out.
"He is gone," they said, "where there 's no returning.
Of the college who is the next to come?"
Then they set the bells tolling, the tapers burning,
And bore him up into Peter's dome.

IV.

And that day the whole world mourned with Rome.

V.

Now, after the organ's drowning note
Grew hoarse, then husht, in his golden throat,
And the latest loiterer, slacking his walk,
Cast one last glance at the catafalk,
And, passing the door, renewed his talk
As to that last raid of Prince Colonna, —
"What villages burned? and what hope of indemnity?"
The Beauty from Venice (or was it Verona?)
With the nimbus of red gold hair, God bless her!
And who should be the late Pope's successor?
I say — that, as soon as the crowd was gone,
And never a face remained in sight,
As the tapers were brightening in chapels dim,
Just about the time of the coming on
And settling down of the ghostly light,
The sudden silence so startled him
That the dead Pope rose up.

VI.

And, first, he fumbled, and stretched his hand,
Feeling for the accustomed cup;
For the taste of the wine was yet in his mouth;
And, finding it not, and vext with drouth,
Feebly, as ever, he called out.
For a Pope . . . . what need has a Pope to shout,
Whose feeblest whisper from land to land
Is echoed, east, west, and north, and south?

But, no one coming to his command,
He rubbed his eyes, and looked about,
And saw, through a swimming mist, each face
Of his predecessors, gone to Grace
Many a century ago,
Sternly staring at him so
(From their marble seats, a mournful row)
As who should say, "Be cheerful, pray!
Make the best of it as you may:
We are all of us here in the same sad case:
Each in his turn, we must one by one die,
Even the best of us, —
God help the rest of us!
Your turn, friend, now. Make no grimace.
Consider *sic transit gloria mundi!*"

He began to grow aware of the place.

A settling strangeness more and more
Crept over him, never felt before,
As he stept down to the marble floor.
He looked up, and down, above him, and under,
Filled with uncomfortable wonder.
What should persuade him that he was dead?
A horrible humming in the head?
A giddy lightness about the feet?
Last night's wine, and this night's heat!
Where were the Saints and Apostles, each
With the bird or beast that belongs to him,
Each on a cushion of cloud, — no film,
But solid and smooth like a pale-colored peach;
In a holy hurry the hand to reach
Down to him out of the glory dim,
Where the multitudinous cherubim,

With wingéd heads, and wonderful eyes
Wide open, are watching in due surprise
How Heaven puts on its holiday trim
To welcome a Pope when he dies?
He could guess by the incense afloat on the air
Some service not yet so long o'er
But what he might have slept unaware,
Nor yet quite waked. What alone made him fear
Was that draperied, lighted, black thing there,
Not quite like a couch, and too much like a bier.
But anyhow, "Wherefore linger here?"
And, pushing the heavy curtain by
That flapped in the portal, the windy floor
Sucking its flat hem sullenly,
He passed out through the great church door.

VII.

So forth, on the vacant terrace there,
Overlooking the mighty slope
Of never-ending marble stair,
'Twixt the great church and the great square,
Stood the dead Pope.
On either side glade heaped on glade
Of colossal colonnade,
Lost, at last, in vague and vast
Recesses of repeated shade
By those stupendous columns cast;
In midst of which, as they sang and played,
(Fire and sound!) the fountains made
Under the low faint starlight, laid
Not far above their splendors bright,
Fresh interchange of laughters light,
Mixt with the murmur of the might

Of royal Rome which, dim in sight,
Revelling under the redness wide
Of lamps now winking from hollow and height,
With a voice of pride on every side
Lay ready to receive the night.

VIII.

Thus, all at once, and all around,
The silence changed itself to sound
More horrible than mere silence is,—
The sound of a life no longer his.
Fresh terror seized him where he stood;
Or the fear that followed him, shifting ground,
Fresh onslaught made; and he rested afraid
To call or stir, like a sick owl, strayed
From a witches' cave back again to the wood
Wherein, meanwhile, the noisy brood
Of little birds, with lusty voice,
Made free of his presence, begin to rejoice,
And he halts in alarm lest, perchance, if he cries out,
Those creatures, fit only to furnish him food,
Already by liberty rendered loquacious,
Picking up heart, and becoming audacious,
Should forthwith fall to pecking his eyes out.

IX.

Indeed, one might fairly surmise
From the noise in the streets, the shouts and cries,
That all the men and women in Rome,
From the People's Gate to St. Peter's Dome,
Though clad in mourning, each and all,
Were making the most of some festival:
Walking, driving, talking, striving,

Each with the rest, to do his best
To add to the tumult; each contriving
To make, in pursuit of his special joys,
Something more than the usual noise.
Since it is not every day in the week
That one Pope dies, and another 's to seek.
Such an event is a thing to treasure:
For a general mourning 's a general meeting, —
A sort of general grief-competing,
Which leads, of course, to a general greeting
(Not to mention the general drinking and eating)
That is quite a general pleasure.

X.

The universal animation,
In a word, you could hardly underrate.
So much to talk of, so much to wonder at!
The Ambassadors, first, of every nation,
Representing the whole world's tribulation,
Each of them grander than the other,
In due gradation for admiration;
How they lookt, how they spoke, what sort of speeches?
What sort of mantles, coats, collars, and breeches?
Then, the Cardinals, all in a sumptuous smother
Of piety, warmed by the expectation
Which glowed in the breast of each Eminent Brother
Of assuming a yet more eminent station, —
Much, he hoped, to each Eminent Brother's vexation.
And then, the Archbishops, and Bishops, and Priors,
And Abbots, and orders of various Friars,
Treading like men that are treading on briers,

Doubtful whom, in the new race now for the State
run,
They should hasten to claim as their hopeful patron.
The Nobles, too, and their Noble Families,
Prouder each than the very devil,
Yet turned, all at once, appallingly civil,
And masking their noble animosities
For the sake of combining further atrocities:
And, after each of the Noble Families,
Each Noble Family's faithful Following;
Who, picking their way while the crowd kept
holloaing,
Stuck close to their chiefs, and proudly eyed them,
Much the same as each well-provendered camel
eyes,
In the drouthy desert, when groaning under
Their pleasing weight of public plunder,
The dainty despot boys that ride them.
A host, too, of Saints, with their special religions,
And patrons, of rival rank and station;
Which, as they passed, the very pigeons
On the roofs uproused in a consternation;
Being deckt in all manners of ribbons and banners,
Painted papers, and burning tapers
Enough to set in a conflagration
The world, you would think by the fume and flare
of them,
And the smoky faces of those that had care of
them;
All marching along with a mighty noise
Of barking dogs, and shouts, and cheers,
Brass music, and bands of singing boys,
Doing their best to split men's ears.

XI.

The excitement was certainly justifiable.
The more so, if, having fairly computed
The importance, necessity, and function
Of a Pope, as divinely instituted,
You consider the fact, which is undeniable,
That, when deprived of its special pastor,
The whole of earth's flock, without compunction,
Must consider itself consigned to disaster.
For, if the world, say,
Could go on as it should,
Doing its duty, fair and good,
Missing no crumb of its Heavenly food,
For even a week or a day
In the absence of Heaven's Representative,
Might it not be assumed from any such tentative
Process, if this each time succeeded,
That a Pope, on the whole, is hardly needed?
And that, if it should ever befall
That Heaven might be pleased, after due delay,
Its Viceroy on earth to recall,
And abolish that post, just as good and as gay
The world would go on in the usual way
Without a Pope at all?

XII.

To this Pope however, yet upon earth,
Who, though dead, knew what a live Pope is worth,
That sight was somewhat provoking:
Millions of men, all jostling, joking,
As merry as so many Prodigal Sons,
Having killed and roasted their fatted calf,
And enjoying the chance to quaff and laugh;

And yet not one of those millions
Who seemed aware of the dead Pope there,
Or even very much to care
What had become of His Holiness,
How he must feel now, or how he might fare;
Who, all the while, was nevertheless
Sole cause of the general joyousness.
This was certainly hard to bear.
His hand he raised: no man lookt to it.
His finger: not a knee was crookt to it.
He raised his voice: no man heeded it.
He gave his blessing: no man needed it.
'T was the merest waste of benevolence,
Since the holiday went on with or without him.
He might have been to all intents
The golden Saint stuck up on the steeple,
Who is always blessing a thankless people,
Nobody caring a button about him.
Bless, or curse, neither better nor worse
For a single word that he said,
On its wonted way a world perverse
Went onward, nobody bowing the head
Either for hope, or yet for dread.

XIII.

Then the dead Pope knew that he was dead.

XIV.

He walked onward — no man stopping him,
Ever onward — no lip dropping him
A *salve:* nobody making way
For the Pope to pass, as the Pope passed on
Through that rude irreverent holiday:

Till the streets behind him, one by one,
Fell off, and left him standing alone
In the mighty waste of Rome's decay.
Meanwhile, the night was coming on
Over the wide Campagna :
Hot, fierce, a blackness without form,
And in her breast she bore the storm.

I never shall forget that night!
You might tell by the stifling stillness there,
And the horrible wild-beast scent on the air,
That all things were not right.

XV.

On Mount Cavi the dark was nurst,
And the Black Monks' belfry towers above :
Then, vast, the sea of vapor burst
Where forlorn Ferretian Jove
Hears only the howlet's note accurst
'Mid his fallen fanes no more divine :
And from the sea to the Apennine :
And swift across the rocky line
Where the blighted moon dropped first
Behind Soracte, black and broad
Up the old Triumphal Road,
From Palestrino post on Rome,
Nearer, nearer, you felt It come,
The presence of the darksome Thing!
As when, dare I say, with outstretcht wing,
By some lean Prophet summoned fast
To punish the guilt of a stiff-neckt king,
Over the desert, black in the blast,
On Babylon, or Egypt red,
The Angel of Destruction sped.

Earth breathed not, feigning to be dead:
While the whole of heaven overhead
Was overtaken unaware,
First here, then there, then everywhere.
Into the belly of blackness suckt,
Sank the dwindling droves of buffaloes
That spotted the extreme crimson glare:
Then the mighty darkness stronger rose,
Swallowing leagues of lurid air,
And crossed the broken viaduct,
Flung forth in dim disorder there
Like the huge spine-bone of the skeleton
Of some dead Python, left to obstruct
The formless Night-hag's filmy path:
Thence on, by the glimmering creeks and nooks
Where the water-flats look sick and white,
Putting out quite the pallid light
Of the yellow flowers by the sulphur brooks
That make a sullen brimstone bath
For the Nightmare's noiseless hoof:
And, leaving the quenched-out east aloof,
The plague, from Tophet vomited,
Struck at the west, and rushing came
Right against the last red flame,
Where in cinders, now, the day,
Self-condemned to darkness, lay
With all his sins upon his head
Burning on a fiery bed,
Helpless, hopeless, overthrown.

XVI.

Now, to all the world it is well known
How the Devil rides the wind by night:

Doing all the harm he can
In the absence of heaven's light
To the world's well-ordered plan,
And with murrain, mildew, blight,
Or thunder blue, or hailstone white,
Marring the thrift of the honest man,
Which much doth move his spite.

XVII.

Certainly, he was out that night,
What time the fearful storm began.
For lo! on a sudden, left and right,
The heaven was gashed from sky to sky,
Seamed across, and sundered quite,
By a swift, snaky, fork-tongued flash
Of brightness intolerably bright;
As, ever, the angry Cherub, vowed
To vengeance, fast through plunging cloud
Wielding wide his withering lash,
That wild horseman now pursued:
Who lurked, his vengeance to elude,
In deep unprobéd darkness still.

Forthwith, the wounded night 'gan spill
Great drops: then fierce — crash crusht on crash —
As it grieved beneath each burning gash,
The darkness bellowed; and outsprang
Wild on the plain, whilst yet it rang
With thunder, the infernal steed,
And dashed onward at full speed,
Blind with pain, with streaming mane,
And snorting nostril on the strain,
Where, dasht from off his flanks, the rain

Through all the desolate abyss
Of darkness, now began to hiss.

XVIII.

And here (for this story is scattered about
The world in dozens of different shapes)
One writes . . . . Some Lutheran lean, I doubt,
Who, nameless, thus from shame escapes.—
Lies thrive and flourish by the score:
Take this for what 't is worth, no more:—

"Out leaping from that riven rack
Of cloud, where night was boiling black,
And so escaping, as God willed,
While, for a time, the storm was stilled,
Satan beheld the face he knew,
Amoris actus impetu.
And to the Shepherd gone astray
Grimly the black goats' Goatherd said:
'Service for service! on their way
To me full many hast thou sped:
And, since it is a stormy night,
Lest thou shouldst lose thine own way quite,
(For how shouldst thou the right way know
Who seek'st it out the first time now?)
Content am I thy guide to be.
Nor marvel that 't is known to me,
The way to Heaven. For who but I
Makes half the ways there, that men try?
Moreover, there 's no jolly sin
Which those I lead may not take in,
If they themselves can pass the gate
Whereat, of course, we separate.
For all the members of my flock

Come furnisht with Indulgences
In proper form, — a goodly stock!
'T is but to pick and chuse from these.
Paid for they are: and, *signo hoc*,
Well paid, if Peter will but please
That wicket to unlock.'"

XIX.

A spiteful fable. Best to own
The truth can ne'er by us be known.
But alas! for any poor ghost of a Pope
In such a night to be doomed to grope,
Blind beneath the hideous cope
Of those black skies without a star,
For the way to where the Blessèd are!
And, if the Evil One, himself,
Was his conductor through the dark;
Or if, dislodged from its sky-shelf,
Some cloud was made his midnight bark;
Or if the branding bolt, that rent
The skies asunder, hewed for him
Through that disfeatured firmament,
Beyond the utmost echoing brim
Of thunder-brewage, and the black
Unblissful night, some shining track
Up to the Sapphire Throne, where throng
The Voices crying, "Lord, how long?"
While the great years are onward rolled
With moans and mutterings manifold;
I know not, for it was not told.

XX.

It would seem, however, all texts agree
(And this should suffice us at any rate)

In assuming for certain that, early or late,
The dead Pope got to the Golden Gate
Where the mitred Apostle sits with the key,—
Peter, whose heir upon earth was he.
And further than this to speculate
I, for one, do not feel justified.
Though a fact there is, I am bound to state:
A renegade Monk avers he descried
In a vision that very night,
When the storm was spending its fiercest hate,—
(And what he saw, so much the sight
Impressed him, he wrote as soon as he woke:—
Was it a dream, or a wicked joke?)
What passed before That Gate.

XXI.

Now, since, after the fashion then in vogue,
He wrote it in form of a dialogue;
Not averring, as he did, the dream to be true,
In all else, as he wrote it, I write it for you:—

VOICE OUTSIDE THE GATE.

"Peter, Peter, open the Gate!

VOICE WITHIN.

I know thee not. Thou knockest late.

FIRST VOICE.

Late! yet, Peter, look, and see
Who calleth.

SECOND VOICE.

Nay, I know not thee.
What art thou?

FIRST VOICE.

Peter, Peter, ope
The Gate!

SECOND VOICE.

What art thou?

FIRST VOICE.

The dead Pope.

SECOND VOICE.

The Pope? what is it?

FIRST VOICE.

In men's eye
Thy successor, late, was I.
What was thine was given to me.

SECOND VOICE.

Martyrdom and misery?

FIRST VOICE.

Nay, but power to bind and loose.
In thy name have I burned Jews
And heretics, and all the brood
Of unbelief . . . .

VOICES FAR WITHIN.

Avenge our blood,
Lord!

FIRST VOICE.

And in thy name have blest
Kings and Emperors; confest
Earth's Spiritual Head, while there
I sat ruling in thy chair.

VOICES FAR WITHIN.

Woe! because the kings of earth
Were with her in her wicked mirth!

FIRST VOICE.

In thy name, and for thy cause,
I made peace and war, set laws
To lawgivers . . . .

VOICES FAR WITHIN.

And all nations
Drunk with the abominations
Of her witchcraft!

FIRST VOICE.

In thy name,
And for thy cause, to sword and flame
I gave sinners; and to those
That feared the friends and fought the foes
Of him from all mankind selected
To keep thy name and cause respected,
Riches and rewards I gave,
And the joy beyond the grave.

VOICES FAR WITHIN.

Souls of men, too, chaffering lies,
Did she make her merchandise.

FIRST VOICE.

By all means have I upheld
Thy patrimony, — nay, 't is swelled.

VOICES FAR WITHIN.

For herself she glorified
In the riches of her pride.

FIRST VOICE.

Wherefore, Peter, ope the Gate!
If my knocking now be late,
Little time, in truth, had I, —
I, the Pope, who stand and cry!
For other cares than those that came
Upon me, in thy cause and name,
Holding up the heavy keys
Of Heaven and Hell.

SECOND VOICE.

If so, if these
Thou hast in keeping, wherefore me
Callest thou? Thou hast the key.
Truly thou hast waited late!
Open, then, thyself, The Gate."

And here the Monk breaks off, to state,
With befitting reflections by the way,

With what great joy the Pope, no doubt,
Soon as he heard the stern voice say
Those words, began to search about
Among his garments for the key;
Which, strange to say, 't would seem that he
Had not bethought him of before.
And how that joy, from more to more,
Waxed most (the historian of his dream
Observes, as he resumes the theme),
"When, after search grown desperate,
A key he found, — just as his need
Seemed at the worst, — a key, indeed!
But, ah vain hope! for, however the Pope
Tried the key in the fastened Gate,
Turning it ever with might and main
This way, that way, every way at last,
Forwards — backwards — round again —
Till his joy is turned to sheer dismay at last,
And his failing force will no longer cope
With the stubborn Gate, — it declines to ope.
A key, indeed! but not, alas,
The Key."

Who shall say *what* key it was?
The Monk, who here, I must believe,
Is laughing at us in his sleeve
(Like any vulgar story-teller,
Fabling forms to vent his spleen),
Surmises that it must have been
The key of the Pope's own cellar.

THOMAS MÜNTZER TO MARTIN LUTHER.

(FROM PRISON.)

KNOW not if what now my spirit doth spend
This tortured frame's last strength in sore endeavor
To write to thee will reach thee, Luther, ever.
For I, whose crime is to have been man's friend,
No friend can claim whose friendship's faith I may
Trust these, my life's last words, to thee to send,
After my death, which thou dost urge, men say.
I know not, Luther, if what 's writ to-night
Be for thy reading, or for any man's.
'T is as God wills. But, since his own eye scans,
And answers, in my heart, what now I write,
Still I write on, while he withholds the end.
And, setting bare my spirit in God's sight,
I summon thine to witness.
'T were in vain
To urge the old sad difference o'er again.
Doomed to an imminent death, — a dreadful one
In all save this, — that death, whate'er the shape
God gives it, is the event of life alone
Graced with God's last great gift to man, — escape
From men's tormenting, — I desire not now
To argue a long-talked theology.
How much mere knowledge with mere life may grow
Concerns not one that, being about to die,

Approaches Truth by no such process slow.
Too near death's hour of certainty am I.
But O the pity! Had we two been one!
As once we might have been: who cannot be,
Henceforth, united, till by God's clear throne
We stand together, with Heaven's eyes to see
What Earth's missed sadly: each, Man's champion,
And, therefore, God's! We, in this dark, abused
By the false glare of midnight watchfires, seen
Across a warring world, where all 's confused,
Mistook for foes each other, who, I ween,
Are soldiers of the self-same King. And so
We fought, and, struck by thee, I fall. Each blow
Of thine, which I must pardon and deplore,
A friend's mistake! though fatal, Luther, more
Than if a foe had dealt it. O why, why
This woful haste, that mars so much? See here
The sad result. For, Luther, while I die,
What ominous, incongruous faces leer
Beside thine own with laughing lip and eye?
What strange unholy helpmates share with thee
The sad bad joy of this false victory
O'er me and man? Error on Error! see,
Beneath the same soiled banner at thy side,
Hand clasping hand, grim Saxon George allied
With him of Hesse! sworn foes erewhile, though now
George, who would think he did God service good
Could he but rend thee limb from limb, as thou
Bid'st him rend me, red with thy brother's blood,
Thy right hand holds: who clasps the other? he,
The Landgrave, who hates him, as both hate me.
And thou, the while, art hugging each red hand!
What glues so fast the fratricidal Three

Together thus? And what of such a band
The shameful central link makes Luther be?
My blood. O shame, shame, shame, my brother, shame!
Is it not sad that God such things should see,
And thou the cause? O worst disgrace of all!
That, when God asks, "Who did this?" men must name
Their noblest, and the blame of such deeds fall
On him whose scorn should brand them with the blame
Such deeds deserve. Error beyond recall!
Yet, think, think, Luther, and be sad 't is so.

Desirest thou man's good? I wot thou dost.
But self hath filmed thy spirit's eagle eye.
Hear him not, heed him not, since cry he must,
The flattering fiend, that in thy heart doth cry!
I hear the plausible serpent tempting Dust
To mimic God! and thou dost taste his lie,
And in the sweetness of it take delight,
Murmuring, "Man's good! for what else have I striven,
Toiled, dared, done battle, conquered? Man's good, ay!
But man's good, by my gift, to mankind given,
Not man's good, man's hereditary right."
Hath it not oft thus whispered thee? and thou
Hast listened till it seemed God's voice! By night,
When thoughts speak loud that scarce dare whisper low
By daylight, — when the Tempter saith his say,
And *will* be answered, — doubtless to me, too,
Would some such wandering whisper steal its way

At times, from the abyss. I thank God, who
Gave my soul strength to answer stoutly Nay,
And foil Pride's prelate-devil of his prey!

Consider, Luther. . . . 't is Paul speaks, not I. . . .
How all are members of the Body of Christ:
Where were the hearing, were the body all eye?
Were it all ear, in what would sight exist?
Were all one member, where the body then?
Many the members, though the body is one:
One Spirit of God in many lives of men:
Can the eye say to the hand, "Need have I none
Of thee"? or can the head say to the feet,
"I need ye not"? Nay, rather they which be
The body's feeblest members most complete
The body's being: rather those that we
Esteem least comely claim the comeliest care,
Those least in honor honor most entreat:
Since to the body these most needful are:
The weaker parts chief cherishing demand:
The limbs crave clothing, — not the head, the hand.

What gleamed on Corinth, in the dawn of Faith,
Is Luther blind to, in Faith's noonday blaze?
To thee, Apostle, still the Poor Man saith
The self-same word that in the old proud days
Paul to the rich Corinthians cried. They heard,
Believed, obeyed, and blest the Preacher's word.

To Corinth God one preacher sent: to thee
A thousand preachers cry aloud, my brother.
The fettered foot rebukes the hand that 's free.
Should not we members cherish one another?
For if one member suffereth pain or wrong,

All suffer with it, and the whole frame ails:
Since each to each the bodily parts belong,
And none without his fellow's help avails
The body's use. But is it so with us?
The Rich oppress the Poor: the Strong the Weak:
The hand lops off the foot. The body, thus
Self-mutilated, suffers, and doth shriek:
But the ear hears not what the tongue doth cry,
And the hand helps not, and Shame shuts the eye!

I sought to heal this sickness into health:
To mitigate, not magnify, man's wrong:
For Want win justice, and give worth to Wealth:
To free the Weak, not to enslave the Strong:
'Mid gifts unequal, 'mid unequal powers,
Secure the equal happiness of all:
Maintain God's law in this mad world of ours:
Replace the force of mere material thrall
By force of love; the old empiry of Might,
Which is imposed upon unwilling hate,
By the serene sweet sovereignties of Right,
That are accepted and secured i' the state
Of man's free spirit, by the loyal love
Of what the soul perceives to be Above.

I sought to attain this by no violent aids:
I preached not Justice from the cannon's mouth.
In humble hearts, not over crownéd heads,
I claimed dominion, and 't was granted. Youth,
Hope's dawn-star trembling in his tear-lit eyes;
Old Age, the twilight of his toilful day
Suffused with solemn joy, — like evening skies
That promise watchful shepherds a fair morn, —
Brightening his grave, calm, satisfied regard;

And Womanhood, — the maiden in her May,
The careworn wife, with hungry eyes, grown hard
From grieving without hope, — pale mothers, worn
With nursing breadless babes; the wan array
Of this world's weary hearts; — all these, no scorn
Could sneer to shame, no cares could keep away,
No want withhold, from Love's new-found domain.
Love showed his face, and was forthwith beloved!
No drop of blood was shed, no victim slain,
For love of all in each loved spirit moved,
And this man's pleasure was not that man's pain;
But in Mulhausen God saw, and approved,
The bloodless triumph that bequeathed no stain
To Love's least soldier. And there rose on earth,
For Heavenly augury of human gain,
A glorious Form of innocent beauty and mirth, —
A little State like one large Family:
All members of one body at one birth:
And all were lowly, because all were high:
None poor: none idle: tyrant none, nor thrall:
Strong labor for the strong: light for the weak:
Labor for all: and food for all: for all
Hope that makes strong, and Reverence that makes meek,
Conscience that governs, Justice that allies,
Love that obeys, and Faith that fortifies.

And so, it grew, and grew: and so, I deemed
It might grow yet, — Earth's fruit of Heavenly seed!
But no! the vulture swooped, the eagle screamed,
The roused hawk hungered, and the dove must bleed!
The banded anarchs of a brutal time
Hated us strongly, and were strong: their greed

Was made earth's god: their lust earth's law sub-
lime:
We loved, and we were weak: that was our crime.
And where was Luther then? From town to town
Chasing gray-headed Carlstadt, his old friend:
Denouncing, persecuting, hunting down,
Down, to a noble life's disastrous end,
The man, to whom, in God's attesting name,
His solemn faith was pledged not long before:
The man he loathed because he could not tame
That old man's fearless spirit any more
To crouch to his! Or to obedience old
Scolding Melanchthon's meeker nature back.
. . . . Ah, dear Melanchthon, loved, though lost!
How, fold
On fold, the blurred Past lifts its vapor black,
To let emerge those melancholy eyes
Once more, which still my wronged heart loves!
Alack,
Love is not always just, nor Memory wise.
May truer friends forgive me, that I cease,
A moment even, to list to their loud woes!
The thought of thee o'er all things breathes sad
peace:
And, for a while, in sorrowful repose
The world's vast wail is husht, to let me hear
The old sweet flute-playing . . . . so faint, so clear!
Melanchthon, never play that flute again!

Back, heart, to Luther! Where was Luther then?
Maligning Müntzer to the magistrate:
The rich man's friend, the friendless people's foe:
With frenzied rail, rebuking hope: elate
To lift the high-born, lay the low-born low:

Now this Elector, now that Landgrave, praising:
Through all Thuringia preaching scorn and strife:
In every Saxon burg crusaders raising
Against the accurséd Anabaptist's life!

Even then, the untaught patient peasant clung
To hope in justice from an unjust power.
Sharp was the cry which misery from him wrung,
But scant his asking even in that last hour.
He asked for leave to labor and to live, —
A free man's life and labor, not a beast's:
To honest Want what honest Wealth may give,
Wages for work: Christ's charity from Priests:
Justice from Law: and man's humanity
From Human Power. His prayer was humbly urged:
Scorn was the guerdon, outrage the reply.
With hoot and howl the importunate wretch was scourged
From field to forest, and from moor to fen.
Then, then at last, lashed, famisht, to its lair,
The frenzied People, raving, rent its den:
Then savageries of nature seethed and surged
In manly breasts unmanned by mad despair:
Brute hardship brutalized the hearts of men:
And beasts of burden changed to wild beasts then.

Ay! then, indeed, another voice was heard:
Not mine: and stormy listeners, lured by hate,
Welcomed the preacher of a wilder word,
With hearts whose love's last cry was strangled late.
Like rainless lightning through a wildwood ran

Stork's fiery utterance: where it dropped it burned:
And all was flame. For each wronged heart of man
Caught fire and flared; and, flaring, backward turned
Before the rushing wind of ruinous Wrath,
And poured that glare upon a blighted Past:
And each beheld, what barred the backward path,
Some mighty image of a monstrous wrong.
Whereon the red revengeful light was cast.
This saw his son's back bleed beneath the thong;
That other his dishonored bride beheld,
Or ravisht daughter: one, the hunter's throng
Trampling his thrifty field: another yelled,
"In Leipheim bleach my boys' unburied bones!"
One saw his brother burning at the pyre:
One caught from bloody racks a comrade's groans:
One saw his father on the cross expire.
Then burst the dreadful shout, the dooming word,
And in the hand of Vengeance flashed the sword.

And peace was passed away. To me, to all,
No choice survived, but action, and a cause
To fight for: man's oppressor, or his thrall:
The makers, or the breakers, of bad laws.
My choice was fixt, my part imposed: in me
No pause disloyal to the past allowed.
Albeit strife's end I could not fail to see:
The certain slaughter of an unskilled crowd,
Disaster, disappointment, death: fit ends
To false beginnings, — war to vengeance vowed,
And valor shamed by violent deeds. My friends
To fancied victory, fooled, with blindfold eyes,
Went forth: unblinded I, to sacrifice.

Yet, when the Armies of the Poor displayed
The Wheel of Fortune on their ensigns borne,
Which, in the turning of her hoodwinked head,
Turns all things upside down with captious scorn,
"Not Chance, but Hope, be our device!" I said,
"For godless Fortune's gifts leave Faith forlorn,
But God's gift Hope stays fast when these be fled."
And on the People's flag I blazoned then
Heaven's rainy bow, first reared o'er rescued men.

Ay! though that banner hath been beaten down,
That symbol trampled out in streams of blood,
While this contented world without a frown
Is praising faithless peace in festal mood;
Though all the friends for whom I hoped are slain
Like shambled sheep, and though myself must die
In some few hours, that hope I still retain:
Not with the same wild moment's flashing joy
That seized my soul when, in war's desperate hour,
I stood on the hill-top, and saw beneath
The all-surrounding hosts of hostile Power,
And mine own helpless sheep, ordained to death,
A faint and weary flock, which to devour,
The herded wolves, hoarse barking, bared sharp teeth;
While high in heaven, athwart the thunder-shower,
Even as I lifted up my voice, and cried
To God, with stretched expostulating hand,
Sprang forth the sudden rainbow, basing wide
O'er battle strewn about the lower land,
Storm strewn in heaven, all its aery pride,
Triumphant on the everlasting hills!
Not thus I hope. No gleam of promise thus
Visits this hour, which Heaven with darkness fills.

For men, must wait. God deigns not to discuss
With our impatient and o'erweening wills
His times, and ways of working out through us
Heaven's slow but sure redress of human ills.
When Christ was in the garden captived, they
That, till that hour, had talked and walked beside
him,
Hoping in him, lost hope, and fled away,
And he that knew him best ere dawn denied him.
What wonder? All seemed lost, i' the very eve
Of an immortal victory. In man's sight,
All *was* lost. What disciple could believe
Love's triumph in Life's failure, that sad night?
But God makes light what men make dark: his
fire
He frees where fall our ashes. And, because
I feel God's power, still doth my spirit aspire:
Not fearing, even now, that unjust laws
By unjust force maintained, rack, stake, or cord,
The signed conventions of convenient wrong,
The tyrant's sceptre, or the hireling's sword,
The servile pulpit, timorous to the strong,
To the weak truculent, or custom tough,
Can crush man's rights forever, or prolong
Man's pain an hour, whene'er God cries, "Enough!"
And for this reason, and because I think
I never cared about myself since first
I cared for man, — from whom I dare not shrink,
Not even though he forsake himself, — nor aught
Hath Fancy nourisht, or Ambition nurst,
That was not featured in the womb of thought
By Hope's keen contemplation of man's face;
Because I cared not ever, care not now,
Which runner's foot be fleetest in the race,

Who, at the goal, assumes to grace his brow
The garland won, who takes the upper place,
Chief at the board, when festal wine-cups flow,
So long as, at the last, the goal be gained,
The garland got, the general table spread; —
Whoe'er the man by whom man's aim attained,
Joy crowns my heart, if victory crowns his head!
Luther, because 't was thus — *'t is* thus — with me,
And because, gazing with intensest gaze
Round each lost field where my life's ruins be,
A gleam of hope for man, in these dark days, —
(His last, perchance, for centuries long!) — I see,
Or seem to see, i' the spirit-power which stays,
Though stained, — like sunrise o'er a stormy sea
Poured from a clouded crag with struggling rays, —
On thy firm forehead's pride, — I write to thee.
Love mankind, Luther, if thou lovest not me!
For thou, great Spirit, art full-armed! a soul
Clothed with strong thunder by the hand of God:
Ardent to combat, potent to control:
Gabriel's spear, John's Angel's measuring-rod,
The Cherub's flaming sword, and Michael's shield,
Were given to thee — to conquer, not to yield.

Yield not the Devil his recaptured prey!
Conquer for all mankind! Complete thy task!
The People thou wast sent to save and sway
Die in the Desert: thirsty lips, that ask
In vain for water! perishing feet, that stray
Farther and farther from the Promist Land,
And sink 'neath weary loads along the way!
Mock not man's thirst with driblets poured i' the sand
From the scant leavings of Wealth's well-drained flask.

Cleave thou the stubborn stone with stern command.
Smite these rich rocks! The rod is in thy hand.

Thou canst. But if thou wilt not . . . .
Hark! give ear
To this sad prophecy of woes to be,
A dying voice to night-winds, moaning here,
Delivers, charging them to bear to thee
The burden of Time's melancholy song:
The Church thou buildest, scorning first to free
Life's cumbered field for Love's foundations, long
Shall be, herself, the slave of Power: and she,
Wed to the World, not Christ, the unchristian wrong
Of worldly Force with worldly Fraud shall share,
And so wax weak by scheming to be strong;
Till there shall be on earth a sight to scare
Earth's holiest hope from human hearts away:
A Priesthood, purchased for complacent prayer,
Leagued with Earth's Pomps, for profit and for pay,
Against Heaven's Love: praisers of things that are,
Scorners of good that 's not: cleaving to clay,
Strangling the spirit; purblind, unaware!
Contracting, not enlarging, day by day,
The charities of Christ, with surly care:
Till man's indignant heart shall turn away,
And chuse the champions of its faith elsewhere.
And champions shall it find. Dread champions, they!
The impatient offspring of prolonged despair:
A prayerless, pitiless, imperious brood,
Whose battle-cry shall be a cry for blood.

It may come soon, come late, come once for all,
Achieve its task, and pass, content, away,
That Hour of Fate, which God to life shall call:
It may come many times, and miss its prey,
And pass, dissatisfied, to come again,
More grimly armed with greed of greater sway,
To rescue from more wretchedness more men:
I cannot tell. For unseen hands delay
The coming of what oft seems close in ken,
And, contrary, the moment, when we say,
"'T will never come!" comes on us even then.
I cannot tell the coming of that day,
If near or far, or how 't will be, or when:
But come it will, and do its work it must,
So sure as moves God's spirit in man's dust.

Men call me Prophet. And thou, too, in scorn.
Prophet I am. For grief hath made me wise.
The night's lone watchman feels far off the dawn,
And, till redressed, all wrongs are prophecies.
This is no tortured fool's despairing curse,
No maniac menace from a murdered man.
Luther, consider, ere man's need be worse,
If thou wilt help it, as none other can.
I claim not justice now, I do beseech
Compassion, for the Poor. To thee, to all,
I would, indeed, my dying cry might reach: —
Place for the People's Cause! in which I fall.

My sands run out. What else my soul would say
Must be said shortly. And these fingers write
But ill the struggling thoughts that force their way
Through tortured nerves, and speak in pain's despite.

Judge if 't is pity for myself I crave.
Luther, one woman lives that loves me : one
Whose life I 'd die ten thousand deaths to save :
I have no friends, and therefore she hath none,
Save God : I cannot shield her, from the grave
To which men doom me : worse than all alone
I leave her, compassed with a world of foes !
That is the wife whose steps with mine have gone
Faithful through life, though led from woes to woes.
I have not breathed one prayer, not made one moan
To thee for her, that 's as myself, Heaven knows !
Much less for this least self, that 's soon to die ;
Though it hath suffered somewhat. Thrice they bound
This body to their rack. Thou wast not by.
Thy friends were. Each dictated some fresh wound,
And all applauded. Let that pass. For man,
Not for myself, I end, as I began,
This letter, and this life.
With failing force,
But not with fainting faith, I lift the cry
That speeds my spirit on its sunward course
Beyond Death's night. And, as I lived, I die,
Man's friend ; imploring — though it be in vain —
From thee, from all — man's pity for man's pain !

ADOLPHUS, DUKE OF GUELDERS.

(FIFTEENTH AND SIXTEENTH CENTURIES.)

ADOLPHUS, Duke of Guelders, having died,
Was laid in pomp for men to see. Priests vied
With soldiers, which the most should honor him.
Borne on broad shoulders through the streets, with hymn
And martial music, the dead Duke in state
Reached Tournay. There they laid him in the great
Cathedral, where perpetual twilight dwells,
Misty with scents from silver thuribles;
Since it seems fitting that, where dead kings sleep,
The sacred air, by pious aids, should keep
A certain indistinctness faint and fine,
To awe the vulgar mind, and with divine
Solemnities of silence, and soft glooms,
Inspire due reverence around royal tombs.
So, in the great Cathedral, grand, he lay.

The Duke had gained his Dukedom in this way:
Once, on a winter night, ... these things were written
Four centuries ago, when men, frost-bitten,
Blew on their nails, and curst, to warm their blood,
The times, the taxes, and what else they could, ...
A hungry, bleak night sky, with frosty fires

Hung hard, and clipt with cold the chilly spires,
Bent, for some hateful purpose of its own,
To keep sharp watch upon the little town,
Which huddled in its shadow, as if there
'T was safest, trying to look unaware;
Earth gave it no assistance, and small cheer,
'Neath that sharp sky, resolved to interfere
For its affliction, but lockt up her hand,
Stared fiercely on man's need, and his command
Rejected, cold as kindness when it cools,
Or charity in some men's souls. The pools
And water-courses had become dead streaks
Of steely ice. The rushes in the creeks
Stood stiff as iron spikes. The sleety breeze,
Itself, had died for lack of aught to tease
On the gaunt oaks, or pine-trees numbed and stark.
All fires were out, and every casement dark
Along the flinty streets. A famisht mouse,
Going his rounds in some old dismal house,
Disconsolate (for since the last new tax
The mice began to gnaw each other's backs),
Seemed the sole creature stirring; save, perchance,
With steel glove slowly freezing to his lance,
A sullen watchman, half asleep, who stept
About the turret where the old Duke slept.

The young Duke, whom a waking thought, not new,
Had held from sleeping, the last night or two,
Considered he should sleep the better there,
Provided that the old Duke slept elsewhere.
Therefore (about four hundred years ago,
This point was settled by the young Duke so)
Adolphus — the last Duke of Egmont's race

Who reigned in Guelders, after whom the place
Lapsed into Burgundian line — put on
His surcoat, buckled fast his habergeon,
Went clinking up that turret stairway, came
To the turret chamber, whose dim taper flame
The gust that entered with him soon smote dead,
And found his father, sleeping in his bed
As sound as, just four hundred years ago,
Good Dukes and Kings were wont to sleep, you
know.

A meagre moon, malignant as could be,
Meanwhile made stealthy light enough to see
The way by to the bedside, and put out
A hand, too eager long to grope about
For what it sought. A moment after that,
The old Duke, wide awake and shuddering, sat
Stark upright in the moon; his thin gray hair
Pluckt out by handfuls; and that stony stare,
The seal which terror fixes on surprise,
Widening within the white and filmy eyes
With which the ghastly father gazed upon
Strange meanings in the grim face of the son.
The young Duke haled the old Duke by the
hair
Thus, in his nightgear, down the turret stair;
And made him trot, barefooted, on before
Himself, who rode a horseback, through the frore
And aching midnight, over frozen wold,
And icy mere. (That winter, you might hold
A hundred fairs, and roast a hundred sheep,
If you could find them, on the ice, so deep
The frost had fixt his floors on driven piles.)
From Grave to Buren, five-and-twenty miles,

The young Duke hunted through the hollow night
The old Duke, like a phantom, flitting white
Through darkness into darkness, and the den
Where great men falling are forgot by men.
There in a dungeon, where newts dwell, beneath
The tower of Buren Castle, until death
Took him, he lingered very miserably;
Some say for months; some, years. Though Burgundy
Summoned both son and father to appear
Before him, ere the end of that same year,
And sought to settle, after mild rebuke,
Some sort of compromise between the Duke
And the Duke's father. But it failed.
This way
The Duke had gained his Dukedom.
At Tournay,
Afterwards, in the foray on that town,
He fell; and, being a man of much renown,
And very noble, with befitting state,
Was royally interred within the great
Cathedral. There, with work of costly stones
And curious craft, above his ducal bones
They builded a fair tomb. And over him
A hundred priests chanted the holy hymn.
Which being ended, ... "Our archbishop" (says
A chronicler, writing about those days)
"Held a most sweet discourse." . . . . And so, the psalm
And silver organ ceasing, in his calm
And costly tomb they left him; with his face,
Turned ever upward to the altar-place,
Smiling in marble from the shrine below.

These things were done four hundred years ago,
Adolphus, Duke of Guelders, in this way
First having gained his Dukedom, as I say.
After which time, the great Duke Charles the Bold
Laid hold on Guelders, and kept fast his hold.
Times change: and with the times too change the men.
A hundred years have rolled away since then.
I mean, since "Our archbishop" sweetly preached
His sermon on the dead Duke, unimpeached
Of flattery in the fluent phrase that just
Tinkled the tender moral o'er the dust
Of greatness, and with flowers of Latin strewed,
To edify a reverent multitude,
The musty surface of the faded theme,
"All flesh is grass: man's days are but a dream."
A bad dream, surely, sometimes: waking yet
Too late deferred! Such honors to upset,
Such wrongs to right, such far truths to attain,
Time, though he toils along the road amain,
Is still behindhand; never quite gets through
The long arrears of work he finds to do.
You call Time swift? it costs him centuries
To move the least of human miseries
Out of the path he treads. You call Time strong?
He does not dare to smite an obvious wrong
Aside, until 't is worn too weak to stand
The faint dull pressure of his feeble hand.
The crazy wrong, and yet how safe it thrives!
The little lie, and yet how long it lives!
Meanwhile, I say, a hundred years have rolled
O'er the Duke's memory.

Now, again behold!

Late gleams of dwindled daylight, glad to go:
A sullen autumn evening, scowling low
On Tournay: a fierce sunset, dying down
In clots of crimson fire, reminds a town
Of starving, stormy people, how the glare
Sunk into eyes of agonized despair,
When placid pastors of the flock of Christ
Had finished roasting their last Calvinist.
A hot and lurid night is steaming up,
Like a foul film out of some witch's cup,
That swarms with devils spawned from her damned
charms.
For the red light of burning burgs and farms
Oozes all round, beneath the locked black lids
Of heaven. Something on the air forbids
A creature to feel happy, or at rest.
The night is cursed, and carries in her breast
A guilty conscience. Strange, too! since of late
The Church is busy, putting all things straight,
And taking comfortable care to keep
The fold snug, and all prowlers from the sheep.
To which good end, upon this self-same night,
A much dismayed Town Council has thought right
To set a Guard of Terror round about
The great Cathedral; fearing lest a rout
Of these misguided creatures, prone to sin,
As lately proven, should break rudely in
There, where Adolphus, Duke of Guelders, and
Other dead dukes, by whom this happy land
Was once kept quiet in good times gone by,
With saints and bishops sleeping quietly,
Enjoy at last the slumber of the just;
In marble; mixing not their noble dust
With common clay of the inferior dead.

Therefore you hear, with moody, measured tread,
This Guard of Terror going its grim watch,
Through ominous silence. Scarce sufficient match,
However, even for a hundred lean,
Starved wretches, lasht to madness, having seen
Somewhat too long, or too unworthily looked
Upon, their vile belongings being cooked
To suit each priestly palate. . . . . If to-night
Those mad dogs slip the muzzle, 'ware their bite!

And so, perchance, the thankless people thought:
For, as the night wore off, a much-distraught
And murmurous crowd came thronging wild to where,
I' the market-place, each stifled thoroughfare
Disgorges its pent populace about
The great Cathedral.
Suddenly, a shout,
As though Hell's brood had broken loose, rocked all
Heaven's black roof dismal and funereal.
As when a spark is dropt into a train
Of nitre, swiftly ran from brain to brain
A single fiery purpose, and at last
Exploded, roaring down the vague and vast
Heart of the shaken city. Then a swell
Of wrathful faces, irresistible,
Sweeps to the great Cathedral doors; disarms
The Guard; roars up the hollow nave; and swarms
Through aisle and chancel, fast as locusts sent
Through Egypt's chambers, thick and pestilent.

There, such a sight was seen, as, now and then,

When half a world goes mad, makes sober men
In after years, who comfortably sit
In easy-chairs to weigh and ponder it,
Revise the various theories of mankind,
Puzzling both others and themselves to find
New reasons for unreasonable old wrongs.

Yells, howlings, cursings; grim tumultuous
throngs;
The metamorphoses of mad despair:
Men with wolves' faces, women with fierce hair
And frenzied eyes, turned furies: over all
The torchlight tossing in perpetual
Pulsation of tremendous glare or gloom.
They climb, they cling from altar-piece and tomb;
Whilst pickaxe, crowbar, pitchfork, billet, each
Chance weapon caught within the reckless reach
Of those whose single will a thousand means
Subserve to (terrible wild kings and queens,
Whose sole dominions are despairs), through all
The marble monuments majestical
Go crashing. Basalt, lapis, syenite,
Porphyry, and pediment, in splinters bright,
Tumbled with claps of thunder, clattering
Roll down the dark. The surly sinners sing
A horrible black santis, so to cheer
The work in hand. And evermore you hear
A shout of awful joy, as down goes some
Three-hundred-years-old treasure. Crowded, come
To glut the greatening bonfire, chalices
Of gold and silver, copes and cibories,
Stained altar-cloths, spoiled pictures, ornaments,
Statues, and broken organ tubes and vents,
The spoils of generations all destroyed

In one wild moment! Possibly grown cloyed
And languid, then a lean iconoclast,
Drooping a sullen eyelid, fell at last
To reading lazily the letters graven
Around the royal tomb, red porphyry-paven,
Black-pillared, snowy-slabbed, and sculptured fair,
He sat on, listless, with spiked elbows bare.
When (suddenly inspired with some new hate
To yells, the hollow roofs reverberate
As though the Judgment-Angel passed among
Their rafters, and the great beams clanged and
rung
Against his griding wing) he shrieks: "Come
forth,
Adolphus, Duke of Guelders! for thy worth
Should not be hidden." Forthwith, all men shout:
"Strike, split, crash, dig, and drag the tyrant out!
Let him be judged!" And from the drowsy, dark,
Enormous aisles, a hundred echoes bark
And bellow, — "Judged!"

Then those dread lictors all,
Marching before the magisterial
Curule of tardy Time, with rod and axe,
Fall to their work. The cream-white marble
cracks,
The lucid alabaster flies in flakes,
The iron bindings burst, the brickwork quakes
Beneath their strokes, and the great stone lid
shivers
With thunder on the pavement. A torch quivers
Over the yawning vault. The vast crowd draws
Its breath back hissing. In that sultry pause
A man o'erstrides the tomb, and drops beneath;

Another; then another. Still its breath
The crowd holds, hushful. At the last appears,
Unravaged by a hundred wicked years,
Borne on broad shoulders from the tomb to which
Broad shoulders bore him; coming, in his rich
Robes of magnificence (by sweating thumbs
Of savage artisans, — as each one comes
To stare into his dead face, — smeared and smudged),
Adolphus, Duke of Guelders, ... to be judged!

And then and there, in that strange judgment-hall,
As, gathering round their royal criminal,
Troopt the wild jury, the dead Duke was found
To be as fresh in face, in flesh as sound,
As though he had been buried yesterday;
So well the embalmer's work from all decay
Had kept his royal person. With his great
Grim truncheon propt on hip, his robe of state
Heaped in vast folds his large-built limbs around,
The Duke lay, looking as in life; and frowned
A frown that seemed as of a living man.

Meanwhile those judges their assize began.
And, having, in incredibly brief time,
Decided that in nothing save his crime
The Duke exceeded mere humanity,
Free, for the first time, its own cause to try,
So long ignored, — they peeled him, limb by limb,
Bare of the mingled pomps that mantled him;
Stript, singed him, stabbed him, stampt upon him, smote
His cheek, and spat upon it, slit his throat,

Crusht his big brow, and clove his crown, and left
Adolphus, Guelders' last own Duke, bereft
Of sepulture, and naked, on the floor
Of the Cathedral. Where, six days or more
He rested, rotting. What remained, indeed,
After the rats had had their daily feed,
Of the great Duke, some unknown hand, 't is said,
In the town cesspool, last, deposited.*

* "Et, comme ecrit Philippe de Comines (qui mêsmes a été employé en ce different par le Duc Charles de Bourgongne) le dit Adolph alla de nuict en plein hyver prendre son vieux pere hors du lict, et lui fit faire pieds nus cincq lieues de chemin, et le detint six mois prisonier en une profonde et obscure prison . . . . Le Duc Charles de Bourgongne tacha par plusieurs fois de reconcilier le pere et le fils, mais en vain . . . . Sur quoy le fils repondit qu'il aymoit mieux jêter son pere en un puits, et s'y precipiter apres luy que de consentir à un tel accord, disant que son pere avoit gouverné 44 ans, et que partant il estoit maintenant temps qu'il gouvernait aussi quelque peu." — D. Emanuel V. Meteren. Traduict de Flamend en Françoys par I. D. L. Haye, 1618.

"Il alla vers Tournay, où il fut tué par les Français en une escarmouche, non obstant qu'il ne fit que crier Gueldre! Gueldre! ce qui luy arriva selon le juste jugement de Dieu pour sa grande rebellion." — *Ibid.*, Fol. 9.

THE DUKE'S LABORATORY.

(A SCENE FROM FLORENCE IN THE SIXTEENTH CENTURY.)*

Persons represented.

FRANCESCO DEI MEDICI. *Grand Duke of Florence.*
PAOLO GIORDANO ORSINI, DUKE OF BRACCIANO. *The Grand Duke's Brother-in-law.*
FRA LUKE. *The Grand Duke's Alchemist.*

(Night. Interior of the Laboratory at the Pitti.)

FRA LUKE.

Another moment, and 't is finisht! Ha,
The white precipitate begins to form!
We 'll set thee there, Death's Angel. Presently
Thou shalt be sphered.

Good ignorant folks believe
The art of kingcraft's writ in histories
By sages, conned from chronicles, and shaped
I' the council chamber. Fools! that wicked craft

* A portion of the dialogue between Francesco and Bracciano is taken from Signor Guerrazzi's Racconto of "Isabella Orsini." The Grand Duke's parting injunction to his brother-in-law is historical. The subject has been incidentally treated, in his "White Devil," by Webster; to whom one of his contemporary eulogists addresses these lines: —

"Brachiano's Ill,
Murthering his Dutchesse, hath by thy rare skill
Made him renowned."

Lies hidden here. And who would study it
Must be content to soil his hands . . . . like these!
(That stain hath never come away, — nor will.
And now the story that it tells is old
As the new fortunes of this House!) . . . . must soil
His hands, I say, as these be soiled, and make
That sort of surgeon's needle of his mind
Which may go through the bloody matter crammed
Into these murtherous manuals of death;
Wherein some monk, among his crucibles,
Hath noted down how such and such an one,
That plotted, prospered, sinned, and still slept sound,
Displeased a Prince on such and such a day,
And presently men missed him: such a lady,
With eyes so lustrous dark, and lips so red,
Wore roses in her bosom at the ball,
On such a night, and whispered one that smiled
Beside her for a moment in the dance,
"To-morrow I await thee," then went home
Happy, and slept, and never waked: or how
On such a day the Conte de Virtù
Poisoned his uncle in a dish of beans,
With something in the salt, — which some surmise,
Erroneously, white hellebore, but he
That writes hath proved it arsenic. This, at least,
Is policy in the school of Cosimo!

And, night by night, I, sitting here, hatch death
For this detested race, whose badge I wear, —
The better to destroy them! who, for this,
Deem me their servant . . . . *me*, pale, patient slave
Of one sublime Idea, that, sitting throned
At God's right hand, looks down and laughs at
kings,

While the slow hours lead on her destined day,
The Nemesis of History! *me,* whose back
Is bent to this, by culling bitter herbs
To swell this scum, till it boil o'er, and purge
The rising caldron of the wrath of God!

O thou, my martyred brother, sainted soul,
Dear murdered ghost, that, unavenged, criest out
To shame Heaven's silence, — Fra Girolamo!
We two were servants to the same Idea:
Thou, in the sun; I, in the shadow; thou
The judge, and I the executioner.
Which chose the surer service? Didst thou deem
Of such vile stuff as these degenerate times
Show all men made of, to rebuild anew
This broken Italy, and transmute to gold,
For Freedom's crown, mixt metal so made up
Of meanest elements? O, too dearly paid,
Error too noble! This flawed crucible,
And these dead minerals which, year by year,
I to ennoble have so idly toiled,
Might teach us both the folly of that dream.
But thou art gone. And still the rabble crowd,
That freed Barabbas and rejected Christ,
Caps to the common tyrant. I work on,
Patient as Death. Because my trust is rather
In man's crimes than his virtues. Rather here,
With Messer Nicolo Machiavelli, brother
(Whose book 's the bible of that bitter faith
Thy life rejected, but thy death confirms),
Than in the force of any single life
To leaven this dead lump, and quicken it
With such a heat as in thine ashes left
The latest human hope of Florence cold,

Lost Savonarola! Let the shames o' the time
Increase and multiply! the swifter speeds
The hour of renovation, summonsing
To the stern sessions of the assembled Fates
Earth's full-grown wickednesses.

Sons of Cain,
Prosper, — and perish! whiles I nurse your race
For condemnation. I, whose eyes have seen
The father buried, and whose hands have hope
To sepulchre the sons! Who takes the sword
Shall perish by it. Be it mine to sow
The cropping seed, whilst thou, dread harvester
Of lusty sins, laborious Liberty,
Whose foison is the full-eared field of Time,
Sett'st to the sickle sharp thy scorned right hand,
Which shall anon with unrelenting swathe
Reap in the ruddy upsprout.
Hist! Who knocks?

FRANCESCO (*without*).

Francesco.

FRA LUKE.

Enter, Highness!

FRANCESCO (*entering*).

Salvum tibi!
Is the stuff ready?

FRA LUKE.

Yes. But it must cool.

FRANCESCO.

O, we can wait. How many drops?

FRA LUKE.

One, Highness.

FRANCESCO.

Is that enough? Well, life 's a vapor, Friar.
Man's flesh is but the flower of the field,
And in the midst of life we are in death.
Last night the Cavaliere Antenori
Expired, at Twelve. He did confess his sins,
And died, I trust, repentant. Heaven have mercy
Upon his soul!

FRA LUKE.

Amen. What died he of?

FRANCESCO.

An apoplexy.

FRA LUKE.

Ah, ... I comprehend!
The cause, — a cord about the jugular.

FRANCESCO.

Peace, Monk! A man dies by the hand of God.
The scandal grew . . . . Why even King Philip
writes, —
But let that pass. *De mortuis*, Fra Luke,
Nil nisi bonum. But for Eleanora . . . .

FRA LUKE.

Is this for her?

FRANCESCO.

What? what? you question me?
Beware! But I have spoken with Don Pietro.
The honor of our brother's wife, Fra Luke!
By Bacchus! and the thing is infamous.
Let him look to it!

FRA LUKE.

Ay.

FRANCESCO.

But he 's so light!
Heady and light. 'T is idle talking to him.
And eaten up with debts. And vices. Zounds,
'T is the most infamous knight in Christendom!
Without a spark of honor — piety —
The most ungodly Good-for-naught . . . . 'Faith,
Friar,
We are not fortunate in our family,
Nothing but scandals! I am all day long
Whitewashing their iniquities; and still
Our House stinks in men's nostrils — and they
know it —
Worse than a plague-pit!

FRA LUKE.

But your Highness soon
Will make it quite a whited sepulchre.
O my good lord, how well this noble zeal

For the fair fame of your illustrious House
Becomes your august father's glorious son!
Could you but know how fervent is my faith
In that vast work, for whose accomplishment
My soul divines in your great daily deeds
The unanswerable warrant of High God!
But shrink not! shrink not! you have far to go,
And much to do, — in furtherance of God's will.
Shrink not, great Master of the Medici!

FRANCESCO.

Fra Luke, Fra Luke! pray Heaven to yield us strength.
We have most painful duties to perform.

FRA LUKE.

My nightly prayer is that your Highness ever
May — as you do — perform them.

FRANCESCO.

I have pledged
The mother of that lad, she shall not lack
Justice. But we must have no public prate.
It must be done discreetly.

FRA LUKE.

What lad, Master?

FRANCESCO.

That — Page of Isabella's — what 's his name?
Lelio, I think — that Troïlo Orsini
Most impudently did assassinate,

With no consideration for ourselves,
Nor for the Church of God. — For, think, Fra
Luke!
The brat was stabbed in our own livery,
And died before he could his sins confess,
In our own sister's house — before her face —
By day — and on a Sunday! What 's the hour?

FRA LUKE.

Nigh midnight, by the Duomo clock. I heard
Three quarters striking to the middle night,
A little while before your Highness knocked.

FRANCESCO.

I 'll see him now, then. Go. The southwest wing,
(But not by the grand staircase, for your life!)
There 's, in the little chamber, where last stood
That vase I sent His Catholic Majesty, —
My porcelain — you remember? — the new shape —
Now waiting — you shall know him by the plume —
A white one — in his hat — a man much injured:
Our sister's husband, Paolo Giordano
Orsini, of Bracciano. Bring him here
By the masked stairway. And be careful, Monk,
To slip the spear back in the Cupid's hand
That 's last of all the group, which, clustered, hides
The spring I showed you, that unlocks the door
Between the two great mirrors. (Twenty Loves
Fighting a hare: Bianca's notion that,
And Venice work.) The Duke and I have business.
And you will find him waiting. Go.

FRA LUKE.

Your Highness,
Like the true artist, no detail neglects,
But your least work is thorough.

FRANCESCO.

Flatterer!
We all must do what little good we can.
Life is so short! Be quick.

FRA LUKE.

(More murder!) Sir,
Your Highness shall not wait. I'll bring the Duke.
[*Exit* FRA LUKE.

FRANCESCO (*alone*).

Ay. Life is short, so short! Brief, brief and evil!
O what a business have I here, to purge
Of its bad blood this fat and pursy time,
And keep a decent cleanness in my Court!
When am I ever idle? Where's the Prince
In Christendom, whatever Philip says,
That's more decorous, or more circumspect
Than I, more nicely careful to maintain
Proper appearances in men and things,
And yet withal, — the shame of it's in that, —
More harassed in his house by kindred more
Disorderly, more thankless! Ferdinand, —
And he a Cardinal, and my heir, — that's worse!
Curse him! he's nothing but a conduit, he,
Perpetually conducting Christian coin
Out of the coffers of my careful thrift
Into the greasy purses of the Jews:

Making himself (a pillar of the Church !)
Chief corner-stone o' the new Jerusalem.
Small thanks to him, if I myself some day
Be not in Abraham's bosom ! Heaven knows how
My substance goes to fatten Abraham's seed.
And the rogues multiply ! Abram begets
Isaac, and Isaac Jacob. Pietro, too,
The most unblushing profligate that breathes,
Connives, unshamed, at his own cuckledom !
And sister Isabella . . . . 'sdeath ! I 'll make
A clean sweep this time. Let them look to it.
'Sdeath ! even Philip shall be satisfied.

[*The clock strikes outside from the Duomo.*

Hark ! there 's another day gone. Coin by coin,
The scrupulous Time tells out his sounding sum,
And rings the tested metal, that he owes
Eternity, that usurer of life,
Which, lending little, takes our all at last,
And gives back nothing got.

Go, coin of time,
No longer current ! pay in part life's loan.
Go, with the image of a Christian Prince
Stamped on thee, to the treasury of Heaven !
Bear witness for me to the King of kings,
That I, Francesco dei Medici,
Grand Duke of Florence by the grace of God,
That grace requite by no disgraceful rule,
Uphold the Church, promote Religion, keep
Morality respected, and pluck off
Even from the cherisht body of my House
Offending limbs. Bear witness there 's no deed
Done in the dark against Heaven's Throne, or mine,

(Which to keep heavenly white is my desire,)
But I have eyes to see it, and no place
On earth so distant, where ill-doers hide,
But I have arms to reach it.

Welcome, Duke!

BRACCIANO (*entering with* FRA LUKE).

Your Highness' humble servant. What strange place
Is this I stand in?

FRANCESCO.

The State's workshop, Sir.
Good simple soldier, in this little cell
The spider, Policy, all arms, all eyes,
Spins, unperceived, the crafty web that takes
That buzzing fool, the world. My father, Duke,
He was a man by all mankind esteemed
Most fortunate. His hair, before its time,
Grew gray with study. Study of what, you wonder?
Chemicals. Studied where? Here, in this cell.
Chemistry, Soldier, trust me, is a science
Which now-a-days we sceptred students need
To study more than your rough art of war.
But that 's beyond. Be seated, brave Bracciano.
We prove our love and confidence in you,
Seeing you here, where few have seen us. Sit.

BRACCIANO.

I wait your Highness' orders.

FRANCESCO.

True. But stay,
You have not slept upon the road from Rome.
For that we thank you. 'T was not without cause
That our despatch was urgent. But, no doubt,
You must be tired and hungry, and in need
Of some refreshment. Ope the door, Fra Luke.
There 's supper in the anteroom.

BRACCIANO.

No, no!
I am not hungry. I have supped elsewhere.
I thank your Highness, but —

FRANCESCO.

Tut! tut! a glass
Of Cyprus wine? a brace of beccafiche?

BRACCIANO.

My Lord, no, thank you. Savory though they be,
These chemicals of yours scarce whet the edge
Of a man's appetite; and as for me,
I have about me no digestive stuff,
No spider paste, no powdered unicorn horn,
Or any other kind of stimulant
Against a too-long after-dinner sleep.

FRANCESCO.

Ha, ha, Bracciano! ever sharp and merry!

BRACCIANO.

No, Sir. Most sad and sober. You were pleased

To invite me hither with some urgency
Which yet I know no cause for. Being come
From Rome in haste to hear them, I now wait
Your Highness' orders.

FRANCESCO.

Leave us, then, Fra Luke.
You shall be satisfied, good brother-in-law.
A word, Fra Luke! Your pardon, dear Orsini.
But if you knew what lovers you have here
(I and Fra Luke. Is it not so, Fra Luke?)
Of the true masters of the Tuscan tongue!
There 's in our private library, Fra Luke,
Fresh from the printer's hand . . . . what type! what type!
The purified and expurgated text, —
'T is by the Cavaliere Leonardo, —
Of the Decameron of Boccaccio.
Be good enough to look at it. One thing
Is sure, at least, — you will admire the type.
And let us know your mind upon the text
Presently. On the whole, it seems to us
The Cavaliere has succeeded well,
And with no common skill, in no slight task.
So many shocking and unseemly parts
In the first nude robustness of the text
Needing to be decorously concealed
In flowers of language carefully arranged,
Or from the body of the book removed
Wholly, with such incision nice as leaves
No beauty blemished. Look at it, Fra Luke.
O, what a fallen thing is Human Nature!
Alas, alas, Fra Luke! is it not sad

That such a genius, such a man as this
Messer Giovanni, should be damned? And yet,
What can we think, Fra Luke? what must we fear?
Such genius with such immorality!
Sad! sad!

FRA LUKE.

The Almighty knows the world too well
To expect five legs of mutton from a sheep.
The best of us, in our imperfectness,
Must largely count upon that tolerance
In him that, having made, best knows, mankind.
But, may it please your Highness, there's no doubt
Messer Giovanni did repent his sins
Upon his death-bed, and so passed in peace.

FRANCESCO.

Are you quite sure of that? I am very glad.
A man of so much genius! And you say
He saw, at last, Fra Luke, and did repent,
The many errors of his pen? Well, well,
Morality thus triumphs at the last.
It comforts me to think he is not damned.
May it be true!

BRACCIANO.

('Sblood! am I his tame hawk?
To be held hooded on the hand of him,
While he — the pepper merchant —) I remind
Your Highness that, not having yet the honor
To be a lackey of the Medici,
I lack that patientness which, as it seems,
Such office craves.

FRANCESCO.

Indeed?

[*In his ear, after surveying him a moment in silence.*

Restrain this fire
A moment. We must fuel it anon.
Off then, Fra Luke, into the Library!
Peruse Boccaccio till we call.

FRA LUKE.

I go, Sir.
(The spider and the wasp. I back the spider.)

[*Exit* FRA LUKE.

FRANCESCO.

Be seated, Duke. Be seated. Now, to business.

[*After a pause.*

Duke of Bracciano, our good brother-in-law,
It needs not now that we remember you
Of our past loves, and care for your good name:
Whose house so neighbors ours, that fire lit there
Must burn ourselves.

BRACCIANO.

I know your Highness' goodness,
And — as it merits — thank it. Pray, my lord,
Come quickly to the matter.

FRANCESCO.

Sir, at once.
Which, were it less notorious than we know it,
I could have fain forgotten. O my lord,

We are the laughing-stock of this lewd town!
I am in you offended, you in me.
Our most unworthy sister — your worse wife —
O'ertasks the common tongue to count up all
Her manifold misconducts.

BRACCIANO.

Isabella!

FRANCESCO.

No better than a strumpet, good Bracciano.

BRACCIANO.

Uncivil Sir, he lives not that dare say it!
Were 't in the Duomo's self, I 'd strangle him.

FRANCESCO.

O much, my lord, I must lament the cause,
As much I do admire your noble anger.
And then, to think the traitor lives —

BRACCIANO.

His name?

FRANCESCO.

Who hath so wickedly abused your faith
Too fondly given — all ties of blood — all titles
That honor 's held by —

BRACCIANO.

Hell, and all its devils!
His name? his name?

FRANCESCO.

Ay, that 's the worst of all.

BRACCIANO.

I am stifling.

FRANCESCO.

Though the town might tell it thee.

BRACCIANO.

The name, Grand Duke of Florence ?

FRANCESCO.

Troïlo
Orsini, and thy cousin.

BRACCIANO.

Troïlo !

FRANCESCO.

Most basely hath betrayed you.

BRACCIANO.

Bear with me.

FRANCESCO.

Ay. Realize that first. It will take time.
For such things toughly task credulity
In all men's natures, but the soldier's most ;
Whose noble wont is never to expect
The blow that stabs behind. But, for the proofs
Of this bad truth . . . . no matter ! they can wait.

Duke, I have brooded on these wrongs of yours
Till . . . .

BRACCIANO.

Yes. I understand. In such a place
As this . . . . what must I call it, Duke of Florence?

FRANCESCO.

Grand Duke, Orsini.

BRACCIANO.

Certainly. Most grand!
In this detestable den of yours, I say,
Where nothing wholesome is, naught 's natural
But what is wholly monstrous. Here you hatch
Each chance-spawned slander of the chattering town,
Shut in this stew where no good air is breathed,
Where each vile fancy cooks her fœtid eggs,
Where all abominable thoughts are brewed,
Until at last, from brooding on these things,
These lies . . . .

FRANCESCO.

Bracciano!

BRACCIANO.

If you spake the truth
Your countenance . . . .

FRANCESCO.

Be still, unhappy man!

By Bacchus! married men are mostly fools,
But you are an amazing maniac.

BRACCIANO.

Troïlo? Now I'll tell you why I know
That is a lie. When he and I were boys —

FRANCESCO.

When you and he were boys! Are you a man?

BRACCIANO.

Ay, and at nature's manly bidding spurn
The lie which wrongs all natural manliness.
You are deceived, my lord. I'll not believe it.

FRANCESCO.

You are deceived. Most wickedly deceived.

BRACCIANO.

I'll not believe it.

FRANCESCO.

Duke, you *will:* though now
You would not. O unhappy infidel,
Already all the town doth pity thee.

BRACCIANO.

That cannot be. Were this the stalèd jest
Of street and tavern, as your talk implies,
I should, myself, have heard it.

FRANCESCO.

What, at Rome?

BRACCIANO.

Why not at Rome? There 's talk enough in Rome
That 's little to the credit, as it goes,
Of the illustrious family of my wife.

FRANCESCO.

My lord, we know it. More behooves it us
To silence this same talk. But married men
Are a strange kind of asses with short ears
That are not quickly tickled by such talk.
It is the mercy, Duke, of Providence
That made them thus.

BRACCIANO.

Prince, you may be deceived.
Even Princes know not everything.

FRANCESCO.

Ay, Duke.
But one — Francesco dei Medici —
Knows everything — at least in Florence. Much
To you and me, my lord, it matters not
If true or false the talk of Florence town.
The talking town talks of us. That 's enough.
The fault of that 's in Isabella now.
If talk goes on, the fault will be in us.
For we are gentlemen and Christians, Duke.
I have a brother's duty to perform,
And you a husband's. But the talk 's all true,

It happens, this time. By and by peruse
These papers, Duke. And learn betimes to know
That I know everything.

BRACCIANO.

Most wretched man,
Thou buyest thy knowledge at too dear a price!
That which we know must make us ignorant
Of happiness forever: ignorant
Of wholesome human faith forevermore.
O God, the misery of knowing this!
The misery of it!

FRANCESCO.

Ay. 'T is bad enough.
You see, that rascal Troïlo has spoiled all
Our care to keep things quiet. But for this
We might have let your Duchess grow in peace
That crop of horns for her wise husband's head,
Which now, I fear, must off with some sharp lopping.
But he, the fool, for stupid jealousy
Of some well-looking lad, a sort of Page
Of Isabel's, I think, — no name, no name, —
Good honest country folk his kindred are,
And scandalized amazingly, — almost
It makes me smile, their infinite surprise
And indignation at what, after all,
Was, though on his part an immense mistake,
Yet, in its way, a kind of compliment
From such a man as your illustrious cousin
To their unlucky kinsman: but, you see,
As I was telling you, from jealousy

This foolish Troïlo has stabbed the youth,
Almost in public. And, in short, the thing
Has made an ugly talk about us all.
And this dead cub's curst dam is shrieking out
For law, and justice, and the devil knows what,
To me, Grand Duke of Florence.

BRACCIANO.

Troïlo!
The gentle, ever-quiet, small, weak boy
I used to carry, when we two were young,
Upon my back — barefooted I, and he
Hugging my neck, while, like a wise church daw,
He chattered, with sagacious spriteliness
(The sagest little man that ever was!)
High up the mountain torrents! Troïlo!
Him that I taught to ride, to fence, to swim,
And never yet could teach an evil thing,
Rebuked, as well my boisterous youth might be,
By that girl's face of his! My Troïlo,
My more than cousin, sister-brother! he
To whose chaste woman-hands I gave in charge,
As to a saint's, my honor and my home!

FRANCESCO.

Most villanously hath betrayed them both.
Bracciano, milk that 's spilt . . . . You know the proverb.
Think only how you best may be avenged.

BRACCIANO.

Avenged? on whom? on what? On all mankind,
For being what I now must deem men all,

Traitors and knaves? No better, sure, the rest,
Than my most trusted friend! All women, too?
For being — what my wife has proved they are,
That was the best of them I ever knew!
Vengeance? on all the world! for all the world
Is my wrong-doer, — suffering such wrongs in it.
Vengeance? on Heaven! that made, and yet maintains,
So vile a world as this. O where, where, where,
In all the armory of human wrath
At most inhuman wrongs, shall I find arms
Enough for such a vengeance?

FRANCESCO.

Stoop thine ear.
Stay! let me first make sure we are unheard.
Keyholes have ears: those ears have tongues: those tongues
Utterance: and I, myself, the great arch spy,
From parasitic spies am never free.
No! I have tried the doors. All 's fast! This way.
Now listen.

[*Whispers.*

BRACCIANO.

Devil! thou has poured hellfire
Into my veins!

FRANCESCO.

Thou hast no choice, Bracciano.

BRACCIANO.

Forbid it, Heaven!

FRANCESCO.

O, Heaven doth forbid it,
But Isabel hath done it.

BRACCIANO.

Misery!

FRANCESCO.

Undoubtedly. But duty, not the less.
Duty, Bracciano, duty!

BRACCIANO.

And my boy,
My innocent brat! When he shall ask one day,
"Father, where is my mother?" God will listen,
And only Hell dare answer!

FRANCESCO.

Bah! Myself,
I 'll answer. Tush, the boy need never know:
Or, knowing it, he shall approve the deed.
I 'll educate him.

BRACCIANO.

You? And after death
Must come the judgment.

FRANCESCO.

She is judged already.
'Sdeath, Duke! What wrongs are mine to match
with yours?

Yet she I sacrifice to your just wrath
And righteous vengeance is my sister.

BRACCIANO.

Ay,
But not the mother of thy children. O,
If they must lose their lives, all they whose names
Are lost in credit by a losel tongue,
There 'll be none living left to slay the rest.
Why should I rashly ratify the word
Of the unthinking rabble?

FRANCESCO.

Cæsar's wife
(Remember, Duke, what Suetonius says)
He suffered not to be suspected even.

BRACCIANO.

Ay, man. But still he did not murder her.

FRANCESCO.

Hush! murder 's not the word.

BRACCIANO.

O, judgment, is it?
Just judges are we, I and thou, Francesco!
Listen to me, Sir. I 'm no hypocrite.
Whose fault was, first of all, this hideous coil?
O, do you think that I deceive myself
Enough to be deceived by you? Sir, hear me.
Here was I, Head of the Orsini, son
Of a long line of ducal sires, whose names

Were old, — incalculably old, I say,
Before the first small Medici was dropt
Into this world, by chance, to make what way
Chance still might help him to find out through it.
So far, so well. What, then, was mine to want?
Money. To get which, what was mine to give?
Just this same ducal name, and lineage old,
With something here and there in men's esteem,
Which, born with these, Wealth, born without it, buys.
You had the wealth, you Medici: and I
What, needing wealth, is still by wealth desired.
So I said, — or, to say the truth, not I —
But all friends said to me, — "This Isabel,
A daughter of the Medici, is rich,
Young, too, and beautiful, as all admit,
Secure the money with the girl, Orsini!"
And you, — illustrious pepper-merchants all,
Pray what said you? O, "Let him take the girl,
And take the money, whereby we take him,
The threadbare duke, with his unbroken line
And broken castles, — just the man we want!"
So much for us. The world, of course, cried, Bravo!
Clapped hands, extolled the "Suitable Alliance."
Which one of all of us once asked himself,
"But what, for her part, does the lady gain?
Has she, by chance, a heart? and what says that?
Well, I believe that I have been no worse,
If, at the best, no better on the whole,
Than other men thus suitably allied.
I liked my wife, admired, respected her;
Took it for granted she should be content

To fill the proper place up in my life
Where she was wanted, and remain therein,
Just as you take for granted the stone saint
Will stay, and decently demean himself,
In that particular cathedral niche
The architect allots him, heeding not
The dulness or the chillness of the place.
And when, to crown it all, there came an heir
Both to the money and the name to boot,
Content with that result, which seemed the end,
Small further care about my wife had I,
Than to select the best man I could find
(He seemed so then) to take up and perform
The *duties* — (mark! not daring to desire
The dear *reward* love's care of love receives) —
Of guardian of the honor of a wife
Whose spouse . . . . O, there's no dearth of weighty cause
For my continued absence: fame, the field,
The Church's banner, then, the friendship vowed
Don John, Lepanto, — man's career, in short!
Of course, meanwhile, with business pleasure goes:
Of course I have my mistresses: my wife
No doubt has heard the Accorombona's name:
But that's a trifle. All's allowed to men.
Of course a wife in fault has no excuse.
Of course, although we rate the women all
As three times weaker than our worthless selves,
We yet expect, we have the right to expect,
That they shall be thrice stronger. Wherefore not?
Man can appeal to man. Woman to whom?
Man's both her judge and executioner.
Woe to her if she slips! Just judges we!

FRANCESCO.

Bracciano, all this . . . .

BRACCIANO.

Interrupt me not!
You 're in the way of it. Your turn is coming.
For what was my worst, maddest, wickedest
Of all mistakes? To dream that I could leave,
Even for an hour, with hope to find again,
Man's honesty or woman's virtue, here
In the foul precincts of this cursèd Court,
Where all the air 's one malady, and all
That breathe it are distempered! here, I say,
Where every shape and kind of wickedness,
For which the name 's to find yet, grows and
thrives,
And at the top of all its hateful growth,
Fed with the sinful sap of all the rest,
Puts forth the crowning vice, — Hypocrisy!
Ha, ha! Grand Duke of Florence, I thank God
For one thing heartily! I have made you wince,
And writhe, like the tormented snake you are.
You hate me; and I know a way to hurt you:
That comforts me a little. Hypocrite!
Do you begin to feel that, after all,
The Devil 's not so safe in Hell, but what
A ray of Heaven gets at him now and then,
And stings him through all custom?

FRANCESCO.

Madman, and fool!
Do you forget that you are in my power?

BRACCIANO.

I forget nothing. But you lie, Grand Duke.
Out of your power I have passed away
Forever, and you know it, this sad night.
How can you hurt me? you have done your worst.
You cannot hurt my wife. I have no wife.
My son? I know not if I have a son.
The adulteress has one. Would you hurt my friends?
There 's no man in the world I love or trust.
My name? Disgraced already, you aver.
My life? What 's life worth, lacking what mine
lacks?
But you 'll NOT take my life. First, for you cannot.
Easier could I kill you than you kill me.
We are alone, just now. Besides, I know,
And you know, that you dare not. Still to you
My life 's more useful than my death can be.
To me 't is useless now. Away with lies,
So thoroughly worn out, they but show the truth
They should conceal! Francesco, to speak plain,
We do not love each other, never did;
But all we ever had in common still
Remains to us. Community of wrong.

FRANCESCO.

Community of interest.

BRACCIANO.

As you please.
And so to finish this vile work of ours.
Only, for Heaven's sake, Sir, no fine names!
If all that you have said be true . . . .

FRANCESCO.

It is.
Convince yourself. The proofs are in your hand.

BRACCIANO.

Presently. 'T is the custom of our House.
And I 'll have surer warrant. Her own lips,
Not mine — not yours — no lips, no lips but hers
Shall sound the sentence, if confessed the crime.
My sentence! For the punishment is mine,
As mine the fault was. She must die.

FRANCESCO.

That 's sense.

BRACCIANO.

Die! yes. And then *my* punishment begins.
For I must live. There 's punishment for both.
Duke, ... *you* have dealings with that sort of
—men
I would not call them: yet there 's ne'er a rogue
In Florence, but, I doubt not he is worth
As much as any other honest man!
Pray, did you ever notice carefully
A hangman's countenance? I try to think
That I am altogether passed away
So far out of all human sense of what
My misery is, that I may dare assume
The inexorably stern judicial mood
Of God's Destroying Angel. You are witness
I have already judged, and have condemned,
Myself, — or rather say, the man I was
Once, and can never be again. Not he,
I try to think, — not he, but that man's judge,

Ascends the justice seat and summons forth
Unhappy Isabella to her doom.
But there 's a something left of man in me, —
I know not what, — 't is strangely out of place, —
That troubles all. And, turn which way I will,
These hands of mine still seem a hangman's hands,
And we two, here, conspirators, — worse, worse,
Cut-throats! and she our victim. Why is that?

FRANCESCO.

Because you are a simpleton. Because
Your mind, just now, puts all things out of place,
And your life's habit has not helped your will
To put them promptly in their places back.
I see in all this, — and see nothing else, —
Plainly, a duty, — painful, I admit,
Painful to me, no less, sir, than to you,
But still a duty, to be done, and done
At once, and, once done, straight from thought dismissed.
The duty 's ours: the consequence is not.
Was Abraham careful of the consequence
When, to please God, he sacrificed his son?
Or did he call himself a murderer?
Yet Abraham's son was guiltless. As for you,
Your wife is guilty. There 's no doubt of that.
You choose to call merely "fine names" what are
Really fine feelings. You are thoroughly wrong:
For are we Christian gentlemen, or not?
That 's the sole point, Duke.

BRACCIANO.

If we be, I say
God help the times!

FRANCESCO.

Amen. God help the times!
God help us all! And most of all, help me!
That have the most to bear of all of you.
And, Duke, you wrong me. Hypocrite I 'm not.
The world leaves its chief actors no such choice
As you may fancy, how to act their parts.
Dissimulation is imposed on us.
And, let me tell you, there are certain signs
Already in the crowd, — I can't say what,
I *feel* them, — that our parts must be played off
Quickly. I think I can, at times, detect
A certain ominous stir about the mass:
Strange faces with uncomfortable eyes:
New-comers, whom their places do not please:
Vague sounds not wholly satisfactory:
A restlessness that . . . . Well, it matters not!
I shall have played *my* part out, anyhow.
Let after-comers manage as they may.
Our stage is old. One of these days, perchance,
It may give way, and there 'll be broken bones.
I shall have strutted off it. Hypocrite
I am not. But profound dissimulator,
Yes. That 's my part. And hypocrite to you!
To you at least I have been frank enough.
Outspoken, like the friendly gentleman
You 'll have occasion yet to find I am.
But your unhappy state excuses all.
You 'll sober, and be sorry by and by.
In thus consulting you, thus timely, thus
Freely and unreservedly, on what
Is after all a matter that concerns,
With or without your leave, or any man's,

Ourselves in chief, (for Isabel 's our stuff,)
We think that we have shown you full regard,
Friendly and honorable confidence,
Deserving recognition. Aught, unknown
To you, we would not willingly have done.
But, knowing what you know, if it would ease
The sort of natural trouble your unuse
To such necessities now suffers, Duke,
We 'll rid your hands of what remains to do,
And undertake . . . .

BRACCIANO.

No, no! not you! not you!
To you 't would be no punishment. To me
'T is punishment already.

FRANCESCO.

As you will.
But you 're so hot! You 'll blunder, I half fear.
I need not say, do nothing unconvinced.
Convinced you will be. But remember, Duke,
No public talk, no scandal! Nothing rude,
Conspicuous, unseemly! What 's to do
Must be discreetly done. Ha, by the way,
My brother Ferdinand writes me word, Bracciano,
That you are much indebted: sorely prest
To make good certain obligations due,
Nor longer now renewable. Is that true?

BRACCIANO.

Pish! yes.

FRANCESCO.

Well, Duke, we 'll settle this for you

Count up your debts. Ah, if you only knew
How you have wronged us! But you 'll find that
out.
Count up your debts. We 'll pay them.

BRACCIANO.

Peace! What 's left
For me to care for? Let the roof-tree fall,
Now all beneath it 's buried! all, all, all!

FRANCESCO.

You must not think of things so sullenly.
But as a man that 's master of his wrongs,
And greater even than the greatness of them.
Rouse! rouse!

BRACCIANO.

Francesco, I will tell you now
A thing will give you pleasure. Take it, fiend!
'T is the last pleasure you will get from me.
I think, if I were capable just now
Of any feeling in the least like joy,
'T would be to know that you were miserable
Beyond endurance: therefore I suppose,
Since no less cordially do you hate me
Than I hate you, 't will give you pleasure, too,
To hear what I shall say. I said erewhile
I liked my wife, admired, respected her.
That 's over. I cannot respect her now,
Admire, or like her. All that 's worlds away!
But what do you suppose I am going to do
Presently, when I leave this den? To murder

The woman that I love! love, love, do you hear?
I never loved her when I thought her pure.
I know her not pure now. I love her now.
And I am going to murder her. Laugh, fiend!
You see that I am miserable enough.
Make much of that. Mine she was yesterday,
And yesterday I was an honest man.
I did not love her then. I loved myself.
All 's changed. She is mine no more: we both
are lost.
For, losing her, I have lost myself. To-night
I, with the murderer's heart in me already,
Love her, the harlot that I go to kill.
Have that writ down by some choice Tuscan
scribe,
A drama for the Devil to chuckle at:
A devil's drama, for a devil's delight,
Acted by devils damned beyond redemption!

FRANCESCO.

The heart of man 's a mystery!

BRACCIANO.

All 's so clear!
The Might-have-been, which never can be now,
The Must-be-now, which never could have been,
Were 't not that knowledge ever comes too late,
And all that 's good is, in this wretched world,
Good missed! Why came I in such haste from
Rome?
Not at your mandate: though your missive seemed
The pretext still. For I was thoroughly tired
Of what had been. 'T is not, I think, in you

To understand how it should come about
That sometimes in the sudden midst of all
The busy so-called waking life of a man,
There slides across the spirit that 's moving it
A silent, instantaneous, dream-like change:
Born, as in dreams such changes are, perchance
Of something, Heaven knows what, so small, so small,
That with a mystic trouble turns aside
Suddenly the main currents of the mind:
The look in a dog's eyes: a stranger's talk:
The death of some man that you never knew:
Less, less than that! chance odors after rain,
Or old-new colors in an evening sky,
And all at once the Present is the Past,
The Past the Present, and the Future all
One nameless yearning to recapture . . . . what?
Ah, that 's the question! But with me 't was Home,
A resting from the nowhere-leading ways
Of feverish Life's sick walking up and down,
Peace, and the quiet-hearted household loves!

FRANCESCO.

Marry again then!

BRACCIANO.

Plaudite! valete!
All 's as it should be here. The play 's complete.
Look round, admire the order of the parts!
Is not all Florence represented here?
The art of murdering and concealing murder,

Called statecraft by this time's complacent voice,
Behold, on yonder silent shelves all round,
Its speechless representatives! The rest?
O, all the rest 's in our two persons played!
Behold the Personages of the Age:
Conspirator, Assassin, Hypocrite,
Prince without truth, and Subject without trust.
As for the People, it is quite as much
Visible here as elsewhere, just at present:
The People's part is properly left out:
The Prostitute 's behind the scenes: the Spy,
The Cuckold, — all are here, I think, and all
Are represented worthily. What else
Is wanting?

FRANCESCO.

Ho! Fra Luke!

BRACCIANO.

True, I forgot.
The Church!

FRANCESCO.

What ho! Fra Luke! Fra Luke, I say!

FRA LUKE (*entering*).

(They have not killed each other? no such luck!
I had a vague sweet hope of some such thing.)
Your Highness called me?

FRANCESCO.

Well? The New Edition?
What of it, Friar?

FRA LUKE.

I like ever best
Each last Edition of what I may call
Your Highness' careful study and extreme care
To improve, suppress, eradicate what needs
The pruning-knife of strict Morality,
This world's rank garden's wary weeder.

FRANCESCO.

Ah!
I am glad that we appear to have done well.
Dear, dear Bracciano! so then you *must* go?
Well, 't were but cruel kindness on our part
To keep you any longer from the home
Where those that love you there have so long missed
Your welcome presence. O, sir, we expect
To hear of famous doings presently, —
Prompt slaying of the fatted calf, — what not?
All sorts of welcomes to this best event!
Heaven bless you, dear Bracciano!

FRA LUKE.

(Strange! He knows
That I know all. Yet, for the life of him,
The habit of hypocrisy so sticks,
He cannot help pretending to deceive me.)

FRANCESCO.

Conduct the Duke, Fra Luke. The Duke 's impatient.
And, dear Bracciano, I 'm so glad, so glad
That, as regards the trifle we discussed,
We are of one mind wholly. And the money,
The money shall be paid. Zounds! it would be
Abominable, unchristian, if we left
In the curst clutches of those rascally Jews
A moment longer our dear sister's husband.
Go! joy be with you. Stay, one parting word!
When of the odious truth you are assured,
I pray you, Sir, remember that you are
A gentleman and a Christian.

BRACCIANO.

Heaven and earth!

FRA LUKE.

(I backed the spider. Well, the spider wins!)
This way, illustrious Senior Duke! this way.
[*Exeunt* BRACCIANO *and* FRA LUKE.

FRANCESCO (*alone*).

Bluster! all bluster! For I hold him fast.
Astonishing! how soon a man forgets
Debts to Despair. Before a month is past
I shall be prayed to pay his other debts,
Almost as desperate. They are all the same.
'T were well to have him watched, though, till he 's tame.

Poor fellow! 't is so fresh to him, all this.
Well, now that 's off our mind which weighs on his.
Suscipiunt montes pacem populo!
Servite Dominum in lætitia. So
Jacta est alea, the bolt is sped.
A litany now: and then, content, to bed!

VANINI*

LECTURES BEFORE THE SORBONNE.

(PARIS, SIXTEENTH CENTURY.)

ELCOME, dear friends! . . . . though to a stranger's heart!
For, 'mid your fair French faces, as they throng
Fast, fast about me, I perceive — if not
The name of Italy encharactered,

* Lucilio (self-styled Julius Cæsar, and Pompeius) Vanini was one of that numerous Army of Martyrs who have been canonized by no church. Murdered by the Parliament of Toulouse upon an infamous and unfounded charge of Atheism, his memory has been calumniated by the few and forgotten by the many. I think that no reader of his "Dialogues" will accuse me of exaggerating the vanity of the man. It was excessive, but not ignoble; and to it I am disposed to attribute much of the heroism with which he endured torture and faced death. When we remember that his martyrdom and murder were justified by their perpetrators on the grounds of the audacious freedom with which Vanini had expressed un-orthodox opinions, the excessive caution and timidity of all his writings significantly illustrate what was considered "freedom of thought" in the sixteenth century. On being accused of Atheism by his judges, he picked a straw from the ground, and proceeded, by arguments which would probably have satisfied Paley, to demonstrate the existence of God from the existence of the straw. Those arguments, however, did not satisfy the tribunal, which condemned him, first to have his tongue cut out, and then to be burned alive. He went through it all, and died "cheerfully for the sake of Philosophy," as he said,

Such as her sultry suns with swarthy finger
Upon my own have traced it — yet the eye
Of keen inquiry, and the eager cheek,
Native to such as Nature's hand hews out
From her unfeatured and inglorious mass,
For common kindred in the shining band
Of those that both desire and dare TO KNOW !
Therefore I take you to my heart of hearts :
High peers, whose brows by Thought are privileged
To owe no homage to the narrow zones
Of partial Place, and casual Circumstance,
But hold high colloquy with those supreme
And solitary Spirits which allow
No bondage of the branding zodiac
To limit their hereditary realms
In universal space ! Therefore, I bid
My best self, freely, to your fellowship :
And as, within the mystic circle traced
By Persic priests, the affable Genius
(Appeased by myrrhy fumes that please him well)
Doth, to delight each mild-eyed Magian,
Unpack the treasures of the ransackt world,
Else hutcht from sight 'twixt either sleeping pole, —
Gold, by winged gryphons for Abassin kings
Guarded in mountain treasure-houses deep,
Great wizard gems from Solomon's thumb ring,
And sea-green marbles from Caucasian mines,
Thick-veined with white fire ; — so, sweet Mages, I,
Lured by your loves, do at your feet lay low

with a heroism never surpassed and rarely equalled by any of those martyrs who are admired as brave men because they died in vindication — not of Doubt — but of a Faith which promised them immediate beatitude. Yet consider the difference !

The spoils from Science filched by stealthy toil;
Rare secrets of the starry universe,
Flying around the centre, and what dwells
Deep in the undivulgéd mind of man.

I mark the wonder widening in your eyes
As they turn to me, wistful what comes next;
And hear you murmuring, as my spirit moves
Among you like the unseen wind that blows
To billowy toil full-bearded harvest fields.
"Can it be true?" ye ask yourselves, ... "The man
Before you, with the scarcely wrinkled brow
And yet unsilvered hair, — can he have reached
So soon the cloudy summits that command
That spacious prospect which the hoary sage
Scarce sees before he sinks into the grave?
How many cycles in the wilderness
Did Moses wander, leading right and left
His puzzled followers, till, fatigued to death,
He, from the top of Pisgah gazing, saw
The Promised Land, and died. Yet hath the man
That stands before you, speaking like a voice
Out of the sundered stars, imperative,
Some years of youth still left to fling away."
And so ye marvel. And I marvel not
That ye delay to put aside all doubt.
Because I know that half the Prophet's power
Upon the multitude (though ye, indeed,
I count not of the many, but the few)
Lies in the lifted rod, the flowing robe,
The hoary beard, and many-furrowed brow.
Yet, friends, 't is true, — all true! The man ye see me,

Such as I am, I have attained the end
And eminence of all the sciences.
A spirit zoned with the nine-folded spheres,
That in his right hand turns the rolling globe
Around, for pastime, — I command the Powers
That hide within the heights and depths of things,
Not easily commanded. In a word,
Whatever may be known by man, I know.

Yes! I, the Italian Doctor, Julius Cæsar
Lucilio Vanini, whom you know
Already by no casual report,
Have, by much study, travel, and strong thought,
Mastered in some few thirty years, or less,
Philosophy and physics; medicals;
Theology; and law, in both its branches,
The civil and the canon; (for who knows not
That *in utroque jure* I am Doctor?)
All schools of East or West; anatomy;
Mechanics; mathematics; music; all
Poets, grammarians, and historians;
Natural magic, and astronomy,
Astrology; with what from these a man
May further fashion, in the advance of time,
By sharp experience of himself, to add
Knowledge to knowledge. Also I have writ
On Free Will, Fate, and Providence, confuting
Whatever was by others said before
Upon these subjects, and constraining those
That read my books to burn their own: besides
Two dialogues on the contempt of glory,
Which, that I do not crave a vain renown,
But have sought Science for her own sweet sake,
Shall witness for me to all candid minds:

And, — so you shall not fear that I indulge
Such froward spirit as our Holy Church
Not seldom in her children hath reproved,
Prodigals that forsake the Father's board
To feed, and starve, on miserable husks, —
A long Apology — *Concilio*
Pro Tridentino — of the Council, and
Decrees of Trent; with many other matters,
Fully discoursed. Which books, whoe'er will read
them,
May at the Fair in Frankfort easily
Obtain, through any merchant of this town.
And I have visited the greater part
Of Europe. I have traversed Italy,
Whereof no city is to me unknown,
Nor I to it. In Holland, Germany,
And England, every University
I have both seen, and sometime studied there.
Nay, was I not the chosen and the chief
Disciple of the English Carmelite,
John Bacon, prince of the Averröists?
So that . . . . albeit I would not have you deem
I in pretension do exceed the pith
And marrow of performance, nor indeed
That, whatsoe'er it may be I have done,
I have done more than any man may do,
Let him but love, as I loved, Learning more
Than house, or lands, or any other good,
(Albeit such fervor is not to be found
In men of insufficient elements,) . . . .
I dare affirm what I erewhile averred,
That whatsoe'er a man may know, *I know.*

And as for Pomponat, men's present Mentor,

He, and Averröes, whom he but follows —
(Although I would not count them less than kings
Whose erudition and audacity
Hath made them half to be esteemed as gods) —
Let these, with Cardan, and I will not name
How many more that be their vavasours,
Sit at my feet forever, and be dumb!
My worst is better than the best of theirs.
(Believe I do not boast!) for they, indeed,
Have but rough-guessed the ways which I have paved
With ponderous fact, and irrefragable
Results, accumulated carefully,
To distances divined not by these men.
Which you shall also, if you will, reach with me:
For what I know I would to all make known:
And what I have would share with who will have it:
Since knowledge by division grows to more.
Is it not written that the Teachers — they
That have turned many to the light — shall shine
Like stars in heaven? Which shine not for themselves
But for the illumination of mankind.
Only believe me!

Yet, for all, I see
That you do think I boast myself beyond
The stretch of my deserving. If, good friends,
You deem it thus, believe me you do wrong
Me first, — and, in the consequence, yourselves!
For I conceive there 's nothing more beseems
A teacher, than assurance of the worth
Of what he teaches, and his own to teach it.
On these two points behooves the man to have

No doubt whatever. If he doubt himself,
Let him be dumb and put belief in others.
For all his right to speak is in the right
Of what he *can* speak to be boldly spoken :
And, therefore, reverently listened to.
Whence, if his worth be furnished with fair titles
Both to his own and other men's good credence,
He cannot too conspicuously show them.
There 's naught but such conviction as rejects
All question of it, that what 's now to say
Is better worth the saying than all else
By others said before it, justifies
Infraction of that silence which befits
A man in presence of the universe,
The stars above him, and the graves below.
Therefore, my masters, I am bold to speak;
This boldness (which, were it less positive,
Would stand in silence) being, as you see,
The only right which I admit myself
To speak at all. Be mine bold speech, or none.

O, I have seen in Professorial Chairs
How much of mock humility, lip-lowliness
Mouthing it thus . . . . "The Grace of God forbid
We should be overbold to lay rough hands
On any man's opinion. For opinions
Are, certes, venerable properties,
And those which show the most decrepitude
Should have the gentlest handling. Yes, good sirs,
We have that sort of courtesy about us,
We would not, flatly, call a fool a fool,
Nor wrong all wrong, nor right entirely right,
Lest we affirm too much. You shall not find us
Of such an overweening arrogance

That we should swear, because we are disposed
To this or that conclusion, that it needs
Must better yours. We think that we are right:
We may be wrong: we doubt you are in error:
You may be right. Civility forbids
Insistance on harsh terms." Civility
Therefore goes sidling, with a glance asquint
'Twixt true and false, along her slippery road,
Which is the road to Hell, the Home of Lies!

Yet will some wise and moderate good man
Make answer, that to no one living soul
Is absolute truth vouchsafed, and this alone
Is absolutely certain. Granted, friend.
Yet he is absolutely right or wrong
That dares, or dares not, follow to the end
And utterly use the whole o' the truth he hath.
For there be many that, in face of Truth
Fear her imperative aspect, and affirm,
"This customary falsehood is a thing
More safe than that uncustomary truth";
Or, "Only thus and thus much of the truth
Is competent of usage," having not
Within themselves true love of truth, nor yet
The courage of the consequence of thought.
This is the approved philosophy of fools,
Of which you shall hear nothing from my lips,
For half-truths need no teaching from this chair.
The craft of cowardice, the world's vile promptings,
The glare of false authority, the fear
Of exile, prisons, halters, and the rack,
These teach the customary compromise
'Twixt true and false; and find in every land
Sufficient school, without the added weight

Of verdict from the lips of men, not vile
By nature, who, though none regard their speech,
Must speak undaunted, or not speak at all.
Most men, indeed, believe in something better
Than their own actions; and conciliate
The world by acting worse than they believe;
And all men even their best actions base
On something worse than is their best Belief;
Yet hope to mollify the scorn of God,
Because their thoughts are better than their acts,
And their beliefs more blameless than their lives.
This needs no teaching. This is the world's wisdom.
But, when the Teacher speaks, he speaks as one
That knows his audience in the universe
Is not of this world only; but perchance
Millions of starry spirits beyond the sun
Pause o'er their planetary toil to lean
And listen to him. If he speak the truth
Truly, his speech is as a trenchant sword
To cut the world asunder to the heart,
And take its stealthy secrets by surprise.
So let him stand up stern, as on a rock,
Like Joshua when he held the sun and moon
In Ajalon and Gibeon, till he ceased
To smite the Amorite before the Lord.
No more ignoble powers, no lesser laws
Can hurt his sacred head whom Nature's own
Eternal and divine supremacies
Safeguard with unseen cohorts to the end.

For wherefore should we call you here, to gaze
In sober earnest, and some shuddering,
Upon this dreadful combat of the gods, —
This conflict of resistant Error armed

Against resistless Truth, on all sides round,
Not ended till the world be won or lost?
Why bid you mark severe Minerva there?
Here snaky Typhon, — both at horrible handgrips?
If, to assuage amazement, and restore
The careless satisfaction we were bold
Thus to break in on with the horrid news,
We lightly whisper, — just when the heart stops
And the veins tighten with the hideous thought
Of what 's depending on the deadly issue, —
"Friends, here 's no cause to fear yon grisly god,
For all his savage show his claws be clipped.
Athene's angry spear can draw no blood,
It being buttoned like your fencing foils.
And this tremendous spectacle, which shakes
The ample theatres of Heaven and Hell,
Is but a mock-heroic at the most."
Ye gods! if this be thus, and only thus,
Why then, I cry i' the name of all men's patience,
You impudent knaves that play the herald's part,
Sound ye your brawling trumpets in our ears
So shrilly? Why do you, unmannerly thus,
Rouse us from slumber, scare us from our business
Of feasting, fooling, and forgetting all things,
To cry the house a-fire? Or why drag hither
Grave men, grown men, gray men, with cares enough,
And griefs enough, and grievances enough,
To try the nerves of those that have the stoutest,
Merely to cheat us of our hard-earned rest
With your preposterous puppetings!

Good friends,
I will not use you thus, I warrant you.

But you shall have hard fighting, and real blows,
Not dealt in vain. For, by the help of God,
We will this day Goliaths more than one
Destroy forever from the Field of Truth. —
If you 'll believe me! —

Nay! but neither think,
Because I have put off humility
Before I stept into this Chair of Doctrine,
That therefore I, with idle arrogance
Aspire to hit the stars; revering not
The worth of modest-mindedness in man.
Not so. I have been humble more than most.
Whiles I was yet a learning, I was humble.
Then, my humility was such as suits
A lover when he sues: which I put off
To clothe me with the pride that lover feels
When afterwards, he having won that wooed,
His love lives in possession. I might tell
Of days and nights of painful patientness
In Padua; when, a beardless boy, I braved
Sharp winter's biting in a threadbare coat,
And, late and early, trimmed a lonely lamp
With toilful tendance; sat at all men's feet;
And read from all men's books right reverently;
And lived to learn; and learned from all that lived;
And held myself the least of little ones,
Not worthy to be seated at the board,
Grateful to cram what charitable crumbs
Fell from o'erflowing trenchers to my lot;
While nothing but the daily doled-out crust
(A frail and miserable alms!) appeased
The begging of the body, barely heard.
But love makes warmth and fulness everywhere.

The lover lives on love luxuriously,
And lacks for nothing. O be very sure
That no man will learn anything at all,
Unless he first will learn humility.
The humblest mounts the highest. Who would
 scale
The skyey Alp must go afoot. The vain
And arrogant man may drive his gilded coach
Across the plain, gazed by the servile crowd,
But, would he mount that mighty eminence,
He must alight, and foot it with slow steps.
Therefore I say, ... Be humble, — to be high!

And I will tell you, — I that have, O friends,
Read many books, and written not a few, —
This is a secret. Tell it not in Gath,
O very reverend Doctors of Sorbonne!
A man may cram his brains with libraries,
And yet know nothing.
 Whence comes Knowledge? think!
By reading? No: by thinking on things read.
By seeing? No: by thinking on things seen.
Nor hearing, but by thinking on things heard.
Yet half the first-class writers I have read
Are merely setters forth — not of their own,
But other men's stale thinkings: second-hand
Employers of spent brains! Is Thought so easy?
Try!
 Take some simple, obvious object here,
And think it. Think the wall.
 What! you are silent?
You cannot?
 Yet although you cannot think
This simple wall that stares you in the face,

You *can* think Plato and Pythagoras,
Zeno, and Aristotle, Epicurus,
Plotinus, Jamblicus, Themistius,
Thales, Parmenides, — and the Lord knows whom.
That is to say, you can think second-hand.
Well then, O friends, now let us learn to think!
Think anything. But only *think.* For, see you?
There 's nothing of so singular, nor mean
Condition in this universe, but what
It doth include, and, in a sort, continue
The fact of something greater than itself,
Nay, of the Very Greatest. Nothing is,
But by the having been of something else,
Which something else, the cause of this thing here,
Is, in its turn, the effect of something elsewhere.
Thus we the higher in the lower perceive;
From each obtain intelligence of all;
And find in all the consciousness of each.
For all which is, by reason that it is,
And is itself, not other than itself,
Defines itself; and, being definite,
Must be perceivable at some one point,
If but no more, on which perception acts,
Whether of bodily sense, or mental force.
Away, then, with the indefinite, from thought,
Which is the non-existent. What exists,
Acts; and what acts gives notice of itself
To all existence, acting thus or thus
Conformably to laws that govern all
Existence. Acts are laws: no law, no act.
Therefore, be sure that whatsoever is
Man's thought is competent, if not to know,
At least to know of. And the Infinite
Appears, reported by its parts, to be

The Finite infinitely multiplied,
Extended infinitely every way.

Think, and all things become confederates
To the thought in you. For the Thinking-Power
Is of such pregnant faculty, it imbues
All things, or can from all things extricate,
And stir to answerable activity,
Some portion of the essential consciousness.
Upon the dumb, long-inarticulate earth
Descends the gift of prophecy and tongues :
The smallest fact, — the last in consequence
Of the supreme procession of events, —
Mere garniture of life's superfluous pomp,
Becomes a willing spy upon the track
Of its more potent predecessor, gone
Most likely in a grand indifference by :
The dust grows dainty with divinity :
The limpet has surmises of the huge
Enormous-backed sea-violencing whale :
He, of Behemoth in the days when God
Held colloquies upon the Chaldee plains
With the vexed Uzzite : the dull-hearted ox
Hath in him legends of his father-race,
Those monstrous and imaginary forms
That frightened Adam when the bitten fruit
Turned sour between his teeth, and thunder lowered.
The sand-grain in his dreams divines the stars.
The very stones are garrulously given,
And babble to each other in the moon
The story of the waters that of old
Rolled Noë's ark on Ararat. Perchance
The poising of a pebble that a child

Sends from his sling in swift parabola,
Interprets in a tongue that 's yet to learn
The fiat that gave motion to the stars.
So that this volatile fluid of the brain,
This flux of thought, like streams compelled to seek
The level of their sources, flowing forth
No matter by what channels, through what fields,
Is by each course constrained towards the height
From whence it issued, and mounts up to God.

Ha! there you smile, and bring your faces all
To bear on mine; like men who, unawares,
And by a sudden happy chance, detect
In some familiar object, grown a blank
By being looked at carelessly too often,
A novel feature, not before divulged.
Why, this is well. And, since we all are here
To use our wits, friends, let us use them sharply
And to some purpose: not as your mere swords
Of ceremony, shut up safe in velvet,
Tawdry and tedious appendages,
Put on for show, and put aside for comfort!
I see you take my humor by this time.
Good! and your faces brighten, and your eyes
Glitter, as stars do in a good sharp wind.
Sharp? why, what else should be the atmosphere
Of vigorous spirits?
You believe me, friends?
You *do* believe me!
Ay, I always felt
That I should find in France my own compeers,
The finest and most eager spirits of men!
Some guiding angel drew me in my dreams
To choose this land for my abiding home.

I loved you ere I knew you; know you now,
And, having known you, love you better still.
Gather, then, close about me, all of you!
You, there, bright youth with sunbeams in your
hair,
And you, grave sir, with eyes like icicles,
Come round me, one and all . . . . close! closer
still!
Let not a word escape!

We will discourse
This day of the Eternal Providence.
Clap all your pens to paper, and write down: —

"*Amphitheatrum Providentiæ*
Eternæ christiano-physicum,
Divino-magicum, astrologico-
Catholicum; adversus veteres
Philosophos, peripateticos,
Epicureos, atheos, stoicos."

Good! Have you written? Now attend.

We thus
Begin with the Beginning. Which is God.

END OF VOL. I.

Cambridge: Printed by Welch, Bigelow, & Co.

www.ingramcontent.com/pod-product-compliance
Lightning Source LLC
LaVergne TN
LVHW021315110826
845150LV00003B/574

* 9 7 8 1 4 2 5 5 5 8 0 8 6 *